Rational Decisions in Organisations

Rational Decisions in Organisations

Theoretical and Practical Aspects

Edited by
Frédéric Adam, Dorota Kuchta, and Stanisław Stanek

Reviewers
Frédéric Adam, Joanna Iwko, Gaye Kiely, Dorota Kuchta,
Ewa Marchwicka, Stephen McCarthy,
Gloria Phillips-Wren, Stanisław Stanek,
Tadeusz Trzaskalik, and Irem Ucal Sari

CRC Press
Taylor & Francis Group
Boca Raton London New York

CRC Press is an imprint of the
Taylor & Francis Group, an **informa** business
AN AUERBACH BOOK

first edition published [2022]
by CRC Press
6000 Broken Sound Parkway NW, Suite 300, Boca Raton, FL 33487-2742

and by CRC Press
4 Park Square, Milton Park, Abingdon, Oxon, OX14 4RN

CRC Press is an imprint of Taylor & Francis Group, LLC

ISBN: 978-0-367-46774-6 (hbk)
ISBN: 978-1-032-19395-3 (pbk)
ISBN: 978-1-003-03096-6 (ebk)

DOI: 10.1201/9781003030966

Typeset in AGaramond
by MPS Limited, Dehradun

Contents

Introduction

Managers in organisations have to make rational decisions. Being the opposite of intuitive decision making, rational decision making is a strict procedure utilising objective knowledge and logic. It involves identifying the problem to solve, gathering facts, identifying options and outcomes, analysing them, taking into account all the relationships, and selecting the decision.

It does not exclude using intuition and other purely human, informal factors, like communication or observing human behaviours and reactions. On one hand, they are an irreplaceable source of ideas, possible scenarios, or solutions. On the other hand, decisions in management concern human beings, so their reactions and feelings cannot be disregarded. In the final analysis, however, all those human and social factors should be woven into the strict rational decision-making procedure.

Rational decision making requires support: methods and software tools. The identification of the problem to solve needs methods that would measure and evaluate the current situation. Identification and evaluation of options and analysis of the available possibilities involves analysis and optimisation methods. Incorporating intuition into rational decision making needs adequate methods that would translate ideas or observed behaviours into hard data. Communication, observation, and opinions recording is hardly possible today without adequate software. Information and data that form the input, intermediate variables, and the output in the decision process have to be stored, managed, and made accessible in a user-friendly manner.

The editors of this book have set the following objective: to present selected recent developments in the support of the widely understood rational decision making in organisations, illustrated through case studies.

Part I of the book (**Human Perspective of Decision Making**) focuses on the human being in the rational decision-making process. Chapter 1, entitled "Intuition in Decision Making – An Investigation in the Delivery Room," describes the problem of observing expert behaviours and their intuitive decision-making process so that they could be translated into a hard decision-making procedure supporting human decisions. Chapter 2, entitled "The Moral Dilemmas Involved in Decisions to Respond to Physical Aggression," explores the problem of rationalising decisions that are difficult to rationalise: those made in the situation of physical aggression. Managers should create conditions that introduce as much rationality as possible even into such apparently uncontrollable decisions.

Part II of the book (**Organisational Perspective of Decision Making**) concentrates on making decisions regarding the improvement of the organisation's functioning. Chapter 3, entitled "Maturity Evaluation in Construction Companies Based on Case Study Research and Fuzzy Set Theory," proposes decision-making procedures to improve the quality of project management in the organisation. Chapter 4, entitled "Corporate Health and Safety Performance Index as a Measure of the Level of Occupational Health and Safety Management in the Company

Based on the ISO 45001 Standard," aims at improving the health and safety aspect of the organisation's functioning. Chapter 5, entitled "The Theoretical and Practical Design Thinking Approach in IT Project – The Remote Human Resource Management System Case Study," contributes to the efficiency of the recruitment process.

Part III of the book (**Uncertainty and Pressure in Decision Making**) addresses the decision making in projects, which are per their nature always linked to risk, uncertainty, and changes. Chapter 6, entitled "Increasing the Efficiency of IT Waterfall Projects Control: Modified Earned Value Analysis Combined with Parametric Estimation," proposes a method supporting decision making with respect to changes in the project under the pressure of time during project execution. Also Chapter 7, entitled "An Application of Decision Support Technique for Global Software Project Monitoring and Rescheduling Based on Risk Analysis," refers to decision making during project implementation in response to risk: the problem treated there is the need for problem rescheduling. Chapter 8, entitled "Type-2 Fuzzy Numbers in Models of Project Time Affected by Risk," proposes a mathematical model of project planning in the situation of risky project duration.

Part IV of the book (**Software Applied to Decision Making in Organisations**) presents three examples of advanced software usage in organisational decision making. Chapter 9, entitled "Socialising Decision Enactment: Living Provenance in Decision Support," describes the usage of software systems supporting social decision making (as opposite to individual decision making), wherein a wide network of partner decisions are made in full transparency, with all the necessary details and aspect accessible any time to anybody. Chapter 10, entitled "Machine Learning Solutions in the Management of a Contemporary Business Organisation: A Case Study Approach in a Banking Sector" describes advanced technology applications in all aspects of organisational decision making. Chapter 11, entitled "Integration of the Decision Support System with the Human Resources Management and Identity and Access Management systems in an Enterprise," presents software support in human resources management related decisions.

We truly hope that the book will open new research and application perspectives to our readers so that more and more rational evidence-based decisions are made in our organisations, producing benefits to all of us.

Editors

Frédéric Adam is a full professor in the Department of Business Information Systems at the University College of Cork's Business School, Cork Ireland. His research interests are focused on decision support systems both in business and in the medical area where he has led several projects aimed at developing decision support artefacts for clinicians. He has also published extensively in the ERP area. He is a principal investigator (PI) in the Financial Services Innovation Centre and a founding PI in the INFANT Research Centre.

Dorota Kuchta is a full professor in the Faculty of Management at the Wroclaw University of Science and Technology, Wroclaw, Poland. Her research interests are focused on management models and methods under uncertainty, ambiguity and incomplete knowledge. She has led myriad research projects in the field of project management. She is the holder of two project management certificates: Certified Project Management Associate and PRINCE2 Foundation.

Stanisław Stanek is a professor in the Faculty of Management at the General Tadeusz Kościuszko Military University of Land Forces, Wrocław, Poland. His research interests are focused on decision support systems. He has designed and implemented computerized decision support systems for businesses across a variety of industries and managed projects in the field of hybrid crisis decision support systems, logistics, IT and construction project management.

Contributors

Edyta Abramek
Faculty of Informatics and Communications
    Department of Informatics
University of Economics in Katowice
Katowice, Poland

Frédéric Adam
Business Information Systems
University College Cork
Cork, Ireland
and
INFANT Research Centre
University College Cork
Cork, Ireland

Biljana Mileva Boshkoska
Faculty of Information Studies in Novo Mesto
Novo mesto, Slovenia
Jožef Stefan Institute
Ljubljana, Slovenia

Eugene Dempsey
Department of Pediatrics and Child Health
University College Cork
and
INFANT Research Centre
University College Cork
Cork, Ireland

Barbara Gładysz
Department of Operations Research and
    Business Intelligence
Faculty of Management
Wrocław University of Science and Technology
Wrocław, Poland

Miljenko Hajnić
Faculty of Information Studies in Novo
    mesto
Novo mesto, Slovenia

Patrick Humphreys
London School of Economics and
    Political Science
London, United Kingdom

Jacek Iwko
Faculty of Mechanical Engineering
Wrocław University of Science
    and Technology
Wrocław, Poland

Joanna Iwko
Faculty of Management
Wroclaw University of Science and
    Technology
Wroclaw, Poland

Ryszard Kałużny
Faculty of Management
General Tadeusz Kościuszko Military
    University of Land Forces
Wrocław, Poland

Mmoloki Kenosi
Department of Pediatrics and Child Health
University College Cork
Cork, Ireland

Agata Klaus-Rosińska
Faculty of Management
Wroclaw University of Science and
 Technology
Wroclaw, Poland

Małgorzata Kochanek
Faculty of Mechanical Engineering
Wrocław University of Science and
 Technology
Wrocław, Poland

Dorota Kuchta
Faculty of Management
Wrocław University of Science and
 Technology
Wrocław, Poland

Ewa Marchwicka
Faculty of Management
Wrocław University of Science and
 Technology
Wrocław, Poland

Tymon Marchwicki
Faculty of Management
Wrocław University of Science and
 Technology
Wrocław, Poland

Aneta Pisarska
Faculty of Management
Wrocław University of Science and
 Technology
Wrocław, Poland

Anna Sołtysik-Piorunkiewicz
Faculty of Informatics and Communications
 Department of Informatics
University of Economics
Katowice, Poland

Stanisław Stanek
Faculty of Management
General Tadeusz Kościuszko Military
 University of Land Forces
Wrocław, Poland

Brian Walsh
Department of Pediatrics and Child Health
University College Cork
and
INFANT Research Centre
University College Cork
Cork, Ireland

Leszek Ziora
Faculty of Management
Czestochowa University of Technology
Czestochowa, Poland

THE HUMAN PERSPECTIVE OF DECISION MAKING

Chapter 1

Intuition in Decision Making – An Investigation in the Delivery Room

Frédéric Adam

Business Information Systems, University College Cork
INFANT Research Centre, University College Cork, Cork, Ireland

Eugene Dempsey and Brian Walsh

Department of Pediatrics and Child Health, University College Cork, Ireland
INFANT Research Centre, University College Cork, Cork, Ireland

Mmoloki Kenosi

Department of Pediatrics and Child Health, University College Cork, Cork, Ireland

Contents

DOI: 10.1201/9781003030966-2

1.1 Introduction

The practice of decision making arguably involves some of the most demanding skills that human beings can acquire. As an activity, it is mostly exclusive to us as a species, insofar as animals are not considered to be able to display the free will that is required to underpin the kind of decision making that we associate with managers, medical doctors, or government ministers, as well as generally with individuals in their personal lives. Damasio et al. (1996) captured this point in their statement that "decision making is, in fact, as defining a human trait as language."

As a result, decision making has received considerable attention from researchers in a variety of disciplines, from psychology to sociology, to management and information systems. In the IS discipline, decision making has been studied in terms of the decision aids or decision supports that can be developed to help decision makers make decisions without replacing them – i.e. in a way that leverages and enhances their decision-making skills. Separately, other domains of research have sought to pursue the artificial intelligence agenda proposed by Simon and Newell as early as 1972, where software artifacts take over specific segments of decision-making processes.

Research in human decision making, however, is complex because the mental activities involved in deciding and the circumstances facing decision makers are themselves complex and varied. It is also difficult because these mental activities are not directly observable for a researcher, not in the way that a physical practice may be visible, and even the closest observation of decision makers can yield ambiguous and incorrect conclusions. In management, we are following in the footsteps of such seminal researchers as Carlson (1951) or Mintzberg (1973 and many other dates) who have explored how to observe managers in a way that can make their reasoning intelligible. Researchers have leveraged this research because developing useful decision supports can only be undertaken on the basis of a stable understanding of human decision making – a science of decision making that delivers some certainties in relation to the mental and organisational processes involved in decision making (Pomerol and Adam, 2008). Without such a scientific base, much of the practice of decision support systems development would need to rely on trial and error, where potential systems are pushed onto managers with varying levels of success. The executive information systems (EIS) period provides examples of this trial-and-error process, with many systems failing to survive the turnover of managers in given positions, leading to systems dis-adoption (Elam and Leidner, 1995; Singh et al., 2002).

However, much progress has been made in relation to the establishment of a science of decision making, with major contributions by such leading scholars as Herbert Simon and Daniel Kahneman who, across a long period and many publications, have proposed some of the theories that still guide us today. Crucially, even they have admitted that we do not understand enough about human decision making to make conclusive observations about its intricacies. As a result of the complexity of the mental processes involved, observation and lab experiments have been the dominant scientific method to learn about decision making, and a rich history of reports on decision making, notably managerial decision making, are available for us to learn from.

One key lesson from this history is that the context and conditions in which a decision takes place and the position the decision maker finds themselves are very important. The more precise the research question, the more useful it is to study a specific type of problem or scenario, rather than attempt to propose generalities that risk providing little actionable understanding of decision makers and their mental processes. Thus, in this paper, we concentrate on a very specific type of medical decision making to try to decipher how a diagnosis is reached, how interventions are designed, and how decision makers could be supported in a very specific scenario: the environment of the delivery room where neonatologists look after the most vulnerable type of patients: premature babies born before 32 weeks of gestation. Our focus on such decision making is justified by the potential to improve health outcomes for these patients with targeted decision support that leverages the expertise of neonatologists and, at the same time, reinforces the evidence-based nature of decision making in a scenario that is characterised by the need for rapid and flawless interventions with very severe consequences. We find that the delivery room is a space where critical decision making takes place under the leadership of an expert and that, although intuition plays a critical role, there is a need to increase the objective nature of some of the observations made during the decision process. We conclude that certain technologies could help in this very special decision-making setting.

The next section reviews relevant observations about the science of human decision making and how it applies to the specific scenario of the delivery room. The paper then presents the methodology we followed, our analysis of five video recordings of deliveries, and our observations and conclusions.

1.2 Researching Human Decision Making

What we know about decision making has mostly been written in the last hundred years, originating in the research conducted by such seminal scientists as Foley, Barnard, Simon, Carlson, Mintzberg, Kahneman, or Drucker, to name only a few of them. Two of them, Simon and Kahneman, received Nobel Prizes for their work on human decision making; this illustrates the excellent research conducted in this domain. In earlier times, Plato had begun our journey of discovery with his observations that the human mind was a tool that could be used to uncover truths and use them to implement positive changes in human society. Thus, the history of research on decision making has been paved by great writers and researchers.

The other side of that coin is more problematic: if the science of decision making has received a lot of attention, from a variety of seminal researchers, this has meant that the decision-making domain is one of the most difficult to penetrate for new researchers within the IS discipline. The volume of material and its diversity are hard to grasp and even more difficult to apply to the analysis of decision making in practice. Yet, this is a requirement if we are to progress in our decision support systems endeavours.

In the context of this research project, the difficulty in studying intuition in decision making comes from a number of specific issues, as discussed in the next sections.

1.2.1 Rational or Not

If we decided to split the science of decision making between two camps, artificial though it may seem, we could oppose those who believed that human decision makers should strive to be essentially rational – that they should seek to optimise their decisions and their outcomes – and those who are more interested in exploring human decision makers as not particularly rational in their decisions, seeking to understand to what extent and why that might be and where and why they might not. The former will consider that deviations from rational orientations are "flaws" in decision making, and the latter will prefer to see these deviations as heuristics and as evidence that human decision makers use their cognitive abilities to adapt to the environment where they operate.

Thus, "classical" economics theories have proposed that human decision makers are rational, seek to maximise their utility by reference to the information they possess about the world around them, and design interventions that maximise the likelihood that their preferences will be achieved. Such theories have been put forward as prescriptions of how human decision makers should behave (Beach and Lipshitz, 2017). Other researchers have provided a rich and ample body of observations and experiments to show that human behaviour often deviates from what rational reasoning may suggest. They have sought to explain why we display such "deviant" behaviour and, furthermore, how we benefit from it as decision makers.

This debate is interesting, but it may be a distraction from the real objective of research on decision making: to understand how decisions are made and, further, how to support them. Clearly, based on seminal research on human decision making, our cognition is characterised by what have been sometimes called "biases" (Samuelson and Zeckhauser, 1988) and sometimes "heuristics" (Busenitz and Barney, 1997). The use of either term reflects a belief that, on the one hand, human decision makers are imperfect (bias) or, on the other hand, that they are well adapted to their environments). Reflecting on the nature of the environment and noting that it was characterised by so much uncertainty, Simon (1986 for instance) referred to Rationality (with a capital "R") as Olympian (by reference to the mountain supposed to the home of the gods in Ancient Greece), and proposed that bounded rationality was the best we could aspire to as decision makers. The future is unknown, the present is a puzzle, and our preferences are often confused: there is much more in human decision making that is not known than that is known. By analogy with the expression "finding a needle in a haystack," Simon (1987a) proposed satisficing as *finding any needle that will do the job*, as against *finding the sharpest one*. Simon's work on bounded rationality remains, to this day, a central theoretical contribution in our understanding of human decision making.

Against this backdrop, it seems a legitimate conclusion to consider that human decision makers, although imperfect in their reasoning, are actually well adapted to their environment and the situations they typically face. Rationality seems well adapted to a situation where many parameters are known and understood, but it is uncertain to what extent it is useful in equivocal situations, where both the diagnosis and the choice of the preferred solution are essentially interpretation-laden.

The crux of the "heuristics-and-biases" debate stems from the consideration of whether human deviations from a rationalistic model are the result of "errors of reasoning" (Keren and Teigen, 2004) and that human decision makers are somewhat "lost in the face of real-world complexity," or, if Simon or Gigerenzer, for instance, are correct and that human cognition, limited though it may be, is essentially a good match for the environment in which we live such that "Human rational behaviour is shaped by a scissors whose two blades are the structure of task environments and the computational capabilities of the actor" (Simon, 1990, p. 7). Keren and Teigen (2004) have suggested that biases are causes in decision-making processes more often than they are effects.

In the context of the delivery room and the decision making faced by neonatologists, it is critical for us to understand the boundary where lifesaving intuition meets the need to be rational at all times and to provide clear evidence (e.g. vital signs and their evolution) to underpin the selection of interventions; the boundaries between the need to react quickly and the need to be able to justify and demonstrate that the right decisions were made in view of the data that was available; the boundaries between relying on experts with huge accumulated tacit experience that cannot be codified and the need to be able to formalise the science of delivery room interventions and make them auditable and repeatable. This is critical in the application of the Hypocratic Oath – First do no harm- and to ensure that all patients are treated in the same best-practice manner, irrespective of where they are born or who is on duty that day.

1.2.2 Thinking Slow and Thinking Fast – Where Intuition Fits

Hogarth (2001) has proposed to define intuition as a "sudden unexpected thought that solve problems" and may require an "incubation period" (p. 251), and Dane and Pratt (2007) have leveraged this definition to differentiate between ***instinct*** ("hardwired" responses or autonomic reflexes to stimuli), ***insights*** (where a decision maker consciously becomes aware of the logical connections supporting a particular answer or solution – a so-called "light bulb" moment) and ***intuition***. Dane and Pratt (2007) also listed "guessing" as a type of decision making because they focus on human decision making in general rather than managerial or clinical decision making, but this is not useful to understanding the context of delivery room decisions (or indeed boardroom decisions), which must have a logical basis and where experts are accountable for outcomes (Feldman and March, 1981). In the medical field, the ever-increasing requirement to be seen to rely on evidence-based decision making makes guessing in either diagnosis or intervention selection even less likely (see Haynes et al., 1997).

There are common elements in many definitions of intuition, and Hogarth (2001) usefully characterised intuition as these responses "reached with little apparent effort and typically without conscious awareness" and which "involve little or no conscious deliberation" (p. 14). This focus on unconscious aspects of intuition is in contrast with the idea that intense cognitive efforts are typically involved in reasoning about complex cases, and this is of great interest to us in our analysis of the delivery room scenario and its intense time pressures. Similarly, Benner and Tanner (1987), who researched decision making by nurses' define intuition as "understanding without rationale" (p. 23) and "synthesis, not analysis... (with) a sense of certainty" (p. 29). Gobet and Chassy (2008) conclude that most descriptions of intuition include "rapid perception, lack of awareness of the processes engaged, concomitant presence of emotions and holistic understanding of the problem situation" (p. 130). This possibly involves the "chunking" of disparate data and its cross indexing, giving decision makers the ability to make holistic association and cross reference experience over hundreds of cases (Hayashi, 2001). All these characterisations are very useful from an empirical viewpoint because they can be used as markers for the use of intuition when talking to decision makers and trying to establish whether they used intuition in given cases.

The reason for us to focus our analysis on the role of intuition is that it has been argued that in business settings, available examples of successful intuition can be matched with examples of catastrophic failures, rooted in intuitive decisions that went wrong. Bonabeau (2003) quotes Bruce Henderson, founder of the Boston Consulting Group, who called intuition "the subconscious integration of all the experiences, conditioning, and knowledge of a lifetime, including the cultural and emotional biases of that lifetime" (p. 118). His issue is that: "Intuition is a means not of assessing complexity but of ignoring it. That's valuable if you're a firefighter in a burning building or a soldier on a battlefield. It's not valuable if you're an executive faced with a pressing decision about investing millions in a new product for a rapidly changing market." This assertion is aligned with the view that decision making is primarily contingent on the situation where the decision maker is placed. Thus, it is critical to analyse and understand what specific decision-making situations are like and not like, and how the trade-off between speed of decision making and the need to consider all variables to the full extent of their implications plays out. This is particularly pertinent to our objective to explore intuition in the delivery room.

To understand where intuition fits in human cognition, Kahneman (2003) has proposed that it can essentially be broken down into two parallel processes, which he labelled system 1 and system 2 (Figure 1.1). Figure 1.1 puts some specific shape on the debate by presenting in the same diagram two different modes of cognition associated respectively with an emotional form of response to stimuli and a reasoned response to stimuli. Intuition – which underpins system 1 – is characterised as fast and effortless, therefore leaving no specific impression on the decision maker other than the positive feeling that comes from recognising familiar objects and patterns – an "aha! sensation" in Hayashi (2001).

There is evidence of this, and Simon (1987b) reported that human decision makers often "make competent judgments or reach reasonable decisions rapidly without evidence indicating that they have engaged in systematic reasoning, and without their being able to report the thought

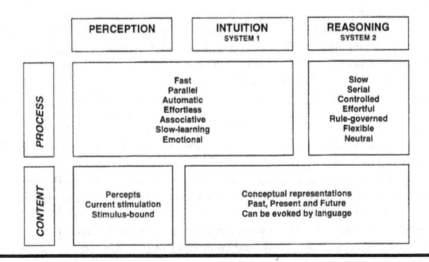

Figure 1.1 Kahneman's parallel cognitive systems (reproduced from Kahneman, 2003).

processes that took them to their conclusion" (p. 58). This rapid, yet precise and accurate decision making is of specific interest to us.

1.2.3 Unit of Analysis

An additional difficulty that we must consider in our research stems from the need to recognise when decision making is no longer an individual pursuit and when it becomes embedded in rich social contexts where the contributions and preferences of a number of contributing individuals must become aggregated. This has given rise to researchers using a number of embedded units of analysis in their research on decision making, from individual decision making (clinicians, managers, political leaders, consumers etc...) to groups of individuals, to organisations, and even to society. On the one hand, it could be considered that only people make decisions (Langlet et al., 1995), but others have argued that large inanimate entities, such as countries, can also "make decisions." In the specific scenario of the delivery room, the unit of analysis is a small medical team collaborating in delivering expert care to an infant. Thus, it goes beyond individual decision making, and yet it does constitute a scenario of tangible decision making observable within a single space and within a limited timeframe. It also entails the need for strong leadership by an expert neonatologist, although communication within the team is clearly paramount. This is an advantage from a research viewpoint, in terms of both observation and designing decision support solutions pertaining to such a scenario: the patient and the decision makers can all be observed at once since their decision making process unfolds over "the first 15 minutes of life."

1.2.4 Decision-Making Process – From Recognition to Intervention

Our focus is on this inherently iterative process where the team investigates a new patient and designs an intervention to facilitate its establishment in extra-uterine life. To explore what happens in such collaborative processes in business contexts, Humphreys (1989) has proposed his representation levels framework (Figure 1.2), where decision problems emerge over time from

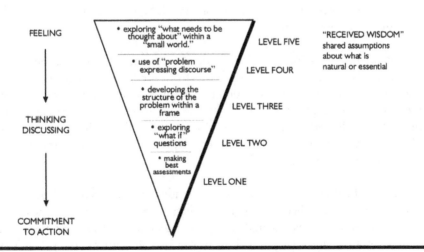

Figure 1.2   Representation levels framework (Humphreys and Jones, 2006).

consideration by high-level managers before becoming increasingly codified and fully described over time, until a clearly implementable solution emerges.

Whereas top managers sense their way through a multitude of complex signals over long periods and reach points of crystallisation where their ideas take shape, care teams in the delivery room are faced with a category of problems that is more clearly identified, but requires immediate diagnosis, with a window of opportunity for intervention that may be measured in minutes if not in seconds. They are concerned with the establishment into extra-uterine life of an extreme preterm infant, struggling with one or more complex pathologies and have a number of interventions at their disposal. We could consider that this decision situation presents an accelerated progression down from level 3 – development of a diagnosis – to level 1 – where an intervention is implemented but we prefer to consider an alternative theoretical lens for our delivery room studies: whereas in the business world, the number of moving parts is considerable, and the variability of many parameters is confounding, the delivery room scenario offers us the opportunity to study the role of intuition in decision making in a real-life, but controlled environment.

Alternative models of decision making exist that are better suited. Gary Klein proposed his recognition primed decision-making model (RPDM) to capture what happens in such rapid decision-making scenarios. He derived this model from his experimentation with naturalistic decision-making (NDM), a paradigm for studying decision makers in the field and systematically learning from them which was quite novel when initially proposed in the 1980's. According to NDM, intuition is "an expression of experience as people build up patterns that enable them to rapidly size up situations and make rapid decisions without having to compare options" (Klein, 2015; p. 164). Our focus on experts leverages NDM to observe how they use this accumulation of knowledge by concentrating on "extreme cases" of decision making (Patton, 1990).

1.2.5 Recognition Primed Decision Making

Klein's (1993) concept of *recognition-primed decision making* (RPDM), where decisions are based on the recognition (total or partial) of previously known patterns and a solution is designed to match these patterns emphasises the importance of the *matching* aspect of decision making in certain situations where speed is critical. According to RPDM, decision makers can be observed to make such extreme decisions in two key iterative stages:

- **Recognition:** the rapid identification, through recognition, of the current situation – a diagnosis of the current state of nature which, as the wording suggests, is all about recognising aspects of the current situation by reference to previously encountered situations.
- **Implementation:** design and choice of an action matching the diagnosis and its implementation, followed by an on-going observation of the evolution of the situation to confirm that the diagnosis was the correct one, based on the emergence (or not) of expected changes within the expected timeframe.

RPDM entails that the decision maker will change or adjust the intervention based on what they see. A fireman might change their strategy for tackling a blaze that is not affected by the water thrown at it because it reveals that the underlying assessment of the blaze is incorrect. In a medical setting, the care to a patient might be adapted or changed altogether if the patient's symptoms don't abate or disappear, or indeed, if the patient's condition worsens. In the delivery room, the neonatologist might decide to intubate if respiratory distress is not solved with manual ventilation or move the baby onto a cooling blanket if it starts seizing.

Klein believes that the mental processes involved in the recognition, implementation, and review of the solution rely on intuition. Pretz and Folse (2011) have noted that intuition is correlated with experience, not only in terms of preferences for certain trialled and tested solutions but also in terms of effectiveness. Intuition is about recognising previously encountered patterns, and experience is correlated with the diversity of patterns previously encountered and their prevalence in a given situation. Pretz and Folse (2011) have insisted that we must be able to show that increasing reliance on experience is not simply a matter of preference, which would deliver no greater accuracy in diagnosis, but is really correlated with competence and accuracy. The concept of "centre of excellence" now favoured by public health experts, where as many cases of a certain kind as possible are channelled through the same facility is born out of this notion (Elrod and Fortenberry, 2017). This is intended to concentrate expertise about the most difficult cases in designated facilities where the level of expertise and effectiveness can rise to unmatched levels. Thus, the neonatal intensive care unit we have studied concentrates care for all the premature babies born in this area of the country, and this means about 100 cases are treated each year. Such level of exposure to difficult cases means that the success rate is extremely high in this facility in comparison to other healthcare settings, where only a few cases would be treated every year. Expertise and experience are concentrated, and clinical decision making gains in accuracy and effectiveness. RPDM provides an adequate theoretical lens to explain this phenomenon, and we are using it as our guiding principle in this research.

1.3 Research Method and Case Sampling

The setting for our investigation of the role of intuition in decision making is neither "a burning building" nor a "multi-million investment": it is a complex scenario of the care for a newborn in the delivery room. It offers opportunities to capture the combination of reliance on both formal medical knowledge and intuition rooted in years of experience of clinical practice, here in the context of a designated centre of excellence. It also offers the opportunity to apply RPDM in a setting similar to those observed by Klein in his work.

In terms of decision making, the delivery room is an extreme case where vital decisions must be made in a compressed timeframe, but it is also a partly controlled environment where the problems facing decision makers are bounded and already bundled into recognisable form: (1) the boundaries of each case are easy to identify for researchers, (2) the decision maker can comprehensively account for the continuity of the care path selected and implemented, (3) documentation exists to catalogue decisions and interventions and (4) the feedback loop on the health outcomes and the impact of care is rapid – a number of days in the first instance (although there can be some longer-term consequences for patients later in childhood and even into adulthood). These four characteristics serve to justify our keen interest in this decision-making setting, but this research study is part of a larger project aimed at developing tangible decision support tools for neonatal care decisions in the delivery room.

A compelling characteristic of this decision-making scenario is the timeframe for making decisions, which is extremely limited, and this reinforces the appeal of, and reliance on, rapid intuition-based decision making.

1.3.1 The Delivery Room Decision Making Scenario

In its fullness, the delivery room environment involves experts from at least two distinct domains of expertise: obstetrics (focusing on the mother) and neonatology (focusing on the newborn). The decision-making scenario explored in this paper is the unique moment where the two patients are separated from each other, and the infant transitions to life in the outside world. The timeframe we are interested in is essentially the first 15 minutes of life, before patients are transferred to either the nursery, special care unit, or intensive care unit where they receive any additional care they need. For instance, the baby may be transferred in the heavily medicalised environment of the neonatal intensive care unit (NICU).

Our focus on newborn care decisions is underpinned by the significant evidence available that a substantial proportion of medical issues in preterm infants, some of which have lifelong implications, occur in these first minutes of life. Most human beings are born in conditions such that they require little or no care in the process of transitioning from intrauterine life to independent life. Births are normal life events and not medical interventions. However, a small proportion of newborns, about 10% in the western world, for instance, require care, some of them intensive, to complete the transition into extra-uterine life. A significant proportion of health issues developed by individuals throughout their lives result from incidents that occurred in the first minutes of life. Furthermore, a small number of individuals carry a disproportionate share of health issues because of incidents that occurred at birth. This is particularly the case for those born before 32 weeks of gestation, most of whom require substantial assistance at delivery, for instance, ventilation, intubation, or even resuscitation.

These interventions must be underpinned by a precise diagnosis, inasmuch as they can improve the prognosis in certain cases but can also be detrimental in other cases. Ventilation, for instance, may be beneficial in terms of oxygen saturation in the blood, but it can also result in lung injury where excessive pressure is applied. A number of specific interventions can be applied to premature babies when they are born, which can reduce or eliminate the long-term impact of difficulties encountered at birth or just after birth; but the current state of knowledge only gives incomplete indications about when or in which case these interventions should be applied. Thus, the diagnosis in the first minutes of life is critical and high impact, with the potential for significant injury, including the very serious possibility of long-term brain injury.

Recent decades have witnessed a significant increase in monitoring options for preterm infants in the neonatal intensive care unit (NICU) setting e.g. cardiac (echocardiography and noninvasive cardiac output monitoring), respiratory (capnography and respiratory function monitoring), and the use of video, yet the monitoring of preterm infants in the delivery room has changed very little over the same period, other than the introduction of pulse oximetry into the delivery room approximately 10 years ago. Experts believe that not enough objective information is permanently recorded about events in these first minutes of life, and tangible learning opportunities are therefore lost. In addition, a certain amount of subjectivity still characterises the initial assessment of at-risk newborns and the determination of which interventions should be undertaken. This evaluation rests on a significant proportion of intuition, tacit knowledge, and accumulated experience by medical staff; hence, our focus on this critical episode of decision making to try to identify the manner in which intuition is used in such extreme cases of decision making.

1.3.2 Our Empirical Study

Our study leverages five in-depth retrospective cases (Koukouris, 1994) where the decision making of neonatal teams was reviewed by three expert neonathologists and their co-author in terms of the evidence available to them and the manner in which they arrived at their diagnosis. Cases were selected where: (1) sufficient time had elapsed to ensure that complete information was available about health outcomes, (2) medical outcomes were generally positive, and (3) case material and participant recollection were available and reliable.

Data collection was carried out using a number of different methods at a large maternity hospital in Ireland. Each case selected involved a review of the documented facts of the case, including case notes, patient health records, medical history, and relevant follow ups and, centrally, the systematic examination of video recordings made in the delivery room. Ethical approval and parental consents were obtained as per the guidelines applicable in both our university and the hospital where the study took place. (They have a collaboration agreement in place between them with specific research protocols already agreed.) Not all births are recorded, but some selected births were recorded for the purpose of research, with the explicit consent of parents involved.

The video recordings are particularly important to show the team dimension of the process, where different actors in the delivery room played different roles. In the case of a preterm baby, in view of the likelihood of complications, a care team of three individuals is always present: (1) a junior doctor (first-year pediatric trainee or registrar), (2) a nurse from the neonatal unit – specialised in the care of infants, and (3) a consultant in neonatology – an expert who gives oversight to the process. The observation of the actions and interactions of these three individuals is a key element in the observation of the decision-making process. Predictably, it is the consultant neonatologist who is most likely to utilise intuition, whereas the junior doctor is mostly following the standard protocol. There is obviously a training and pedagogical element in the process, and this is a key aspect of gaining experience as a healthcare professional. The nurse is typically very experienced as well and carries out a lot of the manipulations that are required on the baby.

Analysis was undertaken by the co-authors based on key elements of diagnosis in part derived from literature and in part identified through observation of the actual decision-making process. These elements were implemented in a new framework to reflect the decision-making conditions in the delivery room, as illustrated below. The framework was used to systematically analyse the facts of the case and to plan for the analysis of further cases in a way that guarantees rigorous replication of the analysis across cases. A data grid was developed based on the framework in which the data from each case were coded.

1.3.3 Data Coding and Analysis

Figure 1.3 shows an abstracted view of a delivery room (without the mother in as much as the neonatologist team has no oversight of the health of the mother, who is cared for by her obstetrician) with currently available data and technologies, and the decision-making team and their patient. The blue and red arrows represent the inputs and outputs of the decision-making process, namely:

1. Inputs
   - Context of the case (characterisation of the issues in the case – e.g. low heart rate)
   - What do the vital signs say / how do they evolve?
   - What are the important observations at birth (e.g. the appearance of the baby)?

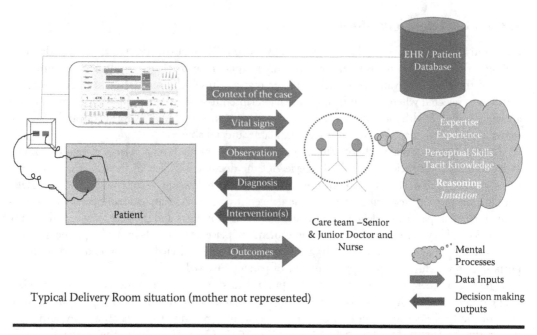

Figure 1.3 Abstracted view of a delivery room and data collection protocol.

2. Outputs
- What is the initial diagnosis?
- What intervention(s) is (are) therefore undertaken?
- What are the observed outcomes immediately after each intervention and after 15 minutes?

The figure also represents our research questions, namely:

- ■ Elements of formal expertise that underpin the diagnosis and choice of care
- ■ Tacit knowledge invoked in the diagnosis and selection of intervention
- ■ Tangible elements of experience which underpin the diagnosis
- ■ Explicit reasoning
- ■ Intuitive elements of decision making
- ■ Communication between the care team (the video recordings also involve an audio recording).

Finally, the figure shows the team element in the process and the importance of the communication between the three members of the care team.

Our study is aligned with NDM research, which probes deeply into the types of cues used by decision makers and the way in which they make their judgments (Klein, 2015). It allows us to focus on the issue of perceptual skills and tacit knowledge, both of which are critical components of intuition in NDM. Our study also leverages RPDM, and Figure 1.3 encapslates the two decision-making stages described in RPDM (Klein, 1993), namely, recognition (here, the diagnosis of the clinicians) and the implementation of interventions (here, the treatment undertaken to help the patient make the transition into extra-uterine life).

Based on this rich dataset, the authors initially discussed the events in the delivery room and used the classification in Figure 1.3 to systematically code the inputs and outputs of the decision-making process in the data grid. They then sought to identify the mental processes involved in reaching and expressing the diagnosis and designing an initial intervention. They also considered the case in a longitudinal fashion where the condition of the patient evolved and provided additional clues that consolidated or changed the diagnosis and, therefore, the chosen care pathway.

One complexity we had outlined earlier is the team dimension, which is captured by the interactions between the members of the care team and the manner in which their different contributions combined in delivering the care to the young patient. This is where the use of the video and audio recording played a critical role in allowing for a complete analysis of the decision-making steps and actions that were revealed by the interactions and the communication between team members. The team element forced the participants to express their opinions and therefore materialise their thought process, which might otherwise have remained hidden from analysis.

The analysis was initially conducted for each case. Each case was considered as a single data set to identify the specific patterns of decision making, followed by the expert neonatologist and their colleagues (see Section 1.4). The interventions were then noted and their impact recorded. In some cases, the care team underook a number of iterations, and these were recorded. The workload involved in analysing this number of cases was significant, and while the analysis of more than five cases may yield additional insight, the substantial nature of our dataset allowed for great insight to be achieved.

The study was concluded with a cross-case analysis, presented in the discussion section, where the observations made across the different cases were synthesised and additional insights were derived from the data. These confirmed our characterisation of delivery room decision making and provided some initial directions for decision support, which we need to experiment with in the next stages in our project.

1.4 Description of the Five Cases

This section presents our analysis of the cases of decision making in the delivery room that we analysed. The families involved in these cases consented to the material being used for research purposes, including a video recording of the birth and any episodes of care in the delivery room; but, of course, the facts of each case are fully anonymized.

1.4.1 Case 1

This case involves a relatively stable preterm baby that required stabilisation due a low initial heart rate (HR) of only 50 bpm at birth. Although her HR increased to over 100 bpm after about 30 seconds, her low oxygen saturation still required an intervention, which was successful.

1.4.1.1 Overview of the Case and Care Dispensed

This case presents an unusual scenario where the baby was presented to the neonatologist in the incorrect position just after birth. The nurse treated the patient as might be done in a normal birth, presenting the baby such that her head was at the wrong end of the resuscitaire – i.e. away from the neonatologist. This was quicky corrected but illustrates the importance of team effort in such cases. The team was unhappy with the baby's "dusky" appearance, and suction was applied to clear the airways. As this was insufficient to improve the respiratory effort, a decision was made to apply intermittent positive pressure ventilation (IPPV) and then move to continuous positive airway pressure (CPAP) as her oxygen saturation began to improve.

1.4.1.2 Analysis of Inputs and Outputs in the Decision Process

The analysis of this standard case of care shows the application of ILCOR principles (International Liaison Committee on Resuscitation). These guidelines chart a care path for infants presenting poor spontaneous respiratory effort, as occurred here.

The application of these guidelines IPPV and then CPAP delivered the improvements in HR and oxygen saturation that were required to satisfy the medical team. The appearance of the baby (colour and skin tone), her low HR, and low oxygen saturation were sufficient to determine the necessity for this treatment.

The impact of the intervention was observable within the timeframe of care delivered in the delivery room, and the baby was deemed to be stable enough to be moved to the neonatal unit.

1.4.2 Case 2

This case involves a relatively stable preterm baby that required stabilisation. After showing good progress initially, despite a "dusky" appearance, his condition deteriorated after about two-and-a-half minutes. His normal HR and good respiratory effort faded after this time, and the team decided to apply ventilation (CPAP) and to escalate to IPPV when his oxygen saturations further disimproved.

1.4.2.1 Overview of the Case and Care Dispensed

This case illustrates the inherent vulnerability of preterm babies and their increased propensity to require help in the first minutes of life, especially in terms of ventilation. Despite showing good signs of progress initially, the newborn required two successive interventions, escalating to the application of IPPV to restore his oxygen saturation.

A key moment in the decision process can be seen in the video recording of the birth when a team member states: "look baby is transitioning."

1.4.2.2 Analysis of Inputs and Outputs in the Decision Process

Understanding of the physiology of transitioning to extra-uterine life is the key in this particular case. Good respiratory effort initially masked difficulties in completing this transition, straight forward for the majority of normal babies, but much more difficult for preterm babies due to the immaturity of some of their organs. The deterioration after two-and-a-half minutes is common and requires prompt intervention when recognised. Pulse-oximetry is the key technology used to make this assessment in an evidence-based manner and to trigger the interventions applied in this case: ventilation. The implementation of this intervention, in line with ILCOR guidelines, may be the difference between a baby at risk of brain damage and a baby who receives prompt help and becomes stable again after a few minutes. This highlights the importance of care teams dealing with premature births on a regular basis – a less-adept care team might have been much slower in implementing the vital interventions that helped this baby's transition.

The impact of the intervention was observable within the timeframe of care delivered in the delivery room, and the baby was deemed to be stable enough to be moved to the neonatal unit.

1.4.3 Case 3

This case involves an interesting decision-making process where good initial progress led to interventions when the heart rate began to deteriorate. The interesting aspect of this case is revealed in the recording of the birth as the care team decided that the measurements provided by the delivery room devices were providing them with incorrect information and chose an intervention based on their intuition and experience.

1.4.3.1 Overview of the Case and Care Dispensed

Similar to Case 2 above, this baby showed good initial progress, although her dusky appearance did raise concern with the team. Her low oxygen saturations had to be addressed, and the team decided to apply CPAP. As her heart rate slowed down, the mask on her face was first repositioned before the ventilation intervention was escalated to IPPV (which gives air, or a mixture of air and oxygen, to the lung between each breath to keep the lungs open and stop them collapsing).

This intervention was successful, and the oxygen saturation reached a satisfactory level after a while.

1.4.3.2 Analysis of Inputs and Outputs in the Decision Process

This case is interesting for this research study because it shows the limits of available technologies and protocols and the need to be able to rely on traditional auscultation techniques to ascertain the effect of interventions. In the case, the available data incorrectly pointed to a normal heart rate, whereas the heart rate clinically was low. This was due to an inadequate seal around the mask on the baby's face and required prompt remedy by the team. This is common enough due to the very small size of some preterm babies and the difficulties inherent in placing some of the equipment on them. This corrective intervention is captured with the acronym MR SOPA, which guides the investigation of any issues that can arise with ventilation in an infant. This is a stark reminder that, notwithstanding decision aids that may be in place, clinical care must always be centered on the observation of the patient. Operators must also understand the technology made available to them in great detail so they can ascertain that it is providing them with accurate data. These are key themes for research in DSS in clinical settings.

The impact of the intervention was observable within the timeframe of care delivered in the delivery room, and the baby was deemed to be stable enough to be moved to the neonatal unit.

1.4.4 Case 4

This case involves a very complex scenario of preterm stabilisation that necessitated many decisions taken within the first 10 minutes of life. The baby's low heart rate and poor oxygen saturation triggered prompt interventions that escalated to her being intubated twice, once by the junior doctor and once by the neonatologist, until her condition improved.

1.4.4.1 Overview of the Case and Care Dispensed

Just after birth, the baby showed signs of poor respiratory effort, and her vitals were a source of concern. The team immediately applied CPAP, but this did not improve her condition, such that IPPV was implemented to seek to increase her fraction of inspired oxygen (FiO2). As this still was not sufficient, the team decided to intubate her. Still the expected progress did not materialise, and the neonatologist decided to re-intubate to ensure the proper insertion of the endotracheal tube. The exceedingly small airways of a preterm baby can prove confusing for anyone other than the most senior neonatologists, and this second intervention finally delivered the expected results. This is a case where learning can only occur "on the job," and the junior staff member must confront the full complexity of each intervention to learn how to cope with it.

After about 10 minutes, the oxygen saturation reached a satisfactory level.

1.4.4.2 Analysis of Inputs and Outputs in the Decision Process

This case illustrates the patterns of decision making that RPDM is intended to capture. A succession of interventions is undertaken, with the team keeping a close eye on the vital signs that they need to improve. The successive interventions are selected based on the response (or lack thereof, as in this case) of the patient until progress is recorded and confirmed. This is the ABC of medical care in such situations.

In this case, a specific piece of equipment is used to help the monitoring: a CO2 tidal flow monitor, which gives a precise reading of the volume of exhaled gases. This is a great example of the intermeshing of real-time data and neonatal expertise in care decisions in the delivery room.

The impact of the intervention was observable within the timeframe of care delivered in the delivery room, and she was deemed to be stable enough to be moved to the neonatal unit.

1.4.5 Case 5

This case involves a scenario of a preterm twin delivery that proved relatively complex. Evidently, this case is complicated by the presence of two patients instead of one, necessitating the addition of an extra junior doctor in the team. In this particular situation, the two junior doctors focused on one of the twins, while the neonatologist focused on the other one.

The babies' low heart rate caused immediate concern and, similar to the case above, the twins required intubation as their HR did not improve for the first three minutes of life. Again, as above, a second intubation was required because the first one was performed incorrectly.

1.4.5.1 Overview of the Case and Care Dispensed

The baby received CPAP initially due to his poor saturation and low HR. The seal between his face and the mask was initially incorrect, delivering no added pressure in the lungs. When this fit was fixed, there was still not improvement, requiring an escalation to IPPV, and, after about four minutes, the intubation of the baby. The use of a tidal monitor showed the lack of progress, and after six minutes, a second successful intubation was carried out.

After this final intervention, the condition began to improve.

1.4.5.2 Analysis of Inputs and Outputs in the Decision Process

The case of the twin shows how complex and high pressure a preterm delivery can become and the absolute necessity to keep decision making timely in the first minutes of life. From a brain oxygenation viewpoint, six minutes is a very long time frame where permanent injuries can occur, and the second intubation could have occurred faster in this case. However, watching the tape shows how tight the decision framework in the delivery room is in such complex cases, and it is hard to imagine a faster decision-making process by the team without cutting corners with the diagnosis.

The tape is indicative of the excellent communication within the enlarged care team in this case. The four team members can be heard to exchange precise details about the condition of the babies and the care provided to them.

The impact of the intervention was observable within the timeframe of care delivered in the delivery room, and the babies were deemed stable enough to be moved to the unit.

1.5 Discussion

Five cases add up to a limited sample to capture the complexity of such a decision-making situation as the delivery room. However, the observation of the video and audio recordings and the facts we analysed yielded some rich observations about the decision-making scenario in the delivery room from a variety of viewpoints.

Firstly, the decision arena in the delivery room is characterised, in the case of complex cases of preterm babies, by an impossibly tight timeframe for decision making, with a sole focus point for everyone in the team: the patient on the resuscitaire and the evolution of their vital signs, particularly HR and oxygen saturation. In this arena, time is counted in seconds and minutes, and there are not many decision-making scenarios that are so constrained in this respect. When vital signs don't improve, further decisions must be implemented until the patient responds.

The reliance on tangible data, heart rate (which is really a surrogate measure for the patient's challenge to adapt and stabilise) and oxygen saturation are the bedrock of infant care, but equally, observation and auscultation are critical elements of the expertise which must be deployed. A common protocol issued by ILCOR guides the interventions, but the interpretation of the vital signs and their evolution are still not completely modelled, and caring for preterm newborns relies heavily on the expertise of the care team.

The mixing of explicit and tacit knowledge is what makes this decision scenario so rich and so interesting to study. While the "rule book" is a necessary starting point, things begin to evolve in unpredictable ways as the first minutes pass. As described in the paper, it is common for premature babies to disimprove after a few minutes, despite adequate initial vitals. The manner of this evolution is what the expert neonatologist must analyse and understand. Thus, from a decision support viewpoint, the delivery room scenario raises critical challenges: the instruments provided must be embedded into the work of the team as we can observe it in the delivery room. Any data stream and any device used to capture them must be unobtrusive, and they must in no any way interfere or compete with access to the patient by team members. Other researchers have already reported that even such basic systems as electronic health records (EHR) are tricky to implement in clinical settings where they are perceived by medical staff to get in the way of their communication with, and examination of, their patients (O'Riordan, 2019). In the tight scenario of the delivery room, this concern is heightened, and the fear of interfering with complex cognitive processes is ever present for decision support developers. This is aggravated by the possibility of instrument and measurement failure, where the apparatus provided is difficult to deploy due to the anatomy of a small baby, and the readings it provides can actually be incorrect in certain cases (e.g. in the case where an incorrect seal is created between the mask and the face of the patient – see Section 1.43). The experts we have studied must not only be able to use the technology available to them, they must understand how it works in great detail so they are able to recognise when it fails instantly.

Thus, our analysis confirms that, despite the science that exists to guide the decision making of neonatologists caring for extreme premature patients, the delivery room is still a decision-making arena where a substantial proportion of elements underpinning decision making are subjective and where the experience accumulated by care teams is paramount. Despite the existence of guidelines and standard codified practices, such as the APGAR test for instance, it is still incumbent on experts to observe, diagnose, and make decisive iterative decisions on interventions and care within a timeframe of a few minutes, which complicates careful longitudinal data collection and rules out long reflective reasoning.

The examination of the baby's appearance to underpin the diagnosis is a clear illustration of this reliance on the expertise of very experienced neonatologists in preterm infant care. While many indicators can be objectivised by the use of technology – ECG monitoring, tidal flows, pulse oximetry – the close observation of the colour, activity levels, and other clues given by the patient's appearance about their condition distinguishes the experienced neonatologist from their novice or even advanced beginner colleague. Cates and Gallagher (2012) have presented a complete analysis of the different stages of expertise decision makers go through in terms of clinical decision making and have presented compelling arguments to explain why the expert can rely on intuition in a manner that is safer than less experienced practitioners.

Certainly, the introduction of technologies, sensors, and scanners of various kinds can objectivise the monitoring of such key parameters as the vital signs. This is associated with improvements in the accuracy of diagnoses and health outcomes in general, but some areas of clinical assessment are likely to continue to defy the implementation of technology (Garingo et al., 2012). Vital clues about the condition of very young and vulnerable patients who cannot express their distress must be found in aspects of the diagnosis which rely totally on the subjective assessment of experts. The appearance of newborns contains many such clues, and it is worrying that a great deal of variability is still found in how different experts assess the same case. Manley et al. (2010) carried out an experiment where video images of 20 babies at age 20 seconds, 2 minutes, and 5 minutes were assessed by a group of experts. Not only were there significant variations in the assessment of the different experts, but in a significant proportion of the cases, the experts markedly misevaluated the chance of survival of the babies. Tellingly, the evaluations were found to include both underestimation and overestimation of positive health outcomes, meaning that incorrect diagnosis is based on incorrect evaluations and not on predictable patterns of biased decision making.

Such results confirm that: (1) medical diagnosis and care to vulnerable patients requires subjective analysis based on expert intuition and (2) expert evaluation faced with limited clues about patients can be erroneous. This dual observation provides an incentive to work harder at understanding the structure of the decision scenario in the delivery room and seek to provide objective measures for the critical indicators and, where possible, to propose decision support artifacts that can speed up or facilitate diagnostic.

1.6 Conclusions and Further Research Steps

This paper is part of a large research project aimed at bringing radical improvement into the decision-making underpinning the establishment of preterm babies by fostering more evidence-based decision making in the delivery room in the first minutes of life. The project will involve developing a prototype mobile application, which will reduce the amount of subjectivity that still characterises the initial assessment of at-risk newborns and the determination of which interventions should be undertaken. As part of this, deep learning on large bodies of data collected in delivery rooms across different hospitals in Europe and their packaging into predictive algorithms will be attempted.

At the stage of the study that is described in this paper, we conducted a review and analysis of five cases of preterm births for which we had access to case notes and video and audio recordings of what happened in the delivery room. Our observations provide a strong incentive to try to help care teams make rapid and robust decisions to maximise the likelihood of positive outcomes for their patients. However, they also highlight the difficulties inherent in trying to do so. Some of these are common to many decision support endeavours, but others are specific to the environment of the delivery room and the nature of the decision problems faced by neonatal care teams. Certainly, these difficulties emphasise that a headlong rush toward placing technology between the patient and the team to somehow moderate the interaction between them would be misguided. The direct contact between carers and patient is a mainstay of modern healthcare, and this is likely to explain why delivery rooms, by and large, have not changed much over the last 100 years, apart from the routine use of pulse oximetric devices.

Our ambition, in the first instance, is to leverage the technologies now available in Neonatal Intensive Care Units (NICUs) to provide better access to real-time data in critical cases, but beyond this, to implement the systematic recording of these data to model the evolution of health outcomes in preterm infants and provide models of care that minimise the chance of complications.

References

Beach, L.R., & Lipshitz, R. (2017). Why classical decision theory is an inappropriate standard for evaluating and aiding most human decision making. *Decision Making in Aviation 85*, 835–847.

Benner, P., & Tanner, C. (1987). How expert nurses use intuition. *AJN The American Journal of Nursing 87*(1), 23–34.

Bonabeau, E. (2003). Don't trust your gut. *Harvard Business Review 81*(5), 116–123.

Busenitz, L.W., & Barney, J.B. (1997). Differences between entrepreneurs and managers in large organizations: Biases and heuristics in strategic decision-making. *Journal of Business Venturing 12*(1), 9–30.

Carlson, S. (1951). *Executive Behaviour*. Stockholm: Strömbergs.

Cates, C.U., & Gallagher, A.G. (2012). The future of simulation technologies for complex cardiovascular procedures. *European Heart Journal 33*(17), 2127–2134.

Damasio, A.R., Damasio, H., & Christen, Y. (Eds.). (1996). *Neurobiology of Decision-Making*. Berlin: Springer.

Dane, E., & Pratt, M.G. (2007). Exploring intuition and its role in managerial decision making. *Academy of Management Review 32*(1), 33–54.

Elam, J.J., & Leidner, D.G. (1995). EIS adoption, use, and impact: The executive perspective. *Decision Support Systems 14*(2), 89–103.

Elrod, J.K., & Fortenberry, J.L. (2017). Centers of excellence in healthcare institutions: What they are and how to assemble them. *BMC Health Services Research 17*(1), 15–24.

Feldman, M.S., & March, J.G. (1981). Information in organizations as signal and symbol. *Administrative science quarterly 26*(2), 171–186.

Garingo, A., Friedlich, P., Tesoriero, L., Patil, S., Jackson, P., & Seri, I. (2012). The use of mobile robotic telemedicine technology in the neonatal intensive care unit. *Journal of Perinatology 32*(1), 55–63.

Gigerenzer, G., & Goldstein, D.G. (1996). Reasoning the fast and frugal way: Models of bounded rationality. *Psychological Review 103*(4), 650.

Gobet, F., & Chassy, P. (2008). Towards an alternative to Benner's theory of expert intuition in nursing: a discussion paper. *International Journal of Nursing Studies 45*(1), 129–139.

Hayashi, A.M. (2001). When to believe instinct. *Harvard Business Review 2*, 71–73.

Haynes, R.B., Sackett, D.L., Richardson, W.S., Rosenberg, W., & Langley, G.R. (1997). Evidence-based medicine: How to practice & teach EBM. *Canadian Medical Association 157*(6), 788.

Hogarth, R.M. (2001). *Educating intuition*. University of Chicago Press.

Humphreys, P. (1989). Intelligence in decision support—A process model. In G.I. Doukidis, F. Land, G. Miller (Eds.). *Knowledge-Based Management Support Systems* (pp. 22–51). Chichester, UK: Hellis Hovwood.

Humphreys, P., & Jones, C. (2006). The evolution of group decision support systems to enable collaborative authoring of outcomes. *World Futures 62*(3), 193–222.

Kahneman, D. (2003). A perspective on judgment and choice: Mapping bounded rationality. *American psychologist 58*(9), 697.

Keren, G., & Teigen, K.H. (2004). Yet another look at the heuristics and biases approach. In D.J. Koehler & N. Harvey (Eds.). *Blackwell Handbook of Judgment and Decision Making* (pp. 89–109). Madden, MA, USA: Blackwell Publishing.

Klein, G. (2015). A naturalistic decision making perspective on studying intuitive decision making. *Journal of Applied Research in Memory and Cognition 4*(3), 164–168.

Klein, G.A. (1993). A recognition-primed decision (RPD) model of rapid decision making. In G.A. Klein, J. Orasanu, R. Calderwood & C.E. Zsambok (Eds.). *Decision Making in Action, Models and Methods*. Nordwood NJ: Ablex, 138–147.

Koukouris, K. (1994). Constructed case studies: Athletes' perspectives of disengaging from organized competitive sport. *Sociology of Sport Journal 11*(2), 114–139.

Langley, A., Mintzberg, H., Pitcher, P., Posada, E., & Saint-Macary, J. (1995). Opening up decision making: The view from the black stool. *Organization Science 6*(3), 260–279.

Manley, B.J., Dawson, J.A., Kamlin, C.O.F., Donath, S.M., Morley, C.J., & Davis, P.G. (2010). Clinical assessment of extremely premature infants in the delivery room is a poor predictor of survival. *Pediatrics 125*(3), e559–e564.

Mintzberg, H. (1973). *The Nature of Managerial Work*. Prentice Hall.

O'Riordan, G.D. (2019). An investigation into the underlying causes of information systems failure and success: case of a national clinical system in Ireland (Doctoral dissertation, University College Cork).

Patton, M.Q. (1990). *Qualitative Evaluation and Research Methods*. SAGE Publications.

Pomerol, J.C., & Adam, F. (2008). Understanding human decision making–A fundamental step towards effective intelligent decision support. In *Intelligent Decision Making: An AI-based Approach* (pp. 3–40). Berlin, Heidelberg: Springer.

Pretz, J.E., & Folse, V.N. (2011). Nursing experience and preference for intuition in decision making. *Journal of Clinical Nursing 20*(19–20), 2878–2889.

Samuelson, W., & Zeckhauser, R. (1988). Status quo bias in decision making. *Journal of risk and uncertainty 1*(1), 7–59.

Simon, H.A. (1983). *Reason in Human Affairs* (pp. 7–35). Stanford, CA: Stanford University Press.

Simon, H.A. (1987a). Making management decisions: The role of intuition and emotion. *Academy of Management Perspectives 1*(1), 57–64.

Simon, H.A. (1987b). Satisficing. In J. Eatwell, M. Millgate & P. Newman (Eds.). *The New Palgrave: A Dictionary of Economics*. Vol. 4. New York: Stockton Press, 243–245

Simon, H.A. (1990). Invariants of human behavior. *Annual Review of Psychology 41*(1), 1–20.

Singh, S.K., Watson, H.J., & Watson, R.T. (2002). EIS support for the strategic management process. *Decision Support Systems 33*(1), 71–85.

Chapter 2

The Moral Dilemmas Involved in Decisions to Respond to Physical Aggression

Ryszard Kałużny and Stanisław Stanek

Faculty of Management, General Tadeusz Kosciuszko Military University of Land Forces, Wrocław, Poland

Contents

2.1 Introduction

Careful observation of people's behavior and an in-depth analysis of press reports and media coverage has probably led many to ask this question: Why is it that some of us, when either threatened by physical aggression or witnessing an assault on another, will remain totally passive, doing nothing to counteract the assault, while others appear to have been waiting for an opportunity to demonstrate their physical strength, dexterity, and ruthlessness and are, in effect, likely to apply excessive measures? Why, in the heat of the moment, does an over-excited defender turn into a violent attacker? At the same time, there are also those who can assess the incident realistically and, whether protecting themselves or other people, will only use measures

DOI: 10.1201/9781003030966-3

commensurate with the threat; in doing so, they stay calm but firm and, rather than provoking or escalating violence, they aim to defuse the attacker. They realize that the attacker is under extreme stress and agitation, and it is all too easy, therefore, to trigger a spiral of violence. It seems, however, that only people with well-established moral attitudes are capable of such behavior in the case of critical incidents.

Those who, seeking no reward and oblivious of hazards to their own life or health, are ready to rescue other people threatened by physical aggression, who will take up the challenge and bear the consequences – they have always been, in the public perception, regarded with esteem, and their attitude has been associated with valor, heroism, and bravery. However, human behaviors can be varied and even unimaginable, the evidence of which can be found in historical records as well as in recent media reports. In some circumstances, humans may be extremely selfish and totally unconcerned with what happens to other human beings.

A spectacular example, one of many, is the shocking case of Kitty Genovese, described by social psychologists. In March 1964, when returning home from work in the middle of the night, she was attacked and murdered by a degenerate individual. One might think that the public has already grown accustomed to hearing news of such crimes. Yet, the distinctive characteristic of this one, and the reason why it has been publicized and analyzed to this day, is the fact that it was committed in front of the building where the victim lived, within earshot and sight of over thirty its residents (Aronson et al., 1994, pp. 453–454). What occurred there, presumably, is known as diffusion of responsibility (Aronson, 2018, p. 57): if a number of people are witnessing a tragic incident, they are less likely to help the victim because each of them hopes that someone else will help. It is just as common that those standing aside will not decide to react because "it's none of our business" or they assume that "I'll be better off if I don't engage" – perfect excuses for remaining passive and indifferent. Alternatively, they will demonstrate a conformist streak, adjusting to the inaction of the other witnesses (more in: Szacka, 2008, pp. 166–168); even more so if they cannot clearly interpret the situation. Their way of thinking and their actions are then based on the touchstone that is wobbly but immediately available: my behavior is right because others are doing the same. Yet, in the context of the Kitty Genovese murder and the behavior of her neighbors, it should be added that the both the decision and the process whereby some victims of physical abuse are delivered from their predicament are complex and determined by many other factors that have not been mentioned above (more in: Aronson et al., 1994, pp. 466–467). And, fortunately, human nature has its better sides, too, that are also frequently illustrated by mass media bringing news of individuals who have rescued helpless strangers experiencing physical violence. The *Daily Mail* published a detailed account of the heroic act of 38-year-old Łukasz – a Pole who, on November 29, 2019, fended off a terrorist attack on passers-by in the streets of London (https://fakty.interia).

It seems that the ability to effectively help those threatened by acts of physical aggression is to a large extent determined by such factors as the awareness of the type and nature of threat being confronted and the prior development of skills relevant to combating it. For example, the military and the police are much more likely to be able to help as they have been trained to respond to such situations (Kałużny and Płaczek, 2011; Kałużny, 2014; Kałużny and Stanek, 2020). In addition to having the requisite knowledge and skills, officers of these services are taught professional ethics that hold it imperative to help others in emergency (Hajduk and Hajduk, 2008, p. 78). Inscribed in the Code of Honor that a Polish professional soldier abides by is that: "[…] he is not indifferent to negative attitudes and actions. He provides help to the needy and acts in defense of the aggrieved" (Kodeks honorowy…, 2008). Hence, defense measures (against physical aggression) declared by candidates for professional military service can be seen as an extremely important object of research. Firstly, because it is a largely unique occupation – a service based on autotelic values embedded in the organization's culture. Secondly, but just as axiologically, because members of the army are constitutionally obliged to act as guarantors of multidimensional security for all population groups making up the country's social system. This would be true not only about the sense of duty inherent in the soldier's profession, but should also be manifest in a natural or internalized need to help people at all times. In the context of issues discussed in this paper, it should be assumed that military universities, besides performing an educational function, are institutions where a certain axio-normative order is inculcated in individuals with a view to forging e.g. altruistic, socially desirable attitudes. At a practical level, these attitudes should be observable in a large variety of real-life situations and result in actions that are not only effective, but also, or above all, righteous.

The question remains whether the behaviors that this paper is focused on, i.e. lines of action chosen in defending against physical violence, can be tested in laboratory conditions and in conformity with scientific standards. The truth is that observation and accurate measurement are practically impossible, given that such measurements should be carried out in a standardized and reproducible environment. Admittedly, it is very difficult to meticulously recreate a situation where defense measures taken against an aggressive attacker, whether in self-defense or in defending another person, are assessed multiple times, each time for a different individual. From the perspective of scientific research methodology, it seems that it is indirect assessments that can best diagnose human behaviors in emergency situations. Thus, any judgments on the actions of individuals, and any quantifications of data to either the class of valorous and righteous or to the class of the dishonorable, are via the interview technique and based on the respondents' inferences about their own actions or the behaviors of people from their environment in specific circumstances. Another method, perhaps even more suitable, would be to evaluate relevant actions through simulation, where specific situations are presented in descriptive form in anonymous questionnaires (Wasyluk, 1998, p. 157). Arguably, the development of simulation research has become an inspiration for scholars, making it possible to examine this difficult but socially vital problem from different angles.

This paper is devoted primarily to learning about the mental predispositions of young people to confront physical aggression – responding to assaults that are, on the one hand, targeted at the respondent or, on the other, at a stranger (another person). Secondarily, it seeks to explore the links between how the respondents react to physical aggression targeted at themselves and others and their previous experience with social activism.

2.2 Theoretical Underpinnings

In the last few decades, an explosive growth of interest in how decisions are made has been combined with an increasing emphasis on researching the issue (cf. e.g. Paradice et al., 2018) and recognition for major contributors (Nobel Prizes awarded to Kahneman and Simon). Research efforts focused on this strand bring together socio-psychologists and decision support specialists sharing the belief that relevant IT solutions must be founded on the observation of practice and must take account of values, ethics, and legal frameworks[1].

Table 2.1 The ethical context in selected decision problems

	Decision problem	*Risk involved*
Ebola Dilemma	Should Dr. Brantley, who has treated Ebola patients in Liberia and contracted this disease, come back to be treated in the US?	Yes. The risk of deaths caused by a potential Ebola outbreak in the United States.
		No. Dr Brantley's chance of surviving in Liberia is extremely low.
Renegade Dilemma	Is it acceptable to shoot down a hijacked passenger plane to prevent terrorists from crashing the plane into a densely populated area?	Yes. The death of people on board the airplane.
		No. The risk of many deaths and considerable damage to property.
Principles that play a central role in research on moral judgment		
DEONTOLOGY		UTILITARIANISM
-the moral status of a behavioral option is derived from its consistency with moral norms		-the moral status of a behavioral option depends on its consequences for overall wellbeing

Source: Own based on Gawronski et al. (2017); Bradshaw (2014).

In today's increasingly diverse societies, ethical decision making is shifting to a central place, highlighting the inclusion of ethical norms as a basis for evaluating and selecting alternatives. Consider, for example, the two decision problems shown in Table 2.1, which are often referred to as the Ebola dilemma and the Renegade dilemma. Each involves a moral choice component that is germane to ethical decision making. Obviously, a number of various value systems can be applied in resolving the dilemma. In the two examples shown at the bottom of Table 2.1, the adoption of utilitarianism as the guiding principle leads to a "no" decision in the Ebola dilemma while yielding a "yes" response to the Renegade dilemma.

What an ethical decision-making process intrinsically entails is the need for a decision support system to embrace values that may not be intelligible or acceptable to it. Clearly, a mature, well-designed decision support system that can accommodate such values must be built around the imperative to act on behalf of the client. The authors' experience indicates, however, that a secondary dilemma might arise where this condition is fulfilled, and time constraints are an important factor in the decision-making process concerning the primary (underlying) dilemma.

Discussing rules governing society, Kenneth E. Boulding (1968) distinguished three mechanisms: threat systems, exchange systems, and integrative systems. In pioneering the Polish school of praxeology, Tadeusz Kotarbiński (1982) differentiated positive cooperation (collaboration) from negative cooperation (rivalry), contrasting these two through the property of compatibility or incompatibility between the goals of the cooperating entities. The history of Poland, a country encumbered with the experience of being stripped of sovereignty, partitioned and occupied, is abundant in commendable instances of negative cooperation. It well may be the reason why so many institutes of the Polish Academy of Sciences, numerous universities, medical and military schools, alongside practitioners and theorists of sports and self-defense throughout the country, have been committed to the study of negative cooperation, traditionally termed as theory of war (agonology)[2]. Agonology provides a conceptual, analytical, and instrumental framework for the study of decision making under threat (there is a significant potential inherent in operations research)[3] (Kałużny and Stanek, 2020).

Agonology is based on a descriptive theory developed by Kotarbiński who used the historical method to review the methods, or stratagems, that effective combatants employ in striving to win (attack) or prevent the opponent from winning (defense). Praxeology is focused on the technical efficiency of combat, taking little interest in the ethical context as long as it does not affect the outcomes of warfare. Some of the stratagems are juxtaposed in Table 2.2.

Most stratagems used in combat situations involve dilemmas related to making a choice between morality and effectiveness. Well aware of such dilemmas, Kotarbiński analyzed relevant

Table 2.2 Some of the stratagems of agonology

Stratagem	Example
Having prevalent resources at the right place and time. Ensuring that your own forces can be easily relocated while restricting the opponents' movements.	Chess. Victory based on a clever deployment of your own forces rather than on outnumbering the opponent.
Exploiting the opponent's functions and resources to your own advantage. It must be borne in mind that your equipment might just as well become the enemy's equipment.	In a dispute, heading toward the opponent's areas of ignorance where they are likely to make gross errors.
Divide and conquer.	A legend inscribed in the history of Rome: the fight of three against three.
Neutralize the opponent's commanders. Make sure your own commanders are replaceable.	David's fight with Goliath.[4] It will suffice to hold back the headwaters of the Nile River to paralyze agriculture in its delta.
Fait accompli tactics.	Unauthorized land development. Capturing and fortifying enemy territory.
Deferment directive.	When in a dispute, be the last one to speak.
Potentialization.	Troops concentrated on the border and ready to invade the area.
Falling back on goals that are shared with the enemy.	An inscription in the Romanian city of Iasi: "Friend, if you take the city, do not destroy this well; remember that its water will be just as useful to you as it is to us."

Source: Based on Kotarbiński (1938, 1982, pp. 221–243).

questions, explored responsibilities, and weighed arguments (Kotarbiński, 1938, pp. 59, 1982, p. 243). The questions included e.g. the following:

- Is it fair to teach dubious artifices and stratagems?
- Those who teach martial arts become indirectly responsible for their potential applications.
- Like any technique, a martial art can be used fairly (righteous behavior) or unfairly abused (dishonorable behavior).
- Righteous people who have learned about stratagems become immune to such methods.

It was in this context and on these assumptions that he founded his original and coherent philosophical concept advocating the real existence of such things only that are directly cognizable (reism), and positing ethics[5] that are independent of religious beliefs, being instead based on the ideal of an active "decent man" – who efficiently pursues decent goals, trying to earn the respect of those around him. He strongly believed that there exists a treasury of ethical truths that have been rationally and empirically proven throughout the history of mankind, and that these now should be exploited by pedagogy. He concluded that any action that causes harm, even if it is efficient or economical, has to be refuted on moral grounds (cf. Sztylka, 2020).[6]

It seems that the ethical norms laid down by Tadeusz Kotarbiński could guide moral reflection across all cultures, ideologies, and religious creeds. Karol Wojtyła (1981), later known as Pope John Paul II, argued that the principles of independent ethics represented by Kotarbiński "are merely the principles and ideals of Christian ethics minus all that relates to God and hence bespeaks their religious nature." A critical and rather comprehensive analysis of Kotarbiński's contributions can be found in the 2019 study by Margaret Fisher (2019). Regretfully, as Polish Socrates and many of his followers published mainly in Polish, a language barrier continues to prevent the international community from discovering and fully appreciating his ideas.

Decision making under threat of physical aggression emerges as a special and important area of agonology applications since, judging by the number of news reports, such threats seem to occur increasingly often. Fair and reasonable self-defense is usually the optimal response to physical violence.[7] In this context, Tadeusz Kotarbiński (1987) recommended that men fight in the defense of themselves and their fellows without hatred and refrain from detriment to the opponent beyond what is necessary to prevail, and that they show generosity to the opponent as soon as the fight is over. The research findings presented further in this paper set off from agonology foundations and address the relationships between praxeological and ethical standards applied to behaviors in either a normative or descriptive context (Smoleń, 2004; Kałużny and Stanek, 2020).

2.3 Methodological Underpinnings

The research involving applicants for military-medical degree programs was carried out in 2019 as part of the enrollment process. The first-year students were surveyed during the basic training period they received at the Wrocław-based University of Land Forces (AWL) in 2018. In both cases, non-probability sampling was used, focusing on prospective officers of the military medical service. The empirical study encompassed 150 individuals who were picked randomly from among 536 applicants. In this sample, 147 questionnaires were eventually qualified as eligible for analysis. The AWL freshmen sample included 116 men who were randomized during their basic

Table 2.3 Characteristics of the respondent groups of military university applicants and students – medical degree

Respondent groups	Gender		Mean age (years)	Prior engagement in social activism	
	F	M		Yes	No
AWL applicants (n = 147)	88	59	19.7	46	101
AWL students (n = 114)	62	52	20.1	28	86
Total, N = 261	150	111	19.9	74	187

training period out of a group of 170 military-medical degree students. Of all the questionnaires completed, 114 were qualified for further processing. The characteristics of the respondent groups are presented in Table 2.3.

The respondents were selected using a combination of random and non-random methods, since the population of upper secondary school graduates was random-sampled across all regions of Poland; at the same time, however, the choice was narrowed down to those upper secondary school graduates who either had applied for admission or effectively enrolled into a military university. Given the approach taken to sampling, the authors will abstain from generalizing their research outcomes to the entire population of upper secondary school leavers. Ideally, any generalizations and conclusions contained in this paper should be deemed applicable, most of all, to youth inclined for military-medical careers.

The central research problem was encompassed in the following general question: *What decisions do the respondents make regarding defense methods when faced with acts of physical violence, whether targeted at themselves or strangers?* In the survey, answers to two specific questions were sought (Table 2.4). It was the authors' intent to validate the research hypotheses via an analysis of the empirical data and the selected variables.

In technical terms, the survey relied on verbal simulation; the reason is that simulation techniques are known to deliver the most likely predictions of what decisions an individual person will make regarding behaviors in difficult and extreme situations while exerting no pressures on the respondents and maintaining a good standard of impartiality and anonymity. In laboratory settings, it is practically impossible to meet certain scientific standards (such as that the key factors underlying the measurement remain consistent throughout the survey, i.e. similar in all instances) in measuring valor, righteous behavior, and dishonorable behavior. It is hardly feasible to reproduce, and do so multiple times, the attack of an aggressive individual along with all factors surrounding it, to the extent that the respondents' effectiveness and ethical profile (valor, righteous behavior, dishonorable behavior, etc.) can be assessed by exposing each of them, one by one, to essentially these same stimuli. Therefore, simulation techniques were considered optimal in assessing the relevant variables (effectiveness, ethics) or, more broadly, in evaluating the outcomes of decision-making processes, i.e. actions undertaken by individuals or groups in response to specific threats.

In collecting empirical data, the K-K'017 anonymous questionnaire was used; it was made up of questions (statements) simulating a variety of situations by providing descriptions of these (Wasyluk, 1998, p. 157). The questionnaire was a modified version of the K-K'98 questionnaire

Table 2.4 Specific research questions

1	When you are the target of a physical assault:
A	you strike back immediately with full force so that the attack is not resumed.
B	you try to restrain the attacker first. If this isn't working, you resort to heavy-handed forms of physical coercion.
C	you don't take any action.
D	you use gentle defense measures, at the same time trying to calm the attacker down.
2	When another person (stranger) is physically assaulted, you will:
A	try to defend the victim within the boundaries of valor.
B	strike back immediately using any available resources.
C	do your best to defend the victim effectively while observing the rules of engagement.
D	not try to defend him/her.

(Kałużny, 2001; Kalina and Kałużny, 2002; Kałużny and Kalina, 2015). The modifications were inspired by conclusions from prior research, chiefly those from a comparative analysis of the findings of two research efforts: the 1999 Kałużny survey of the valor of Polish policemen (Kałużny, 2001) conducted using the KK'98 (Kalina and Kałużny) questionnaire and a similar survey project carried out by Kałużny and Płaczek (Kałużny and Płaczek, 2011).

What remained unchanged relative to the pre-modification version was that the questionnaire had two components. The first one, geared to accomplishing the primary diagnostic purposes, consisted of twelve questions (statements) that are randomly distributed throughout the questionnaire. The questions (statements) described hypothetical situations that likely have happened or could happen to anyone. This paper discusses the findings on the respondents' actions under two simulated threats of physical assault (Table 2.4). The questionnaire included ten more descriptions of hypothetical situations respondents faced or questions probing their attitudes, involving e.g.: an act of physical violence aimed at taking the victim's life; a person about to drown; a group of people to be rescued from an unspecified type and grade of danger; a serious road accident witnessed when hurrying to an important meeting; behavior in combat sports; preferences regarding conflict resolution where a long-lasting effect is a priority; approaches to representing facts in different real-life settings. The second component of the questionnaire included some demographics alongside eight questions addressing the independent variables, including those listed in Table 2.5. Finally, the K-K'017 questionnaire comprised the contact details of the institution responsible for the survey; instructions for respondents on how the questionnaire should be completed; and some information on the aims of the survey and on how the empirical data will be used.

For each of the twelve situations, the respondents were offered four options (alternative courses of action or behaviors) but allowed to select only one; they were instructed to choose the options that best reflected their behavior in the situations described or most closely matched the actions that they were likely to take.

Table 2.5 Research hypotheses and variables

	Research hypotheses
1.	The morality of decisions regarding the defense methods used in the face of a physical assault depends, to a significant extent, on who the assault is targeted at (the respondent vs. a stranger).
2.	Military university applicants do not significantly differ from military university students in their perception of moral decisions in the face of physical aggression.
3.	Gender is a significant factor differentiating the respondents in terms of defense measures chosen.
4.	The respondents' prior engagement in social activism has a significant effect on the choice of defense measures.
	Variables
A	*Dependent variables*: the respondent's declared behavior when facing simulated threats of physical aggression – the morality of decisions made when protecting themselves vs. decisions made when protecting strangers.
B	*Independent variables*: candidates / students, type of degree (medical / command), gender, social activism / social inactivity.

The respondents were supposed to analyze the situation described, assess the intended course of action against their individual predispositions, and indicate (choose) the option that best taps into their experience, knowledge, and skills. Therefore, the decision to act in a particular manner was preceded by a reflection on their responsibility for themselves and others. The outcome of such reflection could therefore be said to reveal the respondents' moral characteristics, as well as their ability to take effective measures in crisis situations, and their confidence in their own agility. By making a specific choice of defense options, the respondents make moral decisions – choices between good and evil. Furthermore, it can be assumed that the behaviors declared in the face of the hypothetical threats are highly indicative of the reactions that the respondents would adopt in real life (Pawłowski, 1978, p. 142; Kalina, 2017).

Using the Delphi technique, three competent referees decomposed diagnostic statements (questions) from the K-K'98 questionnaire and assessed the accuracy of the new statements. The referees affirmed that the relevant criteria were met for all of the twelve simulated situations. An essential modification introduced at this point was shifting from a five-grade (0; 1; 2; 3; 4) to a four-grade scale (0; 1; 2; 3) based on a mix of praxeological and ethical assessment criteria. Options were fine-tuned to make them easy for any researcher familiar with the methodology to align with the following criteria: "effective – ethical (commendable)"; "ineffective – ethical (commendable)"; "effective – unethical (dishonorable)"; "ineffective – unethical (dishonorable)" (Kalina and Barczyński, 2017). The adoption of mixed (praxeological and ethical) criteria for diagnostics on this category of behavior was primarily driven by the commonly perceived brutalization of interpersonal relations.

The use of mixed criteria in assessing human behavior was proposed by Tadeusz Kotarbiński, the founder of modern praxeology. He would attribute the greatest value to those human actions that are not only effective, but that also embody universal humanistic values. Accordingly, in defining "valor," he linked it to values assessed against mixed criteria. Empirical research (using simulation techniques) on this specific aspect of human behavior termed as "valor" was initiated by Roman Maciej Kalina and carried on by Ryszard Kałużny.

To simplify statistical analysis, a unique numerical rating (3; 2; 1; 0, respectively) was assigned to each criterion. Thus, scores assigned to specific courses of action declared by the respondents were to be interpreted as follows: 3 – effective and ethical actions; 2 – ineffective but ethical actions; 1 – effective but unethical actions; 0 – ineffective and unethical actions. Zero points effectively correspond to inaction in the face of a threat since failure to undertake any counter-action is regarded as inappropriate both in terms of effectiveness and ethics. Three points are awarded to ethical behaviors that, at the same time, have good odds for success, and 1 to 2 points represent intermediate evaluations. Actions declared by the respondents were converted into points using a pre-defined coding key. The validation procedure was carried out for the modified K-K'017 questionnaire following its assessment by the competent referees; its reliability was fully confirmed (Kałużny and Kondzior, 2019; Klimczak, 2019).

In analyzing the results, alongside the distribution of response patterns (combined judgments), attention was given to consistency of behaviors and attitudes across the hypothetical situations, i.e. whether similar criteria were met in two simulated situations. Thus, responses declaring "effective – ethical" actions were considered an empirical indicator of "valor." Arguably, actions of individuals can be regarded as valorous if and only if unprovoked by themselves but taken in reaction to a prior attack by an aggressor, and if the countermeasures used are commensurate with the threat encountered (Kałużny, 2018). Declarations of an ethical action in each simulated situation (regardless of effect) were considered empirical tokens of "righteous behavior." This is because a resolve to act in emergency without being mandated to do so by one's professional role does show one as a good, kind, and helpful person, whether or not the intervention was effective (Hajduk and Hajduk, 2008). On the other hand, unethical actions (regardless of effect) were taken to be emblematic of "dishonorable behavior." We thus equated "dishonorable" with unworthy of a human who would meet the minimum conditions of moral recognition (Kotarbiński, 1986). It needs to be emphasized that, in this study, the categories of "valor," "righteous behavior," and "dishonorable behavior" are consistently applied to all of the respondents, across all the constituent groups – whether university applicants or university students, women or men, whether having or not having prior experience with any forms of social activism. Notably, too, the study utilizes statistics capturing relevant distributions and proportions, accounting for the statistical significance of differences – in confidence intervals (0.05 ÷ 0.001) – based on percentage ratios between independent samples.

2.4 Findings

Some 80.4% of all respondents declared behaviors categorized as commendable in simulated situations where physical violence is targeted at themselves, but only 49.8% did so when a similar threat is targeted at another person, opting for behaviors that, albeit compliant with ethical norms, may be effective or not (Table 2.6). Inverse proportions were, as a logical consequence, revealed in declarations of dishonorable behaviors, with 19.6% in case the respondents themselves are threatened by a physical assault, and 50.2% where a similar threat is targeted at a stranger.

Even greater disparities can be noted when it comes to effective and ethical actions, with 42.9% of the respondents choosing such actions where they are themselves targeted by an act of

Table 2.6 Proportions of respondents (N = 261) opting for a specific course of action in two simulations involving a threat of physical aggression

Mixed assessments	Applicants (n=147)		Students (n=114)		Differential	Aggregate (N=261)	
	n	%	n	%	%	n	%
"physical assault on self"							
"effective – ethical"	76	51.7	36	31.6	20.1**	112	42.9
"ineffective – ethical"	41	27.9	57	50.0	22.1***	98	37.5
"effective – unethical"	22	15.0	12	10.5	4.5	34	13.1
"ineffective – unethical"	8	5.4	9	7.9	2.5	17	6.5
"physical assault on another person"							
"effective – ethical"	16	10.9	13	11.4	0.5	29	11.1
"ineffective – ethical"	57	38.8	44	38.6	0.2	101	38.7
"effective – unethical"	71	48.3	51	44.7	3.8	122	46.7
"ineffective – unethical"	3	2.0	6	5.3	3.3	9	3.5

** $p < 0.01$; *** $p < 0.001$.

physical violence, and 11.1% only where aggression is directed at a stranger. Interestingly enough, the percentage of ineffective but ethical behaviors declared was similar for attacks at the respondents themselves and for assaults targeted at a stranger – 37.5% and 38.7%, respectively. Yet, declarations of effective and unethical behaviors were inversely proportional to effective and ethical behaviors (actions) – 13.1% and 46.7%, respectively (cf. Table 2.6).

When looking at the specific samples, that of military university applicants and that of military university students, it could be concluded that, in the event of a physical assault on a stranger, the respondents' choices were roughly similar in both the samples (cf. Table 2.6). No significant disparities were visible in the choice of either righteous or dishonorable options. However, major differences across the breakdown samples can be discovered for the simulated attack on the respondents themselves, albeit for righteous behaviors only. In the latter situation, a statistically significant difference at p<0.01 was revealed for effective and ethical behaviors, whereas for ineffective but ethical responses – at a confidence level p<0.001.

Looking at responses provided by women and men, it is easy to see that the proportions of commendable behaviors are comparable in both the samples as long as the physical assault is targeted at a stranger. Women were slightly more inclined to declare effective and ethical actions, while men were inclined to declare ethical and ineffective ones (Table 2.7). The proportions are similar, too, for behaviors qualified as dishonorable. However, significantly more men (17.2%)

Table 2.7   Proportions of male and female respondents (N = 261) opting for a specific course of action in two simulations involving a threat of physical aggression

Mixed assessments	Women (n=150)		Men (n=111)		Differential	Aggregate (N=261)	
	n	%	n	%	%	n	%
"physical assault on self"							
"effective – ethical"	67	44.7	45	40.5	4.2	112	42.9
"ineffective – ethical"	53	35.3	45	40.5	5.2	98	37.5
"effective – unethical"	15	10.0	19	17.2	7.2	34	13.1
"ineffective – unethical"	15	10.0	2	1.8	8.2	17	6.5
"physical assault on another person"							
"effective – ethical"	19	12.7	10	9.0	3.7	29	11.1
"ineffective – ethical"	48	32.0	53	47.7	15.7*	101	38.7
"effective – unethical"	79	52.7	43	38.7	14.0*	122	46.7
"ineffective – unethical"	4	2.6	5	4.6	2.0	9	3.5

* $p<0.05$

than women (10.0%) favored effective but unethical actions, and, conversely, ineffective and unethical actions were chosen by more women (10.0%) than men (1.8%). Although the differences between women and men advocating dishonorable courses of action might be otherwise important, they are not statistically significant. On the other hand, when facing an incident where others are threatened by a physical assault, more men (56.7%) than women (44.7%) would choose commendable behaviors, and, conversely, more women (55.3%) than men (43.3%) would opt for behaviors categorized as dishonorable. Hence, for commendable – ineffective but ethical – responses, the difference in proportions is 15.7%, while for dishonorable – ineffective and unethical behaviors – it is 14.0%. The differences between women and men shown in this category are statistically significant at a confidence level of $p <0.05$ (Table 2.7).

In exploring the empirical data, the authors also examined the effects of respondents' prior engagement in social activism (Table 2.8). And so, in the face of a physical attack on the respondent, behaviors qualified as commendable were declared by a greater percentage of socially active respondents (87.8%) than of those socially inactive (77.5%). Although the difference is noticeable, it is still within the margin of statistical error. However, the 13.6% difference between socially active and inactive respondents declaring ineffective but ethical actions is statistically significant at $p < 0.05$. Obviously, the percentage of respondents choosing actions qualified as

Table 2.8 Proportions of respondents with varied experience in social activism (N = 261) opting for a specific course of action in two simulations involving a threat of physical aggression

Mixed assessments	Socially active (n = 74)		Socially inactive (n = 187)		Differential	Aggregate (N=261)	
	n	%	n	%	%	n	%
"physical assault on self"							
"effective – ethical"	30	40.5	82	43.8	3.3	112	42.9
"ineffective – ethical"	35	47.3	63	33.7	13.6*	98	37.5
"effective – unethical"	7	9.5	27	14.4	4.9	34	13.1
"ineffective – unethical"	2	2.7	15	8.1	5.4	17	6.5
"physical assault on another person"							
"effective – ethical"	10	13.5	19	10.1	3.4	29	11.1
"ineffective – ethical"	32	43.2	69	36.9	6.3	101	38.7
"effective – unethical"	31	41.9	91	48.7	6.8	122	46.7
"ineffective – unethical"	1	1.4	8	4.3	2.9	9	3.5

* $p < 0.05$.

commendable is in correlation to the percentage of those favoring actions classified as dishonorable. Hence, fewer socially active respondents declared dishonorable actions (12.2%) than those socially inactive (22.5%). Under the threat of a simulated physical attack on a stranger, response options classified as commendable were chosen more often by socially active respondents (56.7%) than by those socially inactive (47.0%). Of course, inverse proportions were seen for dishonorable behaviors, with 43.3% of socially active respondents and 53.0% of socially inactive respondents opting for these. On the other hand, there were no noticeable differences for response options classified into specific categories (commendable – dishonorable) between socially active and inactive respondents (Table 2.8).

What was also analyzed across the empirical data available is the stability, or consistency, of respondents' choices regarding their behavior under both the variants of physical threat. Based on the criteria adopted, it can be stated that 5.4% of military university applicants for the medical program and military university students in this same program could be described as valorous people (Table 2.9). More such people were found in the applicants sample than in the students

Table 2.9 **Proportions of respondents (N = 261) whose actions are emblematic of "valor", "righteous behavior", and "dishonorable behavior"**

Mixed assessments	Applicants (n=147)		Students (n=114)		Differential	Aggregate (N=261)	
	n	%	n	%	%	n	%
"valor"							
"effective – ethical"	9	6.1	5	4.3	1.8	14	5.4
"righteous behavior"							
"ethical – effective, ineffective"	61	41.5	53	46.5	5.0	114	43.7
"dishonorable behavior"							
"unethical – effective, ineffective"	18	12.2	17	14.9	2.7	35	13.4

sample. At the same time, the analysis revealed 43.7% of individuals advocating righteous be-haviors – ethical responses, whether effective or not, under both the simulated threats of physical aggression. The righteousness criteria were met by more students than applicants. What may be disconcerting, though, is that, overall, more than 13% of upper secondary school leavers headed for the career of Polish Army physician and officer favored officer-favored courses of action that were classified as dishonorable, i.e. unethical, with a slightly greater proportion of such choices in the students sample than in the applicants sample. However, none of the differences between applicants and students represents a statistically significant feature.

Looking at the declarations of women and men from the angle of the stability, it could be concluded that a greater proportion of women (7.3%) than men (2.7%) would be described as valorous people (Table 2.10). On the other hand, the proportion of respondents qualifying as righteous was 47.7% in the men sample and 40.7% in the women sample. A larger percentage of women (16.0%) than men (10.0%) favored dishonorable behaviors. The differences between the samples are not, however, statistically significant.

Through comparing the proportions of socially active and inactive respondents (Table 2.11), a conclusion could be drawn that more people exhibiting the empirical characteristics of valor were found in the sample of socially active respondents (6.6%). Further, those meeting the criteria of righteousness were diagnosed more frequently among the socially active (51.4%) than among those inactive (40.6%). Conversely, there were fewer individuals eligible for the dishonorable label in the sample of socially active respondents – 6.8% – than in the socially inactive sample – 16.1%. Wide as they might appear at first, the disproportions between the samples in specific classes of behavior (righteous behavior; dishonorable behavior) remain within the boundaries of statistical error.

Table 2.10 Proportions of women and men (N=261) whose actions are emblematic of "valor", "righteous behavior", and "dishonorable behavior"

Mixed assessments	Women (n=150)		Men (n=111)		Differential	Aggregate (N=261)	
	n	%	n	%	%	n	%
"valor"							
"effective – ethical"	11	7.3	3	2.7	4.6	14	5.4
"righteous behavior"							
"ethical – effective, ineffective"	61	40.7	53	47.7	7.0	114	43.7
"dishonorable behavior"							
"unethical – effective, ineffective"	24	16.0	11	10.0	6.0	35	13.4

Table 2.11 Proportions of respondents having and not having prior experience with social activism (N=261) whose actions are emblematic of "valor", "righteous behavior", and "dishonorable behavior"

Mixed assessments	Engaged in social activism (n=74)		Not engaged in social activism (n=187)		Differential	Aggregate (N=261)	
	n	%	n	%	%	n	%
"valor"							
"effective – ethical"	5	6.6	9	4.8	1.8	14	5.4
"righteous behavior"							
"ethical – effective, ineffective"	38	51.4	76	40.6	10.8	114	43.7
"dishonorable behavior"							
"unethical – effective, ineffective"	5	6.8	30	16.1	9.3	35	13.4

2.5 Practical Applications

The aim of the study, as outlined in the introduction, implies placing the analysis of the authors' research outcomes in the context of their practical applications. The empirical data discussed in this paper form part of the findings of a research project conducted among the students and applicants of the Military University of Land Forces (AWL). By this token, they involve youth intending to pursue professional careers in the Polish military. On the other hand, jobs, such as those performed by army officers and officers of other uniformed services, involve discipline, loyalty and dedication. This is the message stemming from the Rota – the oath taken by the military, as well as from the Polish Army officer's oath, the Polish Professional Soldiers' Code of Honour, and from other normative acts. It was therefore the word "dedication," being at the heart of the fundamental virtues of a soldier (such as valor, sacrifice, responsibility, dignity, courage, and prudence), that was adopted as the semantic key to the discussion over the outcomes of this research.

Once these acts, and the moral-ethical principles that they prescribe, are seen as the cultural DNA of a relatively closed, formalized, and hierarchical organization, it becomes clear that moral behaviors in this professional group will be of a more overtly descriptive nature than is the case with other, less uniform social groups. For the sake of this discussion and analysis, it was also assumed that applicants for a military degree, as well as military university students undergoing their basic training (about a month of service), are characterized by a distinctive set of values distinguishing them from e.g. cadets[8] in senior years at university. This means that the empirical data being analyzed in this study are indicative of their propensity to act (behave) in ways developed in a nonmilitary environment; the effectiveness of their actions and their moral values having been shaped through primary and secondary socialization, and influenced by factors inherent in family, school, and social organizations (Asbury and Plomin, 2014).

The empirical data show that in the face of physical aggression the morality of the respondents' course of reaction depends on who that assault is targeted at. When the respondents themselves are at risk, more than 80% of them will choose countermeasures that are commendable from an ethical standpoint, while less than 20% of them will make a decision to act in ways that, even based on intuition, can hardly be held as ethical. However, where the assault is targeted at another person (a stranger), the respondents' reactions will be significantly different: the ethical options are preferred by less than 50%. Consequently, a similar percentage of the respondents declare reactions that are not socially desirable. There were significant differences at the confidence level $p<0.001$ between the proportions of respondents opting for commendable behaviors in defense of themselves and those declaring commendable behaviors when others are to be rescued. Thus, the hypothesis positing that the morality of decisions depends on the target of aggression (the respondents themselves vs. strangers) has been proven to be right. Not very optimistically, the shift in decisions toward less ethical choices is also observed among those seeking careers in the officer corps of the Polish Army's medical service.

The question could be raised, therefore, how military university applicants and military university students should be evaluated relative to the respondent population as a whole. As a matter of fact, the proportions of those declaring commendable reactions based on valid ethics and those favoring dishonorable behaviors – wrong, despicable and unworthy of a human being – are very similar among the students and applicants groups, with a negligible differential between self-defense and defense of another. Hence, the hypothesis that there is hardly a moral divide between decisions made by military university applicants and military university students is supported by empirical data. Given the fact that the students were at an initial stage of their training when the survey was conducted, it should not be expected that the military university will have had a substantial effect on their mentality. However, the absence of any demonstrable differences between the moral attitudes of students and applicants might indicate that ethical aptitude is not given enough attention in the recruitment process.

In comparing the responses of women and men faced with a physical assault targeted at themselves, no major differences in terms of morality of their decisions have been ascertained. What distinguishes women's reactions from those of men is inaction declared by as much as 10% of the women surveyed, indicative of helplessness that cannot be regarded as commendable when exhibited by persons seeking careers as a military doctor and officer. Daniel Goleman (2018) contends that a propensity for such behavior in candidates for military service poses a danger to their health and may be detrimental to their military career prospects because helplessness in emergency situations plays a decisive role in the formation of post-traumatic shock.

When confronted with a physical attack on a stranger, approximately 45% of women and 57% of men would take a commendable action driven by moral principles. As far the decisions of women and men and their moral assessment are concerned, then, the authors' hypothesis has been partially confirmed since the only statistically significant difference between women and men is the one concerning ineffective but ethical actions taken in defense of a stranger. It should be noted here that the decisions of women seeking medical careers in the military differ from those made by women seeking service as military officers/commanders (cf. Kałużny and Stanek, 2020).

Based on the empirical data, it is easy to see that experience with social activism is the independent variable that most influences the morality of decisions made in the face of danger. When confronted with an aggressive attacker, respondents having such experience are more likely to take commendable actions than socially inactive respondents, whether in self-defense or in defense of another person. Although socially active respondents prevail among those favoring action over inaction in the face of a physical assault, the hypothesis proposing a statistically significant difference has not been fully confirmed. Nonetheless, the survey data seem to provide sufficient evidence that social engagement, and the resulting experience of helping others, may be an accurate predictor of effective and ethical behavior; behavior that manifests in initiatives fuelled by sensitivity to the needs of others and a sense of responsibility for everyone around them, including but not limited to reacting to physical aggression (Kałużny, 2020, pp. 116–118). The positive effects of social activism on the formation of young individuals can be traced back to the fact that in undertaking an activity, a person unveils certain traits of character stemming from education, culture, environment, and hereditary factors (Asbury and Plomin, 2014), while the activity itself reinforces and refines existing talents and abilities.

The effectiveness and, even more so, moralness of measures decided under the threat of physical aggression, under the pressure of time, and under the constraints of one's own physique and moral powers, is accurately judged through the categories of stability/consistency (valor, righteous behavior, dishonorable behavior). In resolving to follow a specific course of action, consistent across all simulated threats, the respondent makes a conscious moral choice – a choice between good and evil. As is often the case, goodness is the perfect motivator for human moral behavior, helping people realize intrinsic virtues and allowing them to perform acts of unsurpassed moral beauty.

A fine exemplification of defensive combat, a method of counteracting physical aggression that has been socially accepted for centuries, is offered by Jarosław Rudniański in his analysis of the biblical story of David and Goliath (Rudniański, 1989, pp. 141–145). As David was facing Goliath – a dreadful Philistine warrior – it was clear to him that he had to win. He had to, because the outcome would decide fate of the entire people of Israel and the lives of many warriors who were too afraid to fight Goliath. The Philistine, on the other hand, obviously wanted to win, but did not have to, not in the sense that David had to win. The difference may seem minor in psychological terms, but it was actually very significant. Goliath was not only very tall and very strong, he was also, as acknowledged by the records, an experienced and skillful warrior who had prevailed in many battles. Seeing David in front of him – a scene portrayed by Michelangelo several thousand years later – he was sure of his victory and slandered David (Scripture…, 17, 9–17). He thus made a fundamental mistake: overconfident in his height and physical strength, he underestimated his opponent. The enemy was naked and almost defenseless, with only a slingshot in his hand and a shepherd's bag over his shoulder containing smooth stones. All that he had was that weapon alone, but he was a master in using it. He knew he could not allow close combat – he would have died, crushed by Goliath's muscles. He could not afford, either, to hurt Goliath without overpowering him, as a wounded giant would be just as dangerous and he would not withstand him.

Thus, Goliath had to be overcome sooner than he could capture David. Goliath's uncommon height – the distinctive feature that his opponents would fear so much and that had given him an advantage in many battles – now led to his defeat. It is much more difficult to hit a short and slender man's forehead with a slingshot stone than that of a tall and massive warrior. They stood facing each other, David choosing the only place that he could strike and win the fight at once. Seemingly, he made a risky decision, as it is easier to hit the chest or stomach than the forehead. In fact, he had no choice, for Goliath wore a scale armor, and he knew that if he did not knock Goliath down on first attempt, he might not have a second chance. And even if he got a second shot, the opponent, if hit anywhere else, would not keep standing up with a forehead open to slingshot stones – the surprise factor would not work any longer. Overall, then, David was not in a worse position than Goliath, because he had contemplated his actions very carefully beforehand. What reduced the risk considerably was his mastery of the slingshot. He did not let the opponent's superior physical strength come into play, and instead, made Goliath's mighty posture into a disadvantage. Finally, when he stood over the powerless enemy, David killed him with his own sword (Kałużny, 2018).

The David-Goliath analysis allows an insight into how effectiveness and morality, the two criteria embraced in the definition of valor, come together to win David an edge over his opponent. When both the conditions are fulfilled, the goals of defensive combat can be best achieved. The Old Testament books are rich in records of David's fitness and preparedness for mortal combat and for resolving matters of life and death. For example, even before fighting Goliath, David told King Saul, "Your servant was feeding his father's sheep, and it happened that a lion or a bear came and took a lamb from the sheep. Then I ran after him, beat him and snatched them from his mouth, if he attacked me, I would grab him by the mane, beat him and kill him" (Holy Scripture…, 17, 34–35). Yet, when the critical moment came for him, as well as for the people of Israel, he was able to make the right choice and stand for the good cause. In addition to physical fitness, he also demonstrated mental resilience, as he did not seek revenge or take pleasure in defeating Goliath, but he took responsibility for the people of Israel and for other warriors.

Obviously enough, respondents seeking careers in the military-medical service cannot be expected to show the same levels of valor as the biblical hero did. However, social expectations regarding their moral standards are much higher than below 44% of decisions to engage in righteous defense and just above 13% of decisions in favor of dishonorable behavior. It could be hoped that, by encompassing the praxeological and ethical facets in the investigation of the empirical data and by including applicants alongside students of a military university in the research, attention has been brought to issues vital to today's society. While it is true that the survey only covered young people and a single military university, the conclusions can be, admittedly, of much wider relevance and just as applicable to people seeking careers in social services or security services. Given the impact that high emotions evoked by dangers and emergencies will make on people's decisions – an excuse most often given for the choice of dishonorable behavior – it well may be well-established moral values that are the only string we can play to resist this impact.

A famous social psychology experiment known as the Stanford Prison Experiment was designed to observe the behavior of student volunteers who were randomly assigned to play the role of prisoner or guard. The team, led by Philip Zimbardo, selected 24 out of 70 candidates from the USA and Canada, having carefully examined them for emotional balance. The experiment, originally scheduled to last two weeks, was terminated on the sixth day due to its detrimental psychological effect on the prisoners. Students playing the role of guards turned evil and began to act like ruthless sadists, while students-prisoners embodied pathologically passive victims (Zimbardo, 2007). During the experiment, dramatic changes occurred in almost every aspect of the students' actions, thinking, and feelings. Human values were suspended, self-esteem was undermined, and the ugliest and darkest side of human nature came to light. Some guards treated the "imprisoned" ones like inferior animals and took delight in being cruel. At the same time, some of the "prisoners" became servile, dehumanized robots, able to think of nothing but escape, survival, and growing hatred for the guards (Aronson, 2018).

Similar to many other research findings of social sciences, notably analyses of the changes of character occurring in people trapped in a melting pot of situational factors, the Stanford Prison Experiment highlights the fact that humans may be capable of any behavior if subjected to overwhelming pressures. Social psychology has accumulated a lot of evidence to support the thesis that, in certain circumstances, situational influences prevail over reason and personal dispositions (Zimbardo, 2007). In April 2004, the media circulated information and photos taken by US soldiers – guards at Abu Ghraib Prison in Iraq – documenting the physical and mental abuses committed by the soldiers (Dougherty and Ghareeb, 2013). The photos showed punching, slapping, and kicking the arrested, [...]; forcing naked prisoners to wear women's underwear over their heads; forcing male prisoners to masturbate [...] while photographing and recording them with cameras, with smiling and encouraging women (soldiers); wandering prisoners on the ground with a leash around their necks and other shameful activities (Zimbardo, 2007). What is perhaps most upsetting about such accounts is seeing how easily most people enter into a role that requires cruelty, or at least moral blindness, if only that role is backed and legitimized by a supreme authority.

2.6 Conclusions

To better address support for decisions involving a response to physical aggression, it is necessary to further knowledge about the sociological, ethical, and moral factors involved. The theoretical foundation for this type of research is provided by agonology initiated by the Polish School of Praxeology. In most cases, righteous self-defense is the best approach to counteracting physical aggression. The authors' hypotheses have been validated and largely confirmed by the findings of their survey-based research discussed in this paper. Other conclusions from the survey are as follows (Kałużny and Stanek, 2020):

- Decision making on effective and ethical courses of action when under the threat of physical violence is conditional on who is targeted by the act of violence (the respondents themselves, or the "alien other").
- In the selection process for the medical faculty of a military university, it is advisable to place applicants' ethical merit over physical ability.
- In making a decision to react to physical aggression, females' emotional attitudes are more diverse, but they are, in percentage terms, more likely than men to take actions emblematic of valor.
- Social activism among youth (at upper secondary school level) is an important factor shaping their moral beliefs and value systems; therefore, it should be included in the selections criteria for military university applicants.
- More than 46% of first-year military university students exhibit ethical behavior. Hence, with the former group, the educational process should ideally be focused on reinforcing their natural aptitude, while with the latter, it should concentrate on developing and consolidating their ethical merit.
- For students, the tertiary study environment should be where they acquire or boost the desirable traits of character. Psychologists argue that certain environmental variables can elicit, constrain, or modify certain behaviors regardless of innate predispositions (Zimbardo and Ruch, 1997).
- To assess the effects of a five-year-long instruction process at a military university on the formation of graduates' physical and ethical aptitude, longitudinal research focusing on this strand is advised.

Recommendation that presents itself on trying to generalize the research findings and the observations of people transforming under the influence of external factors, could be that of giving more attention to moral value systems in recruiting candidates for uniformed services; this would mean that their moral profiles are examined on equal terms with physical strength and agility, intellectual abilities, and mental health. Although candidates join these services voluntarily, they cannot choose if and when tough challenges occur during their years of service. Those who to be effective when confronting an opponent who treats moral norms instrumentally, there are those who will be tempted to reciprocate applying similar unethical measures. People with strong moral beliefs and ingrained values, such as goodness, righteousness, benevolence, dignity, etc., might be, however, able resist to neutralize situational factors and control their emotions enough to observe relevant ethical norms. The authors are more than willing to further engage in research and cooperation in this area.

Notes

1. Cf. the debate around Arnold Kaufmann's book *The Science of Decision Making: An Introduction to Praxeology*, McGraw-Hill, 1968.
2. Notably, modern war doctrines are largely indebted to such early theories as that of Clausewitz (USA) or Sun Tzu (China).
3. The origins of agonology date back to 1938 as the Polish Army's General Staff commissioned Professor Tadeusz Kotarbiński to develop the theoretical foundations for warfare. Among other scholars that ought to be merited for substantial contribution to agonology is Professor Jarosław Rudniański, prisoner of the Soviet Gulag, veteran of Anders' Army (Polish Armed Forces in the East), and member of the Solidarity movement.

4. Discussed at length further in the paper.
5. He understood ethics, in its broad sense, as a wealth of life's wisdom.
6. His personality traits, rigid moral principles, and significant scientific contribution – still relevant and waiting to be discovered – has earned him the nickname of Polish Socrates.
7. Cf. e.g. https://www.bbc.com/news/uk-50870309.
8. The traditional designation of students in higher military education.

References

Aronson, E. (2018). *The Social Animal* (12th edn.). New York: Worth Publishing.

Aronson, E., Wilson, T.D., & Akert, R.M. (1994). *Social Psychology: The Heart and the Mind.* New York: Harper Collins College Publishers.

Asbury, K., & Plomin, R. (2014). *G is for Genes: The Impact of Genetics on Education and Achievement.* New York: John Wiley & Sons, Inc.

Boulding, K. (1968). *Beyond Economics, Essays on Society, Religion and Ethics.* Ann Arbor: The University of Michigan Press.

Bradshaw, R. (2014, April). Hijacked planes and the doctrine of necessity. *The Student Journal of Law* (6) (see https://sites.google.com/site/349924e64e68f035/issue-6).

Dougherty, B.K., & Ghareeb, E.A. (2013). *Historical Dictionary of Iraq.* Lanham: Scarecrow Press.

Fisher, M.W. (2019). Contrasting approaches to conflict. In R.A. Falk & S.S. Kim (Eds.). *The War System: An Interdisciplinary Approach.* London, New York: Routledge, Taylor St Francis Group. ISBN-13: 978-0367312589.

Gawronski, B., Armstrong, J., Convey, P., Friesdorf, R., & Hütter, M. (2017). Consequences, norms, and generalized inaction in moral dilemmas: The CNI model of moral decision-making. *Journal of Personality and Social Psychology 113*(3), 343–376.

Goleman, D. (2018). *Emotional Intelligence: Why It Can Matter More Than IQ.* London: Bloomsbury.

Hajduk, B., & Hajduk, E. (2008). O pomocy skutecznej i nieskutecznej. Wyd. Uniwersytetu Zielonogórskiego. https://fakty.interia.pl/swiat/news-brytyjskie-media-ujawniaja-nowe-szczegoly-na-temat-czynow (accessed January 18, 2021).

Kalina, R.M. (2017). Multidimensional tests as a fundamental diagnostic tool in the prophylactic and therapeutic agonology – the methodological basis of personal safety (Part II: motor and psychomotor multidimensional tests). *Archives of Budo Science of Martial Arts and Extreme Sports 13*, 191–201. http://archbudo.com

Kalina, R.M., & Barczyński, B.J. (2017). Mixed assessments as mental and pedagogic basis of innovative self-defence. *Archives of Budo 13*, 187–194. http://archbudo.com

Kalina, R.M., & Kałużny, R. (2002). Działanie człowieka w sytuacjach zagrożeń. Wyd. Naukowe Novum.

Kałużny, R. (2001). Wykształcenie i nabyte doświadczenia jako kryterium przewidywania sposobów działań człowieka w sytuacjach zagrożeń. [Unpublished doctoral dissertation]. Uniwersytet Opolski.

Kałużny, R. (2014). Idea dzielności w służbie funkcjonariuszy grup dyspozycyjno-mundurowych. In P. Bogdalski, D. Bukowiecka, R. Częścik & B. Zdrodowski (Eds.). *Grupy dyspozycyjne społeczeństwa w świetle potrzeb bezpieczeństwa państwa.* Vol. 1. Szczytno: Wyd. Wyższej Szkoły Policji w Szczytnie, 217–231.

Kałużny, R. (2018). The man's courage and valour in the biblical and contemporary Times. *Scientific Journal of the Military University of Land Forces 4*, 17–29. doi: 10.5604/01.3001.0013.0719

Kałużny, R. (2020). Działania człowieka w sytuacjach zagrożeń zewnętrznych innych ludzi. Wyd. Akademii Wojsk Lądowych.

Kałużny, R., & Kalina, G. (2015). Change of the actions declared in simulated situations involving interpersonal aggression. *Archives of Budo Science of Martial Arts and Extreme Sports 11*, 221–228. http://archbudo.com

Kałużny, R., & Kondzior, E. (2019). Reliability of the KK'017 questionnaire – test-retest military cadets. *Archives of Budo Science of Martial Arts and Extreme Sports 15*, 9–16. http://archbudo.com

Kałużny, R., & Płaczek, A. (2011). "Declared bravery" of Polish police officers (comparative studies of 1998 and 2010). *Archives of Budo 7*(4), 247–253. http://archbudo.com

Kałużny, R., & Stanek S. (2020). Some ethical and moral aspects of decision making in the light of research on physical aggression. *Journal of Decision Systems*. doi: 10.1080/12460125.2020.1848376

Klimczak, J. (2019). Reliability of the KK'017 questionnaire – test-retest female students of tourism and recreation. *Archives of Budo Science of Martial Arts and Extreme Sports 15*, 113–118. http://archbudo.com

Kodeks honorowy żołnierza zawodowego Wojska Polskiego. Wyd. MON, 2008.

Kotarbiński, T. (1938). Z zagadnień ogólnej teorii walki. Wyd. Towarzystwo Wiedzy Wojskowej.

Kotarbiński, T. (1982). Traktat o dobrej robocie. Zakład Narodowy im. Ossolińskich.

Kotarbiński, T. (1986) Medytacje o życiu godziwym. Wyd. Wiedza Powszechna.

Kotarbiński, T. (1987). Pisma etyczne. Zakład Narodowy im. Ossolińskich.

Paradice, D., Freeman, D., Hao, J., Lee J., & Hall, D. (2018). A review of ethical issue considerations in the information systems research literature. *Information Systems 2*(2), 117–236.

Pawłowski, T. (1978). *Tworzenie pojęć i definiowanie w naukach humanistycznych*. Warszawa: Państwowe Wyd. Naukowe.

Pismo Święte Starego i Nowego Testamentu. (1986). Brytyjskie i Zagraniczne Towarzystwo Biblijne.

Rudniański, J. (1989). *Kompromis i walka*. Warszawa: Instytut Wydawniczy Pax.

Smoleń, A. (2004). Prakseologia a etyka walki sportowej: dychotomia czy harmonia? Idō - Ruch dla Kultury: rocznik naukowy: [filozofia, nauka, tradycje wschodu, kultura, zdrowie, edukacja]

Szacka, B. (2008). *Wprowadzenie do socjologii*. Warszawa: Wyd. Oficyna Naukowa.

Sztylka, A. (2020). Etyka – pedagogika – prakseologia: refleksja z myśli Tadeusza Kotarbińskiego, [w:]. In S. Sztobryn & K. Dworakowska (Eds). *Wielogłos w myśli o wychowaniu. 100 lat polskiej pedagogiki filozoficznej*. Warszawa: Wydawnictwo Uniwersytetu Warszawskiego. ISBN 978-8e3-235-4262-9.

Wasyluk, J. (1998). *Podręcznik dydaktyki medycznej*. Warszawa: Wyd. Fundacja Rozwoju Kształcenia Medycznego.

Wojtyła, K. (1981). *Elementarz etyczny*. Wyd. Towarzystwo Naukowe Katolickiego Uniwersytetu Lubelskiego.

Zimbardo, P.G. (2007). *The Lucifer Effect: How Good People Turn Evil? By Philip Zimbardo*. New York: Random House.

Zimbardo, P.G., & Ruch F.L. (1997). *Psychology and life*. Glenview: Scott, Foresman and Company, Illinois, United States of America.

ORGANISATIONAL PERSPECTIVE OF DECISION MAKING

ORGANISATIONAL
PERSPECTIVE OF
DECISION MAKING

Chapter 3

Maturity Evaluation in Construction Companies Based on Case Study Research and Fuzzy Set Theory

Agata Klaus-Rosińska and Joanna Iwko

Department of Management Systems and Organizational Development, Faculty of Management, Wroclaw University of Science and Technology, Wroclaw, Poland

Contents

DOI: 10.1201/9781003030966-5

3.1 Introduction

In the literature on the subject, the term "maturity model" is often found, which allows an organization to assess and compare its own practices with the best practices on the market to identify areas and directions for improvement. Maturity models are designed to assess the company's ability to effectively manage projects to increase the likelihood of repeated success. Each organization should systematically improve project maturity because the higher the maturity in project management, the greater the chance of project success. In addition, the company's success is associated with the growing level of project maturity, which is a condition for successful project management. This seems particularly important for construction companies. Based on the literature research, it was found that many references dealing with project management maturity were developed, based mostly on quantitative research. Qualitative research is very rarely used in research on the project maturity, especially in construction companies. Therefore, the aim of the article is to research a model of project maturity in construction companies with the use of qualitative research strategy and fuzzy numbers. The authors used a single holistic case study in their research strategy. The authors chose a large international construction company for the research because it was assumed that in a large, international company, project maturity would be significant, and the interviewed respondent would be familiar with the nomenclature of project management and able to answer each maturity measure. This is important for testing the model. To gather information, the authors used interviews, document analysis, and audiovisual materials. The authors collected data based on a prepared case study protocol (questionnaire), using a specific project maturity model that was developed by S. Spałek (Spałek, 2013; Spałek, 2015), according to which the project maturity of an organization was assessed in four areas: methods and tools, human resources, the project environment, and project knowledge management. The project maturity model proposed by the article authors aims to assess the project maturity in construction companies, in which the company's project maturity has linguistic value. The study is descriptive and exploratory. The research methods used in the study include critical analysis of the subject literature and logical reasoning. The model proposed by the authors was used to study and assess the level of project maturity in a selected construction company. The use of this model indicated areas for the company to improve in project management so that it will be able to increase the likelihood of project success. Generally, models of project maturity and their use can be a base of information for the needs of making decisions in the field, including: what can the company do to improve its operations? to develop? to implement projects more efficiently and effectively? to improve processes to get higher level of project maturity? Project maturity models can be therefore part of a company's decision support system (DSS).

Figure 3.1 presents the research steps carried out by the authors of the paper (Klaus-Rosińska and Iwko, 2020).

3.2 Review of the Literature on Project Maturity

The concept of "maturity" is often used to describe the state of an organization's effectiveness (Crawford, 2006). Maturity can refer to a state where the organization is in a perfect condition to achieve its objectives. The maturity can be understood as the ability of the organization or/and its processes to improve and thus to achieve better results (De Bruin and Rosemann, 2005). In general usage, "maturity" means fully developed or perfected; it is used in the term "maturity model" (Cooke-Davies, 2004). A maturity model allows an organization to assess and compare its own practices against best practices or those employed by competitors. Project maturity can also

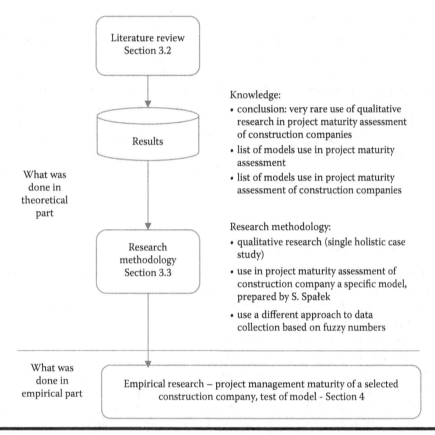

Figure 3.1 Research steps taken by the authors for the purposes of this paper.

Source: Own work.

mean that the organization is perfectly conditioned to deal with its projects (Andersen and Jessen, 2003). Maturity in project management is the position in which the company finds itself regarding the project management processes. Based on this position, maturity models seek to quantify a company's ability to manage projects successfully (Pretorius et al., 2012). Maturity in project management[1] is the implementation of a standard methodology and accompanying processes such that there exists a high likelihood of repeated successes (Kerzner, 2001). Most of the project management maturity models are based on the concept that organizations advance through five stages to maturity; these stages define an ordinal scale for measuring the maturity of an organization's process and evaluating its process capability. The levels also help an organization prioritize its improvement efforts (Cooke-Davies and Arzymanowc, 2003).

There are some results from measuring project maturity within different branches of business; for example, in construction (Klaus-Rosińska and Kuchta, 2016) and engineering companies (Pretorius et al., 2012), in petrochemical and defence industries (Cooke-Davies and Arzymanowc, 2003), and in healthcare (Gomes et al., 2016) or in science (Klaus-Rosińska, 2016). Each organization should systematically improve their project maturity because the higher the maturity in project management, the greater the chance of project success. This thesis has been confirmed in the literature on the subject many times (Haffer, 2013). Moreover, a company's success is connected with an increasing level of project maturity as a condition for a successful project management (Górecki, 2015). Some research indicates a linkage of the benefits of a high level of project management maturity to the degree of complexity of the projects undertaken by industrial enterprises (Albrecht and Spang, 2014). This seems to be particularly important for construction companies. For the purposes of the research, a literature review was carried out to determine the state of knowledge in the area of using qualitative research in the maturity of project management, with particular emphasis on construction companies. Based on this review, it can be concluded that there are many references to the maturity of project management in the literature on the subject. Many of them have been developed mainly on the basis of quantitative research (Górecki, 2015; Spałek and Wolny, 2017; Lianyinga et al., 2012). Only a few cases describe the use of qualitative research to assess the maturity of projects. Taking into account the above information, the authors of this article attempted to use qualitative research in the study of project maturity in construction companies.

3.3 Research Methodology

This section describes the methodology of the empirical research conducted in the context of measuring the project maturity of a selected construction company. The research was qualitative; the research model was the model developed by S. Spałek, with a different approach to collecting data using fuzzy numbers.

As part of **qualitative research**, frequently used strategies are (Creswell, 2013; Czakon, 2011): ethnography, grounded theory, case studies, phenomenological research, and narrative research. For the purpose of research about project maturity in construction companies, a qualitative research strategy was applied – **case studies.** Case study models proposed by R. K. Yin are: single holistic case study, multiple holistic case study, single embedded case study, multiple embedded case study (Yin, 2015). Single and multiple case studies represent different variants of the "case study model" in which it is possible to have one or several units of analysis. A "single case study" is a case study organized around one case. When the case study deals only with the global character (e.g. organization), we deal with a "holistic case study". As part of the qualitative research strategy, one case study model was used – a single holistic case study, where the unit of analysis is a selected construction company in Poland. The authors used a single holistic case study in their research strategy and chose a large international construction company for the research because it was assumed that in a large, international company, project maturity would be significant, and the interviewed respondent would be familiar with the nomenclature of project management and able to answer each maturity measure. This is important for testing the model (see Section 3.1).

Methods that were used to gather information about project maturity in a selected construction company are typical for qualitative research; they include (Creswell, 2013; Czakon, 2011):

- interviews (face-to-face interviews, telephone interviews, focused interview). Interviews will be conducted with people who are responsible for managing construction projects,
- document analysis (public documents such as newspapers, documents of companies such as internal regulations, statutes, procedures),
- audiovisual materials (photographs, video recordings).

The interview had a structured form in which the questions were prepared in advance and were asked to the respondent in a predetermined order (Czakon, 2011). This approach was in line with the recommendation of R.K. Yin according to which, in preparation for data collection, it is important to develop a case study protocol (questionnaire). This is the basic way of increasing the reliability of research, which provides the researcher with tips (Yin, 2015). For the needs of the interview, the case study protocol (questionnaire) was prepared based on specific project maturity model (see Section 3.1). This model was developed by S. Spałek (Spałek, 2013), according to whom the organization's project maturity should be assessed in the context of different areas. The most often assessed areas are: methods and tools, human resources, and organizational context (project environment). The model's author suggests introducing an additional area – project knowledge management. Within individual areas, measures of project maturity are identified, which are the basis for assessment. The structure of the model developed by S. Spałek in empirical research was retained; what was different includes the following: the method of data collection (through qualitative research – interviews, not quantitative – surveys), respondents assessed measures using linguistic expressions (that's why fuzzy numbers were needed), project maturity of construction companies had linguistic not numeric value.

The authors decided to choose the model mentioned above because the role of knowledge management in the project management area is constantly growing (Holzmann, 2013, Bassi and Handzic, 2017). They did not develop a completely new model because it is recommended to use universal models to assess project maturity in various industries; this is evidenced by the works carried out for many years by specialists such as J. K. Crawford (Crawford, 2006) and H. Kerzner (Kerzner, 2001), or conducted literature research (Section 3.2).

3.4 Research About the Model of Project Maturity in a Selected Construction Company

This chapter describes the model used to assess the maturity of a selected construction company. Section 3.1 presents the model itself and explains how to perform a maturity assessment with its use, and section 3.2 describes the company that became the basis for the "single holistic case study" and the results of its project maturity assessment.

3.4.1 General Overview About Project Maturity Model Used in Research

Project maturity was measured in four areas based on specific measures. The respondent (who rated the measures, thus assessing the project maturity) was a person managing construction projects. In this case, this person was the president of the board. The company, which implements construction projects, had a project maturity that resulted in assessing the project maturity in four individual areas A_j, $j = 1, ..., m$ where $m = 4$. The project maturity model is shown in Figure 3.2.

To assess project maturity, one construction company was selected, which is represented by respondent R_1. This respondent assessed maturity in the indicated areas of maturity: area 1 – methods and tools, area 2 – human resources, area 3 – project environment, area 4 – project knowledge management based on specific measures. Examples of measures are entered in Table 3.2. The full set of measures results from the model developed by S. Spałek (Spałek, 2013). The set of these measures in areas A_i will be designated as $S_i = \left\{ S_j^i \right\}_{j=1}^{n_i}$. $M(A_i)$ is a function of S_i with linguistic values. The project maturity of the individual areas will determine project maturity of a company conducting construction projects. Project maturity of a company can be defined as $M(R_1) = \sum_{i=1}^{4} M_1(A_i)$. $M(R_1)$ has linguistic value, which is defined as fuzzy numbers. Thus,

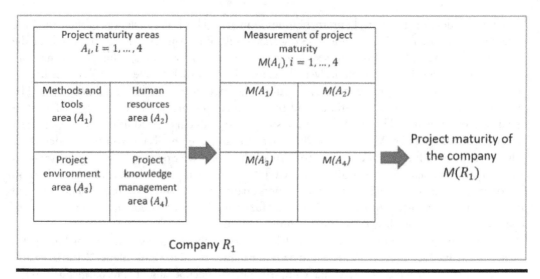

Figure 3.2 Project Maturity Model used in this research.

Source: Own work.

arithmetical operations are defined on them. How to treat variables within linguistic theory is described by J. Collins (Collins, 2014).

3.4.2 Project Maturity in a Selected Construction Company

For the project maturity assessment using the model described in section 3.1, one company was selected; this company was expected to obtain significant maturity results. It was necessary to test the model and use fuzzy numbers, as well as to analyze each of the indicated maturity measures. (In a mature company, there is a high probability that each maturity measure in each area will not be omitted.) After testing the model (what happens in this article), the authors used it to measure the maturity of construction companies in Poland in general (results are not given in this paper).

The collection and analysis of information for the assessment of maturity was carried out in the form of a qualitative research – single holistic case study.

3.4.2.1 Preliminary Information About the Company

The company that was selected for the single holistic case study is a large construction company employing 150 engineers; its revenue exceeds 200 million PLN per year. It performs activity in Poland, Great Britain, and the Czech Republic, and the company's equity comes from Japan. The company started operating before 1990, and has worked in Poland since 2001. Its activity is based on projects. A fragment of the interview questionnaire, on the basis of which it was possible to characterize the selected company, is included in Table 3.1.

Taking into account the company's long period of operation, the origin of its capital, and the size and form of its activity, a high project maturity could be expected. In fact, the application of the model presented in section 3.1 confirmed this hypothesis (see section 3.2.2).

Table 3.1   Fragment of case study protocol (questionnaire) regarding the description of the selected company

1. How many employees does your company employ? (under 50, <u>between 50-250</u>, over 250 people) – 150 people (engineering staff)
2. What is the annual revenue generated in your company (PLN)? (below 40 million, 40-200 million, <u>over 200million</u>)
3. Does your company cooperate internationally? (activity in Poland, within the EU, international outside the EU, global) – England, Czech Republic, Poland
4. How does your company deliver products/ services to customers? (process activity, <u>project activity</u>, both activities)
5. Who is the main owner of your business? (domestic investor, foreign investor) – Japan
6. Since when has your company been operating on the market? (starting operations before 1990, after 1990) – in Poland since 2001
7. Which function do you perform in the organization (choose the closest one)? (Board Member, Business Area Managing Director, Project / Program / Portfolio Manager, Project Office Director, Other) – President of the Board

Source: Own work, based on: (Sońta-Drączkowska, 2007).

3.4.2.2 *Measurement of Project Maturity in a Selected Construction Company*

As mentioned before, the organization's project maturity should be assessed in the context of four areas: methods and tools, human resources, organizational context (project environment), and project knowledge management. Each area consists of groups of measures for assessing project maturity. Area of methods and tools (A_1) contains eight measurement groups, area of human resources (A_2) – three measurement groups, area of organizational context (project environment) (A_3) – five measurement groups, area of project knowledge management (A_4) – four measurement groups. An exemplary set of maturity measures for a selected area is shown in Table 3.2. (This is another fragment of case study protocol (questionnaire)).

The respondent assessed individual measures in particular areas, linguistically, using the phrases like: Rather yes/ Probably not/ It's hard to say/ I think so/ I think not/ I'm sure yes/ I'm sure not that e.g. my company's processes related to information flows are analyzed in terms of potential improvements (measurement one in the first group of measures in area (A_4)). The information led to using fuzzy logic in collecting and counting data from interviews. Table 3.3 indicates how the provided answers were treated in the context of project maturity.

The next part of the paper (section 3.2.3) will describe how the project maturity of the selected area for measurement, which is the area of project knowledge management, was assessed.

Table 3.2 Fragment of case study protocol (questionnaire), which was used in qualitative research about project maturity in selected construction company in the area of project knowledge management

Groups of measures	Area of project knowledge management (A_4) - measures
1	1. Processes related to information flows are analyzed in terms of potential improvements. 2. The processes related to the collection of experiences are analyzed in terms of potential improvements. 3. Processes related to the collection of experiences are analyzed in terms of potential improvements. 4. Processes related to acquiring knowledge analyzed in terms of potential improvements. 5. People with different functions in the company work together to define and agree on common goals. 6. The company applies procedures and mechanisms that ensure that project managers and members of project teams have the appropriate knowledge and experience. 7. The company compares the method of project management with generally accepted standards – it uses benchmarking. 8. The company provides periodic training in methods, tools and techniques in project management. 9. The company uses a formal evaluation system to measure the level of competence of people involved in projects.
2	1. Intellectual capital is accumulated and stored. 2. The company records the knowledge and experience gained during the implementation of individual projects. 3. Intellectual capital is used in subsequent projects. 4. Knowledge and experience from completed projects are used in future projects.
3	1. Project managers understand formal and informal issues related to how projects operate in an organization's environment. 2. Project managers use emotional intelligence to promote a project culture in an organization. 3. Project managers understand the needs of stakeholders.
4	1. The company has created a community of people interested in project management. 2. The company enables project managers to develop their competences. 3. The company has a defined system of cooperation and information exchange between project managers.

Source: Own work based on: (Spałek, 2013).

Table 3.3 Indication of how the provided answers were treated in the context of project maturity

PHRASE – ANSWER OF THE RESPONDENT	I'm sure not	Probably not	I think not	It's hard to say	I think so	Rather yes	I'm sure yes
FUZZY LOGIC – PROJECT MATURITY CONTEXT	Lack of maturity	Low level of maturity	Low level of maturity	Medium level of maturity	High level of maturity	High level of maturity	Very high level of maturity

Source: Own work.

3.4.2.3 Application of Fuzzy Numbers in the Model

At the beginning of this section, the authors present the transformation of linguistic expressions (Lack of maturity, Low level of maturity, Medium level of maturity, High level of maturity, Very high level of maturity) into fuzzy numbers. The transformation is illustrated in Figure 3.3.

In Figure 3.3:

■ the axis x represents the maturity of the company in selected area regarding specific measure (it belongs to the interval [0, 6]);
■ the axis y, limited to the interval [0,1], represents the degree to which the given maturity degree possess the respective feature, e.g. is low, high etc.
■ we can define a set of triangular fuzzy numbers $\tilde{O}_i$, $i = 1, .., N$ representing different features of the maturity degree. In this paper, we assume N = 5 and the respective features are: {Lack of maturity, Low level of maturity, Medium level of maturity, High level of maturity, Very high level of maturity},
■ the fuzzy numbers, representing opinions (assessments) made by respondents, are as follow: $\tilde{O}_1 = (0, 1, 2)$, $\tilde{O}_2 = (1, 2, 3)$, $\tilde{O}_3 = (2, 3, 4)$, $\tilde{O}_4 = (3, 4, 5)$, $\tilde{O}_5 = (4, 5, 6)$.

An example of using fuzzy logic for a selected area, Area of project knowledge management (A_4), is shown in Table 3.4. Fuzzy evaluation for each area is μ_k^j, k = 1, ..K_j.

To determine the project maturity M_j of the selected area A_j, we propose using the following formula, where the standard addition of fuzzy numbers from (Zadeh, 1965) is used:

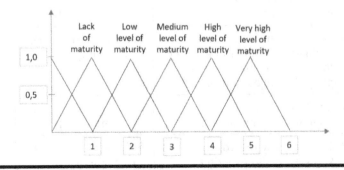

Figure 3.3 The use of fuzzy numbers to describe linguistic expressions.

Table 3.4 Exemplary using of fuzzy numbers in assessment of measures in Area of project knowledge management (A_4)

Group of measures	Area of project knowledge management (A_4) and its measures	Level of maturity regarding each measure	Fuzzy evaluation $\check{\mu}_k^4$, selected form the set $\widetilde{O}_i$, $i = 1, ..5$		
1	1. Processes related to information flows are analyzed in terms of potential improvements.	Very high level of maturity	(4,	5,	6)
	2. The processes related to the collection of experiences are analyzed in terms of potential improvements.	Very high level of maturity	(4,	5,	6)
	3. Processes related to acquiring knowledge analyzed in terms of potential improvements.	Very high level of maturity	(4,	5,	6)
	4. People with different functions in the company work together to define and agree on common goals.	Very high level of maturity	(4,	5,	6)
	5. The company applies procedures and mechanisms that ensure that project managers and members of project teams have the appropriate knowledge and experience.	Medium level of maturity	(2,	3,	4)
	6. The company compares the method of project management with generally accepted standards – it uses benchmarking.	High level of maturity	(3,	4,	5)
	7. The company provides periodic training in methods, tools and techniques in project management.	Very high level of maturity	(4,	5,	6)
	8. The company uses a formal evaluation system to measure the level of competence of people involved in projects.	Very high level of maturity	(4,	5,	6)
2	1. Intellectual capital is accumulated and stored.	Very high level of maturity	(4,	5,	6)
	2. The company records the knowledge and experience	Very high level of maturity	(4,	5,	6)

(Continued)

Table 3.4 (Continued)   Exemplary using of fuzzy numbers in assessment of measures in Area of project knowledge management

Group of measures	Area of project knowledge management (A_4) and its measures	Level of maturity regarding each measure	Fuzzy evaluation $\breve{\mu}_k^4$, selected form the set $\widetilde{O}_i,\ i = 1,\ ..5$		
	gained during the implementation of individual projects.				
	3. Intellectual capital is used in subsequent projects.	Very high level of maturity	(4,	5,	6)
	4. Knowledge and experience from completed projects are used in future projects.	Very high level of maturity	(4,	5,	6)
3	1. Project managers understand formal and informal issues related to how projects operate in an organization's environment.	Very high level of maturity	(4,	5,	6)
	2. Project managers use emotional intelligence to promote a project culture in an organization.	Very high level of maturity	(4,	5,	6)
	3. Project managers understand the needs of stakeholders.	Very high level of maturity	(4,	5,	6)
4	1. The company has created a community of people interested in project management.	Medium level of maturity	(2,	3,	4)
	2. The company enables project managers to develop their competences.	Very high level of maturity	(4,	5,	6)
	3. The company has a defined system of cooperation and information exchange between project managers.	Very high level of maturity	(4,	5,	6)
	Fuzzy assessment of maturity in the area of project knowledge management$\widetilde{M}_4$		**3,61**	**4,56**	**5,50**

Table 3.5 Assessment of the organization's maturity – results

Fuzzy assessment of maturity in the area of methods and tools $\tilde{M}_1$	3,62	4,59	5,56
Fuzzy assessment of maturity in the area of human resources $\tilde{M}_2$	3,59	4,59	5,59
Fuzzy assessment of maturity in the area of the project environment $\tilde{M}_3$	3,50	4,50	5,50
Fuzzy assessment of maturity in the area of project knowledge management $\tilde{M}_4$	3,61	4,56	5,50
	14,32	18,24	22,16
		4	
Fuzzy assessment of the company's maturity $\tilde{M}$ (R_1)	**3,58**	**4,56**	**5,54**

$$\tilde{M}_j = \frac{\sum_{k=1}^{K_j} \check{\mu}_k^j}{K_j} \qquad (3.1)$$

for j = 4 we get the following value $\tilde{M}_4$.

The remaining three areas (A_1), (A_2), (A_3) were assessed regarding their maturity in the same way. The results are as follows (Table 3.5):

$\tilde{M}$ will stand for the overall maturity of the organization and will be calculated by the following formula:

$$\tilde{M} = \frac{\sum_{j=1}^M \tilde{M}_j}{M} \qquad (3.2)$$

The fuzzy maturity of the organization, calculated by above formula, is (3.58, 4.56, 5.54). How can the result be interpreted? The authors suggest the use of one available approach, which consists in setting threshold values from which the organization's maturity levels are expressed. The following thresholds can be used:

5	which means "high maturity"
3,5	which means "medium maturity"
2	which means "low maturity"

The calculated fuzzy maturity for the selected construction company is illustrated in Figure 3.4. It can be seen that the company is "high mature" in 14% (it was computed by the following formula: $\frac{S(DEC)}{S(ABC)}$). It means the company has a good, mature attitude to manage its projects, but it still has room for potential improvement. How can this be done? It can be done through a detailed analysis of individual project maturity areas (A_1), (A_2), (A_3), (A_4) and measures

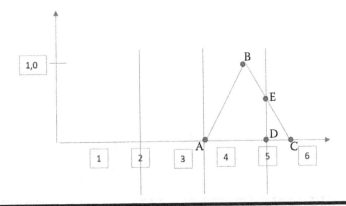

Figure 3.4   Fuzzy maturity for the selected construction company.

assigned to them. The fields for improvement are the measures rated at the lowest level (for example measure: "The company has created a community of people interested in project management" (see Table 3.4).

The large construction company with foreign capital was taken into account when testing the project maturity model. A high level of maturity in the company's project management could be expected, which was confirmed. Instead, let's look at some other hypothetical sample results that can be obtained.

Figure 3.5 shows a situation where the (hypothetical) fuzzy maturity of project management in an organization is (2.4, 3.3, 4.4). Taking into account the introduced thresholds, the obtained fuzzy value means that the company in 0% did not reach the "high maturity" level in project management (because it did not exceed the threshold – 5), but it reached "medium maturity" in some percentage, possible to calculate according to the formula indicated earlier ($\frac{S(DEC)}{S(ABC)}$.). Comparing this result to the result obtained in the single holistic case study (Figure 3.4), we can see that the project maturity of a real organization is much higher than in the case of the introduced hypothetical example. From a practical point of view, this means that in the simulated case, we have more fields for improvement that would be visible with the measures at the lowest levels.

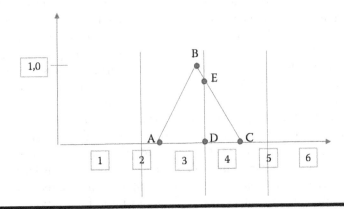

Figure 3.5   First hypothetical sample results - fuzzy maturity for the company.

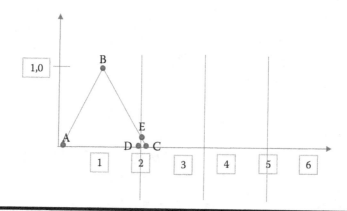

Figure 3.6 Second hypothetical sample results - fuzzy maturity for the company.

Let's consider one more hypothetical situation. Figure 3.6 shows the organization's project maturity with the fuzzy number (0.1, 1.1, 2.1). The adopted thresholds for the maturity assessment indicate that in this simulated example, the organization achieved 0% of "high maturity" in project management (the fuzzy value did not exceed the threshold – 5) and 0% of "medium maturity" (the fuzzy value did not exceed the threshold – 3.5). It has, however, reached a small percentage of "low maturity" (once again, we should use here the formula: $\frac{S(DEC)}{S(ABC)}$). With this kind of result, the organization has a tremendous amount of work to do to improve its maturity areas and project management processes.

3.5 Conclusions

In conclusion, for the purpose of empirical research about project maturity in construction companies, a qualitative research strategy was applied – case studies. The authors used a single holistic case study in their research strategy. The authors chose a large international construction company for the research because it was assumed that in a large, international company, project maturity would be significant, and the interviewed respondent would be familiar with the nomenclature of project management and be able to answer each maturity measure. This is important for testing the model. In preparation for data collection, the authors prepared a case study protocol (questionnaire) based on a specific project maturity model that was developed by S. Spałek (Spałek, 2013). According to this model, the organization's project maturity should be assessed in the context of four areas: methods and tools, human resources, organizational context (project environment), and project knowledge management. Within individual areas, measures of project maturity are identified, which are the basis for assessment.

The fuzzy maturity of the large international construction company is (3.58, 4.56, 5.54). It can be seen that the company is "high mature" in 14%. It means the company has a good, mature attitude to managing its projects, but it still has room for potential improvement. How can this be done? Improvement can be achieved through a detailed analysis of individual project maturity areas and measures assigned to them. The fields for improvement are the measures rated at the lowest level. Moreover, the respondent assessed the linguistic formulations as convenient and sufficient in determining the maturity level of project management of their organization.

The authors of this chapter realize that their research has some limitations. These were preliminary studies to test the model that will be used to assess the project maturity of construction companies in Poland. In this situation, the used single holistic case study was justified, but the use of single holistic case study in the research of the project maturity of construction companies in Poland would not provide reliable results. The difficulty is due to the limitations of this type of study: it isn't possible to generalize the conclusions of this study to other construction companies in Poland. Therefore, a multiple holistic case study was used in the target study of project maturity of construction companies. (This research isn't included in this paper.)

The use of project maturity models has its justification in decision-making processes, as mentioned earlier; thanks to them, it is possible to give answers for questions: what company can do to improve its operations? to develop? to implement projects more efficiently and effectively? how to improve processes to get higher level of project maturity? So, managers in construction companies can use research result in a decision support system (DSS).

Based on the model tested in this article, the project maturity of construction companies in Poland was measured using multiple holistic case studies. To measure this maturity, the opinions of project managers were taken into account and expressed in the form of linguistic expressions; fuzzy numbers type-1 were used to measure maturity. In the future, it is planned to expand these studies by using the opinions of stakeholders other than project managers, also using linguistic formulations. In this case, the authors will use multiple embedded case studies in their research strategy and fuzzy numbers type-2.

Acknowledgements

This work was supported by the National Science Center (Poland), under Grant 394311, 2017/27/B/HS4/01881 "Selected methods supporting project management, taking into consideration various stakeholder groups and using type-2 fuzzy numbers".

Note

1. In project management, the most commonly described maturity models include: OPM3 – Organizational Project Management Maturity Model, PMMM – Project Management Maturity Model, Capability Maturity Model (CMM), Capability Maturity Model Integration (CMMI), Prince2 Maturity Model (Spałek, 2014).

References

Albrecht, J.C., & Spang, K. (2014). Project complexity as an influence factor on the balance of costs and benefits in project management maturity modeling. *Procedia – Social and Behavioral Sciences 119*, 162–171.

Andersen, E.S., & Jessen, S.A. (2003). Project maturity in organisations. *International Journal of Project Management 21/6*, 457–461.

Bassi, M., & Handzic, A. (2017). *Knowledge and Project Management*. Geneva, Switzerland: Springer International Publishing.

Collins, J. (2014). The nature of linguistic variables, https://www.oxfordhandbooks.com/view/10.1093/oxfordhb/9780199935314.001.0001/oxfordhb-9780199935314-e-004 (accessed April 17, 2020).

Cooke-Davies, T.J., & Arzymanowc, A. (2003). The maturity of project management in different industries: An investigation into variations between project management models. *International Journal of Project Management 21*, 471–478.

Cooke-Davies, T.J. (2004). Project management maturity models. In P.W.G. Morris & J.K. Pinto (Eds.). *The Wiley Guide to Managing Projects*. Hoboken, NJ: Wiley, 1234–1264.

Crawford, J.K. (2006). The project management maturity model. *Information Systems Management 23/4*, 50–58.

Czakon, W. (2011). *Podstawy metodologii badań w naukach o zarządzaniu*. Warszawa: Oficyna a Wolters Kluwer Business.

Creswell, J.W. (2013). *Projektowanie badan naukowych, metody jakościowe, ilościowe i mieszane*. Kraków: Wydawnictwo Uniwersytetu Jagiellońskiego.

De Bruin, T., & Rosemann, M. (2005). Towards a business process management maturity model. In D. Bartmann, F. Rajola, J. Kallinikos, D. Avison, R. Winter & P. Ein-Dor (Eds.). *ECIS 2005 Proceedings of the Thirteenth European Conference on Information Systems*. London: Verlag and the London School of Economics, 1–12.

Gomes, J., Romão, M., & Carvalho, H. (2016). Successful IS/IT projects in healthcare: Pretesting a questionnaire. *Procedia Computer Science 100*, 375–382.

Górecki, J. (2015). Maturity of project management in polish and foreign construction companies. *Foundations of Management 7*, 521–532.

Haffer, J. (2013). Model skutecznego zarządzania projektami w świetle badań empirycznych. *Zarządzanie i Finanse 2/4*, 95–105.

Holzmann, V. (2013). A meta-analysis of brokering knowledge in project management. *International Journal of Project Management 31*(1), 2–1.

Kerzner, H. (2001). *Strategic Planning for Project Management Using a Project Management Maturity Model*. New York: Wiley.

Klaus-Rosińska A. (2016). Maturity model of project management in research projects: a synthesis of project management literature and directives for future research, 8th International Conference on Education and New Learning Technologies (Edulearn), 445–454. doi: 10.21125/edulearn.2016.1083

Klaus-Rosińska, A., & Iwko, J. (2020). Research in the field of project maturity in construction companies. *Journal of Decision Systems*, 1–14. doi: 10.1080/12460125.2020.1862987

Klaus-Rosińska, A., & Kuchta, D. (2016). Maturity of project management in construction companies with the use of fuzzy numbers. International Conference of Numerical Analysis and Applied Mathematics 2016 (Icnaam), pp. 230003-1–230003-4. doi: 10.1063/1.4992388

Lianyinga, Z., Jinga, H., & Xinxinga, Z. (2012). The project management maturity model and application based on PRINCE2. *Procedia Engineering 29*, 3691–3697.

Office of Government Commerce (2010). P3M3 v2.1 Self-Assessment. Instructions and Questionnaire.

Pretorius, S., Steyn, H., & Jordaan, J.C. (2012). Project management maturity and project management success in the engineering and construction industries in Southern Africa. *South African Journal of Industrial Engineering 23/3*, 1–12.

Sońta-Drączkowska E. (2007). Wpływ zarządzania projektami na tworzenie wartości przedsiębiorstwa, Rozprawa doktorska pod opieką prof. M. Trockiego, SGH, Warszawa.

Spałek, S. (2013). *Dojrzałość przedsiębiorstwa w zarządzaniu projektami*. Gliwice: Wydawnictwo Politechniki Śląskiej.

Spałek, S. (2015). Establishing a conceptual model for assessing project management maturity in industrial companies. *International Journal of Industrial Engineering 22*(2), 301–313.

Spałek, S. (2014). Zwiększanie stopnia dojrzałości w zarządzaniu projektami. Koncepcje, uwarunkowania i możliwe zastosowania praktyczne, Marketing i Rynek, 5.

Spałek, S., & Wolny, M. (2017). Zintegrowana ocena stopnia dojrzałości w zarządzaniu projektami, *Zeszyty Naukowe Politechniki Śląskiej, seria Organizacja i Zarządzanie 10*, 331–343.

Yin, R.K. (2015). *Studium przypadku w badaniach naukowych, Projektowanie i metody*. Kraków: Wydawnictwo Uniwersytetu Jagiellońskiego.

Zadeh, L.A. (1965). Fuzzy Sets, Information and Control, no 8.

Chapter 4

Corporate Health and Safety Performance Index as a Measure of the Level of Occupational Health and Safety Management in the Company Based on the ISO 45001 Standard

---

Jacek Iwko

Departament of Lightweight Elements Engineering, Foundry and Automation, Wrocław University of Science and Technology, Faculty of Mechanical Engineering, Wrocław, Poland

Aneta Pisarska

Department of Management, Calisia University, Faculty of Social Sciences, Kalisz, Poland

Joanna Iwko

Department of Management Systems and Organizational Development, Wrocław University of Science and Technology, Faculty of Management, Wrocław, Poland

Małgorzata Kochanek

Wrocław University of Science and Technology, Faculty of Mechanical Engineering, Wrocław, Poland

DOI: 10.1201/9781003030966-6

Contents

4.1 Introduction

The growing interest in safe working conditions causes not only the need to adapt the company's activities to the changing legal requirements and standards provisions, but also the need to look for ways to measure the health and safety level at work. Independent occupational health and safety management systems (OHS management system) (Pacana, 2016) are created, as well as those integrated with other systems, such as quality and environment management. The most effective way to ensure occupational safety is the proper management of occupational safety – a systematic approach to OHS. To examine the level of health and safety management, many indicators have been developed, which can be divided into two groups: result indicators related to the effects of improper working conditions, and leading indicators reflecting the health and safety area of the organization – or working conditions (CIOP, 2014). Economic practice shows that organizations have the greatest problem with the availability of data necessary to determine the value of a given indicator. A good indicator should be simple to use and easy to calculate (Kubista, 2019). The Corporate Health and Safety Performance Index (CHaSPI) is a quite new, interesting numerical indicator in Europe that assesses the effectiveness of OSH management in an enterprise (Pawłowska, 2006; Mardsen et al., 2004b). In addition, CHaSPI can be the basis for the implementation of the ISO 45001 standard. This indicator can be used to assess the current situation in the field of health and safety management, including a gap analysis against the above standards, and to determine the strengths and weaknesses of health and safety solutions used in organizations.

Considering the above, the research problem undertaken in this study is the answer to the question: how does CHaSPI support occupational health and safety management in organizations? The purpose of the article is to present CHaSPI as a measure of the level of occupational health and safety management based on the ISO 45001 standard and to study CHaSPI in a manufacturing company from the soft-plastic packaging industry. The research methods used in the study include a critical analysis of the literature on the subject, international standards, and logical inference. Moreover, a case study was used to achieve the research objective (questionnaire and in-depth interviews). In the future, results of this research may be used in a decision support system (DSS) in the area of OHS management.

4.2 Occupational Health and Safety Management

Occupational health and safety management should be a priority for every enterprise. As stated on its website by the International Organization for Standardization (ISO): Latest estimates from the International Labor Organization (ILO) show that more than 6,300 people die each day (that's over 2.3 million people each year) as a result of work-related activities, and in total, over 300 million accidents occur on the job annually. The burden to employers and employees alike is immense, resulting in losses to the wider economy from early retirements, staff absence, and rising insurance premiums (Gasiorowski-Denis, 2017).

Occupational health and safety management is often associated with the fact that a company has an implemented occupational health and safety management system. Nevertheless, it is not legally required in Poland, but taking into account the large number of legal provisions that employers have to follow, sooner or later, such a system may prove very helpful. The larger the enterprise, the more people it employs, which in turn may increase the probability of non-compliance in the area of health and safety. Occupational health and safety management looks a bit different in each enterprise. The results include the size of enterprises, employment structure, working conditions, or the specificity of activity (production or services) (Chomątowska, 2011). Its shape is also influenced by the highest management and its involvement in the area of enterprise security.

Enterprises have different approaches to the subject of health and safety. Some treat OHS as a necessary evil, a set of regulations that they must comply with and the fulfillment of obligations imposed by law, while striving to minimize efforts; others, on the contrary, assume that work safety is a very important aspect of the company's operation and are guided by continuous improvement, development of new, more effective methods of protecting the health and life of their employees. Table 4.1 presents four levels of OHS management in workplaces distinguished by M.B. Weinstein(Chomątowska, 2011).

The table shows factors motivating enterprises to undertake activities in the field of health and safety at individual management levels, type of activity, basis for evaluation, methods and purpose of OHS training and the results of these activities. It follows that on the 3rd and 4th level, there are enterprises that approach occupational health and safety management in a systemic way (as opposed to the 1st and 2nd level enterprises, which treat this area as secondary). This may result from a change in the way of thinking about health and safety and the implementation of an occupational health and safety management system. Safety is on a par with areas such as the quality of goods and services provided, customer service, and environmental protection. Such workplaces are motivated by profit opportunities resulting from minimizing the number of accidents and noncompliance. They are focused on continuous improvement in the area of health and safety, so they can implement the best methods to improve the health and safety at work (Chomątowska, 2011).

The essence of health and safety management covers not only material factors, such as hazardous materials or workplace equipment. It is primarily the participation of employees in developing safe work methods. Health and safety management should also focus on developing safe and ergonomic solutions to reduce the exposure of employees to nuisance and harmful, hazardous factors for their health. The participation of the top management and their commitment is also very important, which should guide the company's health and safety policy. In order to comprehensively manage occupational health and safety, many aspects should be considered, including the idea of continuous improvement. The essence of OSH management is presented in Figure 4.1 (Berkowska et al., 2013; Chomątowska, 2012).

Table 4.1   Occupational health and safety management levels in enterprises according to M. B. Weinstein (Chomątowska, 2011)

Level	Motivation to act	Type of action	Typical evaluation method	Typical training method	Typical OHS goals	Results achieved in the area of OHS
I	Fear	Passive	Only inspections of supervisory institutions	Basic courses only	Avoidance of penalties and fines	Incomplete compliance, results worse than average
II	Penalty	Reactive	Documentation analysis, inspections	Courses, instruction and checking	Avoidance of Incompatibilities	Legal compliance, no improvement, average results
III	Prize	Active (understanding and trust)	Observation of work stations, audits of the health and safety management system	Thorough instruction and support	Performing all work correctly	Correct behavior, better than average results
IV	Internal motivation	Proactive (passion and commitment)	Reviews and interviews, work results	Based on examples, self-improvement	Zero accidents, the best methods	Continuous improvement, leadership, excellent results

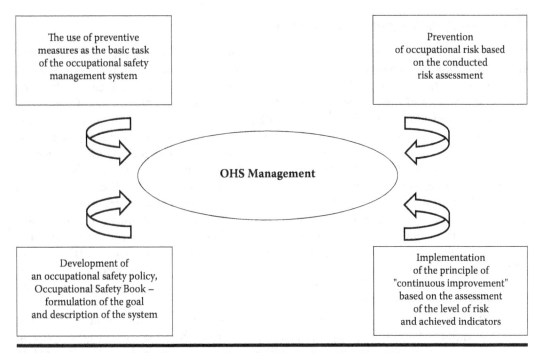

Figure 4.1   The essence of work safety management (Berkowska et al., 2013).

Along with the change in the approach to the issues of occupational health and safety management, with the help of scientists and practitioners, systems supporting OHS management began to be created. Occupational health and safety management is becoming an inseparable element of a comprehensive management system based on the quality criterion. An effectively functioning health and safety management system influences both the improvement of the economic results of the enterprise due to the management of processes, where health and safety hazards may occur, and the improvement of the quality of life of employees (Zymonik et al., 2013). This view is also reflected in one of the principles of the safety management system developed by D. Petersen (Markowski, 1999), where safety management should be treated on an equal footing with other departments of the company, such as quality or costs, and the OH&S area should be integrated with the company's operational strategy.

Recently, a significantly changing perspective can be noticed in the approach to the area of occupational health and safety management. More and more often, it is no longer a separate area of company operation. It becomes an integral part of the management of the entire enterprise, closely harmonized at various levels, which should contribute to sustainable development by providing people with safer and healthier jobs. The introduction of the international ISO 45001 standard in 2018 (ISO 45001, 2018) can be considered an expression of this approach. It will be discussed more detail in the next part of the study.

4.3 OH&S Management System

The constant growth of interest in the systemic management of occupational health and safety means that the legal requirements in individual countries in this area are constantly changing. New guidelines for occupational health and safety management systems are constantly being developed. The first of these standards – BS 8800 – was created in 1996 in Great Britain. The International Organization for Standardization (ISO) in 1997 decided not to work on a single, universally recognized standard due to legal differences in the field of health and safety in different countries. In Poland, in 1998, work began on the standardization of the OH&S management system. Standards PN-N of the 18000 series were established[1] in the field of occupational health and safety management. They were adjusted to the international OHSAS 18001 standard. In accordance with the requirements of the PN-N-18001: 2004 standard, the occupational health and safety management system model was based on the concept of continuous improvement,[2] which is a formal requirement to be implemented in standardized management systems. It is also the principle that most closely approximates these standards to the TQM concept (Ejdys et al., 2012). The effective operation of such a system depends on the involvement of all employees, including management, as well as linking the system with the organization's goals and development strategies (Wyrębek, 2012).

In 2013, an attempt was made to develop an international standard in the field of health and safety management due to the ever-increasing interest in the health and safety management system in the world and the increasing number of different systems. The general standard ISO 45001 should have been published in 2016 (PKN, 2019). It was finally published in 2018. ISO 45001:2018 (ISO 45001, 2018) provides OH&S management system requirements and application guidance to enable organizations to provide safe and healthy workplaces by preventing work-related injuries and illnesses, and proactively improving business performance in the field of occupational health and safety. It can be used in any organization, regardless of the size, type, and type of business. Ultimately, it should replace national standards based on the OHSAS standard, including the Polish standards of the 18000 series.

In accordance with the ISO 45001:2018 occupational health and safety management system is a management, or a part of a management, system used to achieve the OH&S policy. The implementation of an OH&S management system is a strategic and operational decision for an organization. The operation of the OH&S management system depends on leadership, commitment, and participation from all levels and functions of the organization. However, the success of an organization's OH&S management system will also depend on a greater number of factors, such as (ISO 45001, 2018):

- the organization's context (e.g. number of workers, size, geography, culture, legal requirements, and other requirements),
- the scope of the organization's OH&S management system,
- the nature of the organization's activities and the related OH&S risks.

In this standard, the approach to an OSH management system, as with other standards that underpin the certification process, is based on the PDCA cycle. Sections 4 to 10 of this standard can be assigned to this cycle (PKN, 2019; BSI, 2018). This relation is presented in Figure 4.2 (ISO 45001, 2018).

As ISO 45001: 2018 is an international standard with a standardized structure, it is easier to recognize and identify risks. Other potential benefits of establishing this standard are (BSI, 2018):

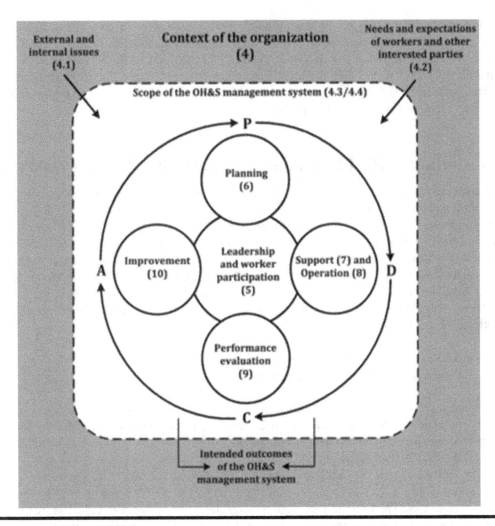

Figure 4.2   Relationship between PDCA and the framework in ISO 45001 (https://www.iso. org/obp/ui/es/#iso:std:iso:45001:ed-1:v1:en).

- reducing the number of deaths, illnesses, and work-related injuries;
- elimination or minimization of health and safety risks;
- improving health and safety performance and efficiency;
- meeting supply chain requirements and demonstrating corporate responsibility;
- protection of the brand's reputation;
- engaging employees and motivating them through consultations and their active participation in the implementation of the ISO 45001 standard.

Comparing the OHSAS 18001 standard and the ISO 45001:2018 standard, it can be concluded that they are very similar to each other because they both use the PDCA model. The structure of the new standard corresponds to other international standards. It places greater emphasis on the responsibility of management, which plays a key role in building an effective health and safety management system and active involvement of employees. It emphasizes that health and safety at work does not depend only on the responsibility of one person or department. According to the ISO standard, each employee should focus on safety issues in their daily tasks (ISO-U, 2018). It is process-based and considers the risks and opportunities that arise in them. This standard pays particular attention to defining the scope of the occupational health and safety management system, considering the analysis of the nature of the organization[3] and the need to understand the needs and expectations of interested parties.[4]

4.4 Corporate Health and Safety Performance Index (CHaSPI)

Occupational health and safety management in enterprises should contribute to the creation of safe working conditions and the development of a system supporting their supervision, control, and continuous improvement. But the proper operation of this system is also related to the performance of appropriate analyses, as well as the assessment of the organization's functioning in the area of health and safety. According to Kaplan, you cannot manage something that cannot be measured (Pawłowska, 2006). Therefore, a number of indicators for measuring occupational safety have been developed. To examine the condition of the working environment, traditional measures of health and safety at work are used, among others, reflecting the effects of poor working conditions, i.e.

■ accident frequency and severity index,
■ indicator of the number of occupational diseases.

Other measures concern the number of people working in hazardous or harmful conditions. The others are related to the level of knowledge of health and safety by employees and the level of motivation or safety culture (Smoliński and Solecki, 2015; CIOP, 2014; Iwko and Iwko, 2018a; Iwko and Iwko, 2018b; Ejdys, 2010).

The measurement of the health and safety in an enterprise is a process that consists of three basic stages (Figure 4.3). The first step is collecting data on the OH&S management system and all its components. Then, the collected information should be analyzed and documented in the form of reports. A properly conducted process of measuring the functioning of the enterprise in the area of health and safety enables a reliable assessment of the level of health and safety management and the correct interpretation of the results (Smoliński and Solecki, 2015; CIOP, 2014).

The research carried out by CIOP (CIOP, 2014) shows that Polish entrepreneurs most often use three indicators to assess the health and safety at work:

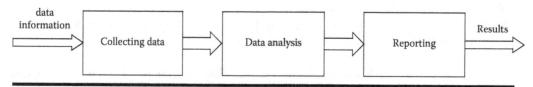

Figure 4.3 Measurement of health and safety in the enterprise (CIOP, 2014).

- number of accidents at work
- number of people employed in hazardous conditions
- number of days of absence due to sickness

The reason is the necessity to prepare annual reports for ZUS and GUS. Enterprises with a high level of health and safety management use a larger number of indicators, but their use can be cumbersome, and the selection of an indicator appropriate for a given type of enterprise is often a big challenge.

Because many indicators are used to assess the efficiency of the OSH management system, and some of them cannot be expressed in the form of a numerical value, it is very difficult to compare different enterprises in terms of their functioning in the area of OSH, as well as evaluate these activities. Therefore, an attempt was made to develop one integrated health and safety management indicator. This effort was done by a team of British specialists from the Health and Safety Executive (HSE) in 2002–2004 (Pawłowska, 2012). One of its goals was to encourage management to better manage health and safety. As a result of the conducted research, it turned out that investors have a keen interest in the OHS indicator. Many of them understood the issues of health and safety management and indicated the need for specialists to develop a group of relevant indicators. On the other hand, senior managers needed an effective tool for measuring changes in the OHS area and more efficient planning of improvements. Based on the commissioned research and feedback from entrepreneurs, experts from HSE determined that there is a need for an indicator that would meet the requirements and be determinable. Such indicator should (Mardsen et al., 2004b):

- fit into the patterns of corporate social responsibility;
- contain both standardized performance and process measures;
- allow comparisons between companies;
- reflect the global nature and needs of businesses;
- provide a variety of usage options depending on user resources;
- not invest a lot of resources;
- be adjusted to the realization of broader goals and objectives;
- be rewarding for shareholders.

The integrated occupational health and safety management index was created based on the above assumptions. It is a set of result and process indicators, so it presents a balanced picture of the occupational health and safety area in enterprises. It does not consider financial outlays and performance measures in adapting to changes because it is very difficult to assess to what extent the money invested in health and safety directly affects the improvement of working conditions. More money spent does not always result in greater safety.[5] As for the success rate, it was not included due to its values. They are too low in relation to the other measures considered and could distort the proper picture of the health and safety condition. This is due to the fact that the health and safety law does not change often, which means that there are few changes (Mardsen et al., 2004b). Research on the level of health and safety management using the CHaSPI indicator can therefore be part of a company's decision support system (DSS).

Decision support system (DSS) is an important tool that helps decision makers take accurate, unbiased, and insightful decisions from the available data in the area of health and safety management. For example, when analyzing accidents at work, decision making should be effective and, more importantly, prompt. Managers can use DSS to obtain such decisions (Sarkar et al., 2018).

The practice of enterprises shows that the cause of most accidents at work is the human factor, which is expressed as people making wrong or illogical decisions. They result from the influence of factors of the working environment and the work process itself, as well as the lack of sufficient information support. These problems are particularly evident in extreme situations and in the absence of time to make a decision. To meet these challenges, expert decision-making systems are created in the area of occupational health and safety management, which use various models to make optimal decisions (Semeykin et al., 2019). CHaSPI can provide managers with a complex data necessary in the process of making accurate and quick decisions.

The integrated occupational health and safety management index can be determined independently using simple formulas and using statistical data on the number of accidents at work in the entire country (national average). For this purpose, a website has been developed in Great Britain with a tool for calculating this indicator (HSE, 2021). It has been called the CHaSPI acronym (*Corporate Health and Safety Performance Index*) (Williams and Shahriyer, 2010). In Poland, such a tool was made available on a website by the Central Institute for Labor Protection – National Research Institute in Poland (CIOP, 2021).

The integrated occupational health and safety management index is calculated as the weighted sum of its individual elements. The integrated occupational health and safety management index consists of five sub-indicators (Pawłowska, 2006; Mardsen et al., 2004b; CIOP, 2021). Each indicator can get a rating from 0 to 10, where 10 means the best rating. Index 1 receives a weight of 0.5 as the most important component, while the remaining four indexes recieve a weight of 0.125 each (Pawłowska, 2006; Smoliński and Solecki, 2015; Mardsen et al., 2004b) (Figure 4.4).

The integrated indicator also considers three issues that are not included in the evaluation of an enterprise in the area of health and safety on a point scale. The first one is occupational risk

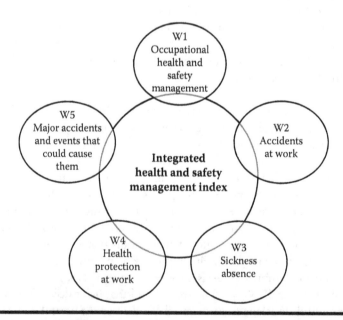

Figure 4.4 The integrated occupational health and safety management index (Pawłowska, 2006; Mardsen et al., 2004a, 2004b).

assessment and proper management in the form of management's declaration of conducting such an assessment and implementation of appropriate actions, as well as employee compliance with occupational health and safety rules and principles. The second issue is to determine whether the organization is subject to special regulations in connection with its activities of a hazardous nature, such as activities involved with chemical warehouses or chemical production plants. These regulations are included in national legal acts that implement the provisions of the Seveso III Directive into Polish law (EUR-LEX, 2020). Such companies are then required to establish a Major Accident Prevention Program (PZA) (CIOP, 2020). In the UK, these are COMAH regulations (ang. *Control of Major Accident Hazards Regulations*), whose main goal is to reduce the risk of major accidents (HSE, 2019). The third issue is the presence of major accidents in the past or the existence of premises signalling the possibility of such event. When this situation has happened, these enterprises receive flag "under observation" and are committed to take action to prevent the formation of disasters (Mardsen et al., 2004b).

The following part of the article presents the results of the research on the level of occupational health and safety management in the company based on the ISO 45001 standard using the integrated occupational health and safety management index in the selected company from the soft-plastic packaging industry. The study was conducted based on the procedure for determining CHaSPI in the Mardsen report (Mardsen et al., 2004b).

4.5 Research on the Integrated OHS Management Index in a Selected Production Company

A small manufacturing company was selected to study the integrated occupational health and safety management index,[6] which produces soft packaging for the chemical, hygiene, food, construction, and specialist industries. It has a production hall, a warehouse, and social and office rooms. Dynamic development, favourable market conditions, and the commitment of employees allowed the company to achieve success and consolidate the position of one of the leading producers of soft packaging in the entire region. The company's goal is to produce legal and safe packaging, compliant with the law and meeting the highest quality standards and customer requirements. In addition to production, it also offers professional advice in the field of plastic packaging. The company uses the requirements of the British BRC/IOP standard regarding the quality and safety of packaging, which complies with the requirements of ISO 9001 and HACCP. The state of occupational health and safety in the enterprise meets the legal requirements related to this area. The company employs 35 people. Health and safety tasks were entrusted to an external company.

Each newly hired employee undergoes mandatory health and safety and fire safety training, completed with a short exam. Additionally, before starting work, he or she is required to undergo preliminary medical examinations. Employees employed directly in the technological process must also undergo sanitary and epidemiological tests and repeat them periodically. Employees recruited to work in positions requiring specific authorizations, e.g. forklift operators, are required to present such permits, and in the absence of such permits, they are directed to the course.

The company regularly assesses the occupational risk in new jobs. Employees are informed about the risk and are also presented with the rules of protection against threats. Each employee is equipped with personal protective equipment, such as gloves, safety shoes, or work clothes, and where necessary, each employee is additionally equipped with masks that filter out harmful vapours. All protective measures used, as well as tools and auxiliary materials used by employees, are specified in the work regulations. The company has safety data sheets (SDS) for all hazardous substances used in the production of packaging. Each employee who comes into contact with hazardous substance is obliged to read the appropriate SDS. Additionally, the employer tests the concentrations of these substances and defines protection measures to prevent exceeding the permissible concentration.

The audited enterprise does not use indicators for the assessment of the area related to occupational safety and health, except for the mandatory ones related to reporting to the Central Statistical Office and the Social Insurance Institution. The owner of the company considers the work safety to be very good, but there are some irregularities. To assess the health and safety condition in the enterprise and to identify possible areas for improvement, an integrated occupational health and safety management indicator was established.

4.5.1 The Integrated OHS Management Index Analysis

The study of the integrated occupational health and safety management index in the selected enterprise began with getting acquainted with the specificity of the company and the current state of health and safety management. To determine the partial indicators concerning OHS management and health protection, an in-depth interview was carried out with the person responsible for this area. To obtain data on the rates of accidents at work and the occurrence of major accidents in the past, the accident records kept in the company, as well as the knowledge of the management, were used. Data on employee absenteeism due to sickness was obtained from a report generated from a computerized HR program.

First, answers were obtained to three questions dealing with issues that did not affect the final value of CHaSPI. The first question concerning the occupational risk assessment was positively answered. Regarding the following issues, it should be noted that the audited enterprise is not subject to any specific regulations, nor is it under the supervision of external institutions.

4.6 W1 Indicator – Health and Safety Management

Appropriate formulas were used to calculate the values of individual partial indices. This is due to the fact that the form published on the CIOP website did not contain the statistical data needed for the calculations. The values of the components that make up the W1 index are presented in Table 4.2. Component values were calculated based on the distribution of responses to the questions contained in the Mardsen report (Mardsen et al., 2004b).

The value of the W1 index is calculated as

$$W1 = \frac{\sum_1^n W_{1.n}}{11} \times 10 \tag{4.1}$$

$$W1 = \frac{4,68}{11} \times 10 = 4,25$$

where: n – number of components <0; 11>

$W_{1.n}$ – value of the partial index

Table 4.2 The values of the W1 indicator components

Partial index	Value
1.1 How are health and safety targets formulated?	0,67
1.2 How is health and safety represented at the board (or equivalent)?	0,50
1.3 What is the level of health and safety reporting to the board?	0,69
1.4 What is the level of public health and safety reporting?	0,50
1.5 To what extent has the company selected or formulated health and safety performance standards and requirements?	0,80
1.6 To what extent are health and safety plans developed?	0,50
1.7 To what extent are the workforce involved in health and safety?	0,40
1.8 How is health and safety management performance verified?	0,33
1.9 How is health and safety performance monitored and reviewed?	0,29
1.10 To what extent is there a health and safety management system?	0,0
1.11 Procurement Indicator – do you require good health and safety performance of those who supply to you goods and services?	0,0
SUM	**4,68**

Source: Own work.

4.7 W2 Indicator – Accidents at Work

The W2 index is considered by large organizations as the most appropriate, and even ideal, index in the range of occupational health and safety assessment. It is assigned to both permanent employees and subcontractors. There are only permanent employees in the surveyed enterprise. The company does not use subcontractors; therefore, when calculating the W2 index, the formulas for accidents at subcontractors were not used and there was no need to determine the employment and subcontractor coefficients (percentage of permanent employees index WZ = 1, percentage of subcontractors index WP = 0, subcontractors accidents index LWPO = 0).

In the analyzed period, the company had one accident at work and the company employed 35 people. The accident index in Poland (SWW) in the analyzed period was 6.84 per 1,000 employees (GUS, 2018).

The permanent employees accident index LWPR in the described enterprise is

$$LWPR = \frac{number\ of\ employees\ accidents}{number\ of\ permanent\ employees} \times 1000 \tag{4.2}$$

$$LWPR = \frac{1}{35} \times 1000 = 28{,}57$$

The overall weighted accident index (OWW) should be calculated as

$$OWW = WZ \times LWPR + WP \times LWPO \qquad (4.3)$$

Due to the assumptions presented above, it can be seen that this index is equal to permanent employees accident index LWPR.

The value of the w2 index is obtained by comparing the calculated overall weighted accident index (OWW) with the average number of accidents in the country. Thus, the value of the OWW indicator should be divided by the average national accident index SWW in the country:

$$w2 = \frac{OWW}{SWW} \qquad (4.4)$$

$$w2 = \frac{28,57}{6,84} = 4,18$$

The value of w2 obtained in this way should be found in the comparative table (Mardsen et al., 2004b), and the value of the W2 index achieved by the enterprise should be read from that table. A fragment of this comparative table (selected values of w2 and W2) is presented in Table 4.3. If the result of w2 index is 0.1 or less, the index W2 has a maximum value of 10; however, when w2 index is greater or equal to 10, the index W2 equals 0. Comparing the obtained result w2 with the comparative table, the value of W2 index was read:

$$W2 = 1,9$$

4.8 W3 Indicator – Sickness Absence

This indicator was included in CHaSPI as a result of consultations that showed a need to include the absence of employees due to their health condition related to the performed work. It was found that these absences could be related to the health and safety in the enterprise. However, it is very difficult to determine which periods of sickness absence are clearly related to work. When determining the W3 index, the number of days of sickness absence of all employees was summed

Table 4.3 The values of the W2 indicator components (Mardsen et al., 2004a, 2004b)

w2 index	W2 index	w2 index	W2 index	w2 index	W2 index
0,1	10,0	1,5	4,1	6,0	1,1
0,2	8,5	2,0	3,5	7,0	0,8
0,3	7,6	3,0	2,6	8,0	0,5
0,4	7,0	4,0	2,0	9,0	0,2
0,5	6,5	4,2	1,9	9,5	0,1
1,0	5,0	5,0	1,5	10,0	0,0

up, not taking into account the absence related to the employee's time on sick leave due to the child's illness. The total number of days of absence of employees in the analyzed period was 548 days. The rate of absence, WN per 1 employee, is calculated as

$$WN = \frac{548}{35} = 15,66$$

As this index is greater than 15, it means, as shown in Figure 4.5, that the value of the W3 index is 0.

4.9 W4 Indicator – Health Protection at Work

Due to the lack of the existing measurable indicator of health protection at work, a set of questions and statements was developed aimed at the status of occupational risk management. It covers issues related to the broadly understood assessment of health protection at work. These include dangers such as work stress and physical injuries.

When determining the value of the W4 indicator, the answers given by a person with knowledge in the studied area were used. The $W_{4.0}$ value was calculated based on the distribution of answers to the questions included in the Mardsen report (Mardsen et al., 2004b). The value of the W4 index was determined based on these responses by multiplying the $W_{4.0}$ index by 10:

$$W_{4.0} = 0,21$$

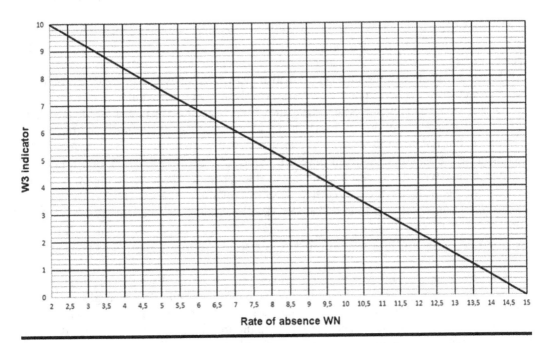

Figure 4.5   The value of W3 indicator (Mardsen et al., 2004a, 2004b).

$$W4 = 0,21 \times 10 = 2,1$$

4.10 W5 Indicator – Serious Failures and Events that May Cause Them

This indicator was taken into account due to the authors' view that managing the risk associated with hazards such as slips, trips, and falls does not mean good management of the risk of major accidents. The W5 indicator considered the number of events of a given category that have taken place in the enterprise in the last three years. The following categories of events are distinguished:

1. major accidents of international scope
2. major national accidents
3. major accidents resulting in fatalities
4. failures that do not pose a threat to the environment, causing death, injuries, or sickness of several people
5. serious incidents
6. incidents
7. anomalies
8. deviations

When determining the value of the W5 indicator, the knowledge of people employed in the enterprise for at least three years was also used. No major accidents or incidents have occurred. Therefore, the W5 index has a maximum value of 10. It should be emphasized, however, that the assessment of this parameter is subjective because it is not based on any documents, but only on the employees' memory.

Summarizing the obtained results of partial indicators and multiplying their values by their weights, the value of the integrated indicator of occupational health and safety management in the examined enterprise was obtained. These values are presented in Table 4.4.

The calculated value of the integrated occupational health and safety management index in the selected enterprise is 3.876 points. This result is only 38% of the maximum number of points that can be obtained. This proves that there are several areas of occupational health and safety management in the company, which should be given special attention and opportunities to improve the functioning of these areas. The analyzed enterprise carries out an occupational risk assessment, which is nothing unusual since it is required by Polish law. The appraisal report is available to employees in the positions subject to this appraisal. There are no objections to the operation of the plant in this respect. The specificity of the company's production does not require any specific legal regulations. The plant does not conduct any activity considered to be dangerous. In addition, the company has not experienced catastrophic events in the past, and there are no indications that such events would take place in the future. Therefore, the company is not "under surveillance."

When analyzing the responses to individual components of the W1 indicator, it can be noticed that the company does not have an implemented health and safety management system based on the ISO 45001 standard and does not assess the performance of its subcontractors and sub-suppliers in the area of health and safety at all (indicators $W_{1.10}$ and $W_{1.11}$ assumed the value 0). The index $W_{1.5}$ concerning procedures received the highest grade. This proves a good basis for

Table 4.4   Calculation of overall CHaSPI index

overall index			**3,876**
Has a director's declaration been made?			Yes
Does this organization conduct major hazard operations that would be covered by regulations such as COMAH, Nuclear Site Licenses, aircraft licensing, etc.?			No
"Under Watch" due to major event?			No
Indicators	*Rating (0 to 10)*	*Weight*	*Weighted rating*
W1. H&S management system	4,25	0,5	2,125
W2. Employee injury rate	1,90	0,125	0,238
W3. Employee absence rate	0,0	0,125	0,0
W4. Occupational health management	2,10	0,125	0,263
W5. Major incident rating	10,0	0,125	1,250

the implementation of a health and safety management system. It is also related to the performance of the obligations incumbent on the employer. The company also has partially formulated goals in the area of safety ($W_{1.1}$), and the level of informing the top management about the health and safety status ($W_{1.3}$) is high. This may be the result of a hierarchical structure and a high degree of centralization. Every significant decision made in the company must be considered by the CEO. On the other hand, the commitment of the top management, the level of information on health and safety to external organizations, and the development of plans are at an average level (values of the relevant indicators equal 0.5). The managing director is kept informed of any problems, but he is not provided with periodic health and safety reports. Health and safety management reviews are carried out sporadically, and the CEO does not always take part in them. Due to the fact that the company does not regularly conduct audits, external organizations are not informed about their progress; therefore, the evaluation of $W_{1.4}$ indicator was average. As for health and safety plans, they are not updated by the company. Changes are made very rarely, mainly for reasons generated by legal restrictions, e.g. in the case of limiting the concentration of a given substance at the workplace. Monitoring and assessment of the OHS area in the enterprise is at a low level, which is indicated by $W_{1.8}$ and $W_{1.9}$ indicators, because of the lack of established rules for these activities and the person responsible for this area.

To summarize, the level of occupational health and safety management is not high. The company did not receive even half of the points in this area (4.25 out of 10 possible). This low score is due to the lack of strictly established rules for monitoring this area, and the main reason for this score is that the company has not implemented an OH&S management system that would greatly facilitate these tasks. A company that wants to minimize costs should think about solving this problem because the costs related to health and safety are also funds intended to cover losses related to possible accidents at work. The situation in the company is also not good from this point of view. There was one accident at work in the analyzed period. It would seem that one accident per year is very little. However, considering the number of employees (35 people), the result is quite a high accident rate, which is more than four times the national average. CHaSPI takes into account the national average when examining the accident rate. So, the W2 index calculated in this way can be considered measurable for further comparison with other organizations in the country. The low value of this partial indicator may result from incomplete health and safety management in the enterprise.

When analyzing the W3 indicator result, it can be concluded that high sickness absence may be related to improper health and safety management. Employees are exposed to stress at work, which may be the reason for such high absence. Some people have sick leave with the duration longer than seven days of the average cold. According to experts, stress can cause many work-related health problems. The percentage of absenteeism related to this factor may be 45%, and even up to 60% (Gratka, 2017). Stress factors are not considered when conducting occupational risk assessment and planning activities in the area of occupational health and safety in the examined company. Perhaps if they were considered, the absence would be several dozen percent lower.

Healthcare in the analyzed enterprise is also a weak point in the assessment of health and safety performance. The W4 index score obtained by the plant is slightly more than 20% of the maximum score. Employees only undergo mandatory periodic tests required for individual work positions. The risk of nuisance factors such as stress or monotony is not limited in any way. Employees often do the same job all day long. The company does not guarantee the employees any training that would enable them to take up another job if they become unable to perform the current job, e.g. due to an injury resulting from an accident at work. Sickness absence is monitored only by employees of the HR department, and it has nothing to do with health and safety.

When analyzing the results of the study of the integrated occupational health and safety management index in the surveyed company, it can be concluded that the state of safety meets all legal requirements related to this area. However, the enterprise does not undertake actions aimed at continuous improvement of safety or work ergonomics. The obtained result is low, but it is difficult to clearly state the level of the company's functioning in the area of occupational health and safety, because in Poland the CHaSPI indicator is not very popular. There are no data with this indicator in the Polish literature. Therefore, it is not possible to compare the obtained CHaSPI value with the results of other Polish companies.

4.11 Conclusion

Issues related to occupational health and safety are the subject of many considerations by both scientists and practitioners. One of the ways to ensure occupational safety is proper management of occupational health and safety based on the international ISO 45001 standard. The level of occupational health and safety management should be measured. There are many measures to assess the health and safety condition, but they are not easy to use, especially if they are not required by law. Entrepreneurs are reluctant to use these indicators due to difficulties in determining them. The Corporate Health and Safety Performance Index (CHaSPI) examines many areas related to occupational safety. This indicator enables the most comprehensive analysis of this area among all known indicators. Its use can be considered justified in the study of the level of health and safety management based on the ISO 45001 standard, and it can play an important role in the effective process of its implementation.

Finally, it is worth noting that the main barrier to the use of CHaSPI may be its low popularity. Based on research commissioned by the Health and Safety Executive (HSE), CHaSPI was reported as being mainly used for benchmarking, as an internal tool to identify strengths and weaknesses and to report back on organizational health and safety performance. Many users felt that CHaSPI currently had limited impact due to levels of awareness and number of users. For those who had used CHaSPI, it was considered to have had a very positive impact for their companies (Williams and Shahriyer, 2010). The literature contains very few studies on the subject of the CHaSPI (Marsden et al., 2004a; Walker, 2006). This makes it difficult to compare the performance of different companies in the area of occupational health and safety with this indicator.

Notes

1. They included the following standards: PN-N-18001:2004, *Systemy zarządzania bezpieczeństwem i higieną pracy – Wymagania*, Polski Komitet Normalizacyjny, Warszawa 2004; PN-N-18002:2011 – *Systemy zarządzania bezpieczeństwem i higieną pracy – Ogólne wytyczne do oceny ryzyka zawodowego*, Polski Komitet Normalizacyjny, Warszawa 2011; PN-N-18004:2001 – *Systemy zarządzania bezpieczeństwem i higieną pracy – Wytyczne*, Polski Komitet Normalizacyjny, Warszawa 2001; PN-N-18011:2006 – *Systemy zarządzania bezpieczeństwem i higieną pracy – Wytyczne audytowania*, Polski Komitet Normalizacyjny, Warszawa 2006.
2. Continuous improvement is repeated action to improve the effects of an action (ISO 9000, 2015).
3. The context of the organization is a combination of internal and external factors that may influence the organization's approach to setting and achieving its goals according to (ISO 9000, 2015).
4. The interested party is a person or organization that can influence, be influenced by decisions or actions, or who is considered to be influenced by decisions or actions by (ISO 9000, 2015).
5. On the one hand, frequent inspections of machines and devices affect the safety of the operators' work, and on the other hand, investing in systems supporting accident investigation may contribute to detecting more of them, for example when employees do not report minor accidents, which would lower the safety index.
6. The study was conducted in 2017 in a family company established in 1989.

References

Berkowska, A., Drzewiecka, M., & Mrugalska B. (2013). Analiza obszarów techniczno-organizacyjnych wpływających na zarządzanie bezpieczeństwem pracy. *Konferencja IZIP Zakopane*, Część X, 1052.

BSI. (2018). https://www.bsigroup.com/pl-PL/ISO-45001-Bezpieczenstwo-i-Higiena-Pracy (accessed July 18, 2019).

Chomątowska, B. (2011). Zarządzanie bezpieczeństwem i higieną pracy. *Nauki o Zarządzaniu 8*, 162–163.

Chomątowska, B. (2012). Zarządzanie bezpieczeństwem i higieną pracy – istota i współczesne wyzwania. *Prace Naukowe Uniwersytetu Ekonomicznego we Wrocławiu 274*, 29–30.

CIOP. (2014). Wytyczne do oceny funkcjonowania przedsiębiorstwa w obszarze bezpieczeństwa i higieny pracy z wykorzystaniem wskaźników wynikowych i wiodących. https://m.ciop.pl/CIOPPortalWAR/file/71799/wytyczne_oceny_funkcjonowania_bhp.pdf (accessed February 13, 2021).

CIOP. (2020). https://www.ciop.pl/CIOPPortalWAR/appmanager/ciop/pl?_nfpb=true&_pageLabel=P15000156221346925948558&html_tresc_root_id=25314&html_tresc_id=3001032&html_klucz=25314&html_klucz_spis=25314 (accessed December 17, 2020).

CIOP. (2021). https://m.ciop.pl/CIOPPortalWAR/appmanager/ciop/mobi?_nfpb=true&_pageLabel=P40200299501486654454849&html_tresc_root_id=300004907&html_tresc_id=300004904&html_klucz=300004907&html_klucz_spis= (accessed February 20, 2021).

Ejdys, J. (2010). *Kształtowanie kultury bezpieczeństwa i higieny pracy w organizacji.* Białystok, Poland: Oficyna Wydawnicza Politechniki Białostockiej.

Ejdys, J., Kobylińska, U., & Lulewicz-Sas A. (2012). *Zintegrowane systemy zarządzania jakością środowiskiem i bezpieczeństwem pracy.* Oficyna Wydawnicza Politechniki Białostockiej.

EUR-LEX. (2020). Dyrektywa Parlamentu Europejskiego i Rady Europy 2012/18/UE z 4 lipca 2012 r. *w sprawie kontroli zagrożeń poważnymi awariami związanymi z substancjami niebezpiecznymi, zmieniająca, a następnie uchylająca dyrektywę Rady 96/82/WE;* https://eur-lex.europa.eu/legal-content/PL/TXT/PDF/?uri=CELEX:32012L0018&from=EN (accessed December 12, 2020).

Gasiorowski-Denis, E. (2017). *Moving Ahead with iso 45001 for Safety and Health at Work.* International Organization for Standardization. https://www.iso.org/news/Ref2180.html (accessed February 19, 2021).

Gratka (2017). https://gratka.pl/regiopraca/portal/rynek-pracy/wiadomosci/stres-jest-przyczyna-60-proc-nieobecnosci-w-pracy (accessed May 22, 2018).

GUS. (2018). https://stat.gov.pl/obszary-tematyczne/rynek-pracy/warunki-pracy-wypadki-przy-pracy/wypadki-przy-pracy-w-2017-r-dane-wstepne,3,30.html (accessed May 20, 2020).

HSE. (2019). Health and safety eExecutive, http://www.hse.gov.uk/comah/ (accessed July 17, 2019).

HSE. (2021). https://www.hse.gov.uk/ (accessed February 24, 2021).

ISO 45001:2018. (en). *Occupational Health and Safety Management Systems — Requirements with Guidance for Use.* Geneva, Switzerland: International Organization for Standardization, 2018.

ISO 9000:2015 – *Systemy zarządzania jakością. Podstawy i terminologia.* Warsaw, Poland: Polski Komitet Normalizacyjny, 2015.

ISO-Update (2018). http://isoupdate.com/resources/introducing-iso-45001-affects/ (accessed December 11, 2020).

Iwko, J. & Iwko, J. (2018a). *Badanie poziomu kultury bezpieczeństwa w wybranym przedsiębiorstwie. Zeszyty Naukowe Politechniki Śląskiej, Seria Organizacja i Zarządzanie, zeszyt 131,* 149–166. doi: 10.29119/1641-3466.2018.131.11

Iwko, J., & Iwko, J. (2018b). *Znaczenie kształtowania kultury bezpieczeństwa w przedsiębiorstwie,* Zeszyty Naukowe Politechniki Śląskiej. *Seria Organizacja i Zarządzanie, zeszyt 131,* 167–182. doi: 10.2911 9/1641-3466.2018.131.12

Kubista, M. (red.) (2019). *ISO 45001 – System Zarządzania Bezpieczeństwem i Higieną Pracy,* Quality Austria-Polska, Mikołów.

Markowski, A. (1999). *Zapobieganie stratom w przemyśle. Część II. Zarządzanie bezpieczeństwem i higieną pracy.* Wydawnictwo Politechniki Łódzkiej.

Marsden, S., Wright, M., & Shaw, J. (2004a). Measuring corporate health and safety performance and corporate social responsibility – latest developments, *Greenstreet Berman Ltd, Symposium Series No. 150,* IChemE.

Marsden, S., Wright, M., Shaw, J., & Beardwell, C. (2004b). *The Development of a Health and Safety Management Index for Use by Business, Investors, Employees, the Regulator and Other Stakeholders. Research Report 217.* Health and Safety Executive.

Pacana, A. (2016). *Synteza systemowego zarządzania bezpieczeństwem i higieną pracy.* Oficyna Wydawnicza Politechniki Rzeszowskiej.

Pawłowska, Z. (2006). Jak oceniać funkcjonowanie przedsiębiorstwa w obszarze bezpieczeństwa i higieny pracy?. *Bezpieczeństwo Pracy 2,* 5–7.

Pawłowska, Z. (2012). Wskaźniki do oceny skuteczności zarządzania bezpieczeństwem i higieną pracy. *Bezpieczeństwo Pracy 8,* 32–34.

PKN (2019). https://wiedza.pkn.pl/web/wiedza-normalizacyjna/zarzadzanie-bezpieczenstwem-i-higiena-pracy (accessed March 2, 2021).

PN-N-18001: 2004, *Systemy zarządzania bezpieczeństwem i higieną pracy – Wymagania,* Polski Komitet Normalizacyjny, Warszawa 2004.

PN-N-18002:2011 – *Systemy zarządzania bezpieczeństwem i higieną pracy – Ogólne wytyczne do oceny ryzyka zawodowego,* Polski Komitet Normalizacyjny, Warszawa 2011.

PN-N-18004:2001 – *Systemy zarządzania bezpieczeństwem i higieną pracy – Wytyczne,* Polski Komitet Normalizacyjny, Warszawa 2001.

PN-N-18011:2006 – *Systemy zarządzania bezpieczeństwem i higieną pracy – Wytyczne audytowania,* Polski Komitet Normalizacyjny, Warszawa 2006.

Sarkar, S., Chain, M., Nayak, S., & Maiti, J. (2018). Decision support system for prediction of occupational accident: A case study from a steel plant. In Abraham A., Dutta P., Mandal J., Bhattacharya A., Dutta S. (Eds.). *Emerging Technologies in Data Mining and Information Security. Advances in Intelligent Systems and Computing,* vol. *813.* Singapore: Springer. https://doi.org/10.1007/978-981-13-1498-8_69

Semeykin, A., Kochetkova, I.A., Klimova, E.V., Nosatova, E.A., & Drozdova, A.O. (2019). Decision-making process modeling for occupational safety management system based on a fuzzy analysis of production incidents, *Journal of Physics 1333,* 072021. doi: 10.1088/1742-6596/1333/7/072021

Smoliński, D.R., & Solecki L. (2015). Mierniki stanu bezpieczeństwa i higieny pracy na stanowiskach pracy. *Medycyna Ogólna i Nauki o Zdrowiu 21*(2), 208–214.

Walker, D. (2006). Measuring corporate health and safety performance – the value of a universal indicator, *Centre for Hazard and Risk Management,* Symposium Series No. 151, IChemE.

Williams, N., & Shahriyer, A. (2010). *Review of CHaSPI,* Research Report RR813, Health and Safety Executive, 2010.

Wyrębek, H. (2012). Zarządzanie bezpieczeństwem pracy. *Zeszyty Naukowe Uniwersytetu Przyrodniczo-Humanistycznego w Siedlcach.* Seria Administracja i Zarządzanie *95,* 472–473.

Zymonik, Z., Hamrol, A., & Grudowski, P. (2013). *Zarządzanie jakością i bezpieczeństwem.* Polskie Wydawnictwo Ekonomiczne.

Chapter 5

The Theoretical and Practical Design Thinking Approach in IT Project – The Remote Human Resource Management System Case Study

Anna Sołtysik-Piorunkiewicz and Edyta Abramek

Faculty of Informatics and Communications, Department of Informatics, University of Economics in Katowice, Katowice, Poland

Contents

DOI: 10.1201/9781003030966-7

5.1 Theoretical Background

Most modern companies envy others' ingenuity and innovation. Therefore, in order to innovate and win with competitors, companies need a so-called design-thinking approach (Abramek and Sołtysik-Piorunkiewicz, 2020), (Figure 5.1).

Design thinking (DT) allows knowledge to transform and go through subsequent stages, i.e. secret -> heuristics -> algorithm -> code, which provide groundbreaking innovation and competitive advantage (Martin, 2009). In implementing projects, more and more companies recognize the importance of people's creativity and ingenuity (Stanek and Sołtysik-Piorunkiewicz, 2011a; Stanek and Sołtysik-Piorunkiewicz, 2011b).

The idea of design thinking was initiated in California, USA. One of its creators is D. M. Kelley (Kelley and Kelley, 2012), founder and owner of a company implementing projects using DT called IDEO (1991) and the d.school institute (2005). D. Kelley's brother – T. Kelley (Kelley 2012) and T. Brown (Brown, 2019), A. Osborne and D. Norman were also famous as creators or propagators of this approach in the process of creating innovative solutions. In Europe, the HPI School of design thinking, based in Potsdam, Germany, is responsible for the promotion of DT (since 2007). The University of Economics in Katowice is one of many centers that actively use the DT approach in Poland.

Design thinking is a method of creative problem solving (Abramek and Sołtysik-Piorunkiewicz, 2020). Its goal is to create innovative solutions that fully meet the needs of users (Brenner and Uebernickel, 2016), (Kolb, 1984; Li et al., 2016; Liu et al., 2017). It is a universal and very intuitive method that can be used by small and large corporations. T. Brown claims that **"the mission of design thinking is to turn observations into ideas, and ideas into solutions that make life better"** (Brenner and Uebernickel, 2016). This confirms that the method, by discovering, researching, and creating new solutions, and forgetting about established patterns, improves the quality of life, work, products, or services. This method places great emphasis on thorough knowledge and understanding of users and their needs (Hoover, 2018). In the business approach, it also focuses on the possibilities of subsequent implementation of the invented solution.

The translation of the name of this method into Polish may suggest that it is a method used only for project management. However, this is not the case. This approach should be understood more broadly because DT helps, above all, to change the way of thinking during project implementation (the problem is seen from the customer's perspective) and to change the way of working (interdisciplinarity, trusting the ideas of employees in the company). DT works very well in solving the so-called difficult, complicated, "wicked problems."

DT is a method that leads to the generation of innovative ideas for a product, service, or process, and, most importantly, it helps to create solutions that are needed and useful. The

LEAN	Build **the right things**
AGILE	**Build** the thing **right**
DESIGN THINKING	**Explore the problem**

Figure 5.1 Comparison of the Lean, Agile and DT methods in project implementation.

Source: Schneider (2017, p. 2).

resulting solutions must be functional and user-friendly, technically feasible, and economically justified.

Design thinking is divided into five main stages: empathization, problem definition, idea generation, prototype building, and prototype testing (if necessary, you can return to previous stages). The DT approach teaches you how **to focus primarily on the problem and not on the solution when implementing projects**. Many IT projects fail because IT specialists focus mainly on the solution and not on analysing the needs of their clients (the empathy stage is key to project implementation). Problems are either complex, complicated, or have many solutions, and it is difficult to find one solution for them. That is why DT encourages creative problem solving through action, in particular through prototyping and testing (feedback is key to these stages). DT shows how to do something better. From the very beginning, DT teaches that you should not focus solely on the product or service, but on how "to love" the problem, not only recognize it, recognize the situation, look at it systemically and from different perspectives.

The design-thinking process combines divergent and convergent thinking (Figure 5.2).

Divergent thinking, in this case, looks for many possible solutions, viewing the problem from a wide perspective, which allows you to find many unusual solutions. DT is one of those methods that affect the creativity of solutions (Stanek and Sołtysik-Piorunkiewicz, 2011a). On the other hand, convergent thinking allows you to analyze a problem to find the one, the best solution using available resources. Figure 5.2 shows DT as a process from a problem to solution. Each rhombus is divided into two phases: divergent thinking – wide to best identify a given research topic, and convergent thinking – in which we narrow down the way of thinking, striving to infer specific conclusions.

DT as a method involves creative trust (Kelly and Kelly, 2013). People lose their creativity as a result of inappropriate teaching methods or, just simply, with age. Therefore, the goal of DT is to encourage people during the implementation of the project to use various, additional working methods that stimulate creativity, such as SCAMPER. This method was developed in the 1970s by B. Eberle, but its propagation is attributed to A. Osborn. It tries to transform a given thing in seven ways: S (substitute), C (combine), A (adapt), M (modify), P (put to another use), E (eliminate), or R (reverse). The brainstorming stage generates a huge amount of ideas. Next, we choose the best one.

The use of DT methods and tools in project implementation is aimed at thoroughly identifying the causes of observed problems and discovering gaps in knowledge about users of products or services, and, as a result, it provides useful and creative solutions. The advantage of the design-thinking approach is focusing on the needs of the recipient, effective knowledge sharing, and focusing on quick implementation, as well as comprehensive and contextual preparation to solve the problem.

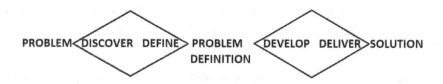

Figure 5.2 The problem-solving process takes into account the divergent and convergent thinking phases.

Source: Own elaboration based on stages of design thinking.

5.2 Integration of Design Thinking Methods into the IT Project Life Cycle

The creativity in an IT project-designing approach is now one of the critical factors of the IT project life cycle. The design-thinking method is universal, so it can be easily applied in companies, projects, or everyday life, developing a way of thinking for IT project development. This is undoubtedly an advantage of this method, but not the only one. Another advantage of design thinking is looking at the problem from the user's perspective (the so-called persona). It is for the customer that a solution is invented and designed, so the better we understand their needs, the better solution we will offer them, the better we will meet their requirements. That is why it is so important to spend as much time as it takes to thoroughly understand the needs and problems of customers, recipients, or users.

Design thinking is also a process, one that brings results quickly. It all depends on the complexity of the challenges faced by the designers, but usually, a few or several days pass from the idea to the solution. However, remember that you should not rush, skipping or neglecting individual stages of the process; doing so may result in proposing an ineffective solution, and the entire process may have to be carried out from the beginning.

The DT approach involves the following steps:

1. **Empathize** – This phase is when we carry out interviews, surveys, observations, and conversations, and we analyze literature. It is important to identify your best interlocutor. To sum up, at this stage, we answer the question: **Who are we doing it for?**
2. **Define** – Defining the problem is the phase during which we prepare: user persona, user stories, and empathy maps. Goals, challenges, opportunities, and risks are defined at this stage. To sum up, at this stage, we answer the question: **For whom and why do we do it?**
3. **Ideate** – This stage is when ideas are generated. The best-known tool in this case is brainstorming, during which everyone has the right to speak. Her or his ideas will not be negatively assessed. It is important to remain objective and not attach too much to your idea because this stage should end with the emergence of the best idea, by e.g. voting brainstorm participants. Generating ideas should take place in multidisciplinary teams, based on co-operation. They do not criticize, ridicule, or analyze other people's ideas. The DT connects perspectives – each member of the team has different knowledge and experience, and it is worth using them. There is no such thing as a "stupid" idea at this stage. The emphasis is on quantity, not quality. Even irrational ideas can lead the team to a valuable idea. The ideas are presented in a clear and understandable way to other members. To sum up, at this stage, we answer the question: **What can we suggest?**
4. **Prototype** – At this stage, a prototype is developed based on the idea. To sum up, at this stage, we answer the question: **What does it look like?** In a word, we visualize our idea.
5. **Test** – At this stage, we test prototypes. To sum up, this stage is when we answer the question: **How does it work? Is it useful?**

Research thesis: We can state, considering the above literature survey and our own observations and experiences, that *the use of the design-thinking approach in the implementation of the projects facilitates making project decisions thanks to precisely defined stages of the process and knowledge of what to do at each stage.*

The following parts of the work are presented:

- What stages does the human resource (HR) management process consist of?
- What selected models are used in the recruitment process (HRM models)?
- What problems in the HR area can be solved using the DT approach?
- How do we apply the DT approach to solving the problem of remote recruitment of employees?

5.3 The Human Resources Management (HRM) Models Review

The human resources management process is divided into several stages, among which we can distinguish:

1. human resources planning and acquiring employees,
2. recruitment and selection,
3. hiring, introducing new employees (onboarding), and training,
4. evaluation of work results,
5. employee development and motivation,
6. collecting employees' experiences and their insights (prosumption).

Planning and acquiring employees are key elements of human resources management; these goals can be met only when we have an appropriate number of employees with the required predispositions. Personnel planning should precede recruitment because, thanks to planning, we know how many employees the company needs to hire and what qualifications should be sought (people with what qualifications does the company need). It is important to have a good foundation; for example, a "humanist" will not learn analytical skills just like that, if he does not show such skills during recruitment. Therefore, the acquisition of employees itself is an extremely important task because if you want to have a highly qualified staff, you should hire employees with specific skills, important from the company's perspective, that can be improved in the subsequent human resources management process.

Persons involved in the preparation of a competency profile of employee should know what "hard" requirements the organization desires (i.e. education, experience, and skills), but also be aware of what features a candidate should have, the so-called "soft" skills (mental and physical requirements). Such a profile should comply with the requirements for a given job.

There are several models in the recruitment process (that an organization can adopt in remote human resource management) (Leśniewski and Morawska, 2012):

1. **The sita model** is based on the competition and competition between candidates and employees. At the recruitment stage, it consists of accepting only the best candidates whose usefulness is supported by their education, documented diplomas, and certificates. However, the competition does not end at this stage. With employees, those with the best results are promoted, and those with the weakest ones are dismissed to replace them with new, more effective ones. This model makes employees feel constantly at risk, so they work at top speed to obtain the best results and avoid being laid off. This model allows you to minimize the expenditure on human resources management by verifying the skills of employees in their daily work; however, it creates an unpleasant atmosphere at work, leading to many conflicts between the staff.

2. **The human capital model** is people-oriented (for employee development). Candidates do not necessarily have to be highly educated with the best diplomas, but they must show willingness to develop and collaborate in a team, and above all, willing to develop their skills and cooperate. This model assumes hiring an employee for a long period. In the organization, people should feel good and not worry about layoffs, as they happen very rarely. If an employee cannot cope with a specific position, it is preferable to transfer him/her to another position first, until he finds something suitable. This model assumes overcoming the employee's weaknesses and reaping the benefits of his strengths. The model promotes a good atmosphere at work; however, it is highly expensive due to the investment in human development.

3. **The Harvard model** (HRM, "employees as assets, not costs") consists of four areas of human resource management: employee participation, employee rotation, employee motivation, and work organization. This model is characterized by a system of mutual dependencies. The implemented in company tasks are significantly influenced by, among others, employment structure, strategy, market situation, and all situational factors. The decisions made have not only direct effects (such as commitment and productivity), but also indirect effects (such as employee well-being, social well-being, and the high/good company's performance). The creators of this model distinguish three ways of managing human resources. The bureaucracy method characterizes the existence of a hierarchy, where the employee is a subordinate and his participation in the life of the organization takes place only through the official route. In the market method, employees or groups of employees are assigned tasks. The employee participates in the life of the organization in accordance with the provisions of the contract. Employee rotation takes place when necessary. In the clan way, employees participate in the life of the organization by creating project groups; the employee is part of the organization, part of the project team.

4. **The Michigan model** assumes that human resource management should be like any other resource (resemble the management of other resources in the organization, e.g. material, financial, information). It assumes minimizing the costs of acquiring employees and maximizing the use of employees and their skills. This model includes four steps: employee selection, efficiency assessment, employee motivation, and development. These steps create a process that allows you to achieve the intended goals of the organization, but they are also identified as important issues in strategic, tactical, and operational management. This model places great emphasis on recruitment since it allows for effective human capital management.

5. **Models of managing the personnel function** (HR function management models) include three sample models. Under the traditional model, an employee needs motivation, clear orders, and work control. The model of interpersonal relations uses the idea that a human being is a social being (group work, respect, and acceptance). A model of human resources is one in which a person strives for self-realization, where he can demonstrate creative invention or initiative that will bring benefits to the organization.

The decision to choose a given model is influenced by many factors, including the market strategy pursued by the company, the conditions prevailing in the nearby market, relations with trade unions, and the competences of potential employees in the company's region.

An interesting example of a company that, influenced by the expectations of its employees, changed the model of human resources management is Deloitte. Deloitte's experience shows that traditional HR solutions (business-focused) built around the recruitment process, forms, formal training, and events are over. Recruitment processes need to be remote and more interactive (talent-focused). Deloitte has applied design thinking to transform traditional HR solutions and move from a **process developer** to an **experience architect**, and from **redesigning the physical work environment** to **optimizing the digital workspace** (Chatterjee, 2020).

5.4 The Online Recruiting Model in Remote Human Resources Management

Recruitment is aimed at attracting candidates to the organization, people who will be selected and then the best of them hired as employees. This process will allow the organization to acquire employees meeting certain requirements, with the help of whom the organization will be able to achieve its strategic goals.

The stages of recruitment can be divided into (Szałkowski, 2000): (1) determining the requirements and competences of the candidate, (2) attracting candidates, and (3) selecting them.

After preparing the employee's professional (ideal) profile, you should start looking for candidates for the position. Recruitment can be carried out among employees of a given company or among new candidates. In the case of a pandemic, the pool of candidates in internal recruitment is made up of employees of a given company. Enterprises often collect information about their employees and their potential in advance, in order to focus on their development, if necessary, to transfer them to another position, promotion, or retraining without any problems. This method is generally less time-consuming and cheaper than external recruitment. Also, candidates do not have to go through a long adaptation process, and the possibility of promotion additionally motivates them and increases loyalty to the organization. However, the method of internal recruitment may also spoil the atmosphere at work when there is competition between employees. In the case of external recruitment, there are two types of recruitment: broad, i.e. targeted at the labor market, or segmented, i.e. targeted only at the market segment.

There are a lot of methods of informing about recruitment, and the most popular of them include:

- Internet tools, where there is a wide audience, and offers can be posted, among others on portals (e.g. Pracuj.pl, Olx.pl, LinkedIn), on the company's website, on social networks,
- Notification of the demand for employees at the labor office, which will pass the offer on to jobseekers,
- Discernment among friends and relatives,
- Posting the offer on the notice board in public places and institutions,
- Placing an advertisement in a newspaper,
- Organizing job fairs at universities to attract graduates of a given specialization,
- Employee leasing, i.e. "loaning" a given employee for a specified period.

When recruiting, it is very important that the information about the opportunity is concise and encourages the potential candidate to take an interest in it and apply for an offer. The job offer should contain basic information about the features of the job, i.e. the name of the position, the employee's obligations, the required skills and education, the company's location, and the method of applying for the job. It is also worth adding what the company offers on its side to encourage as many candidates as possible to apply.

5.5 The Users' Needs Analyzes of Online Recruiting System in the Context of IT Company Example – Case Study

The characterized online recruiting system solution was created based on IT company in Poland in Katowice, which is a world leader company in the IT industry. The company deals with business consulting in the field of IT solutions, as well as providing software and hardware to its clients. The case was studied in context of IT IBM Poland.

At the beginning of its activity, the company operated under the name of Computing Tabulating Recording Corporation; with time, and with the acquisition of the company by James Watson in 1924, the name was changed to International Business Machines Corporation (IBM), which operates to this day. IBM is recognized as one of the largest and most profitable enterprises in the world, with highly skilled employees and one of the most sought-after companies in the labor market. Due to the size of the company, it is also struggling with various internal problems, such as cultural and geopolitical barriers. Employee rotation is also an important issue, which on the one hand brings benefits, as frequent refreshment of the staff motivates employees to transfer to the company as much as possible, but it also exposes the company to the costs associated with training new employees.

IBM focuses on continuous development by cooperating with enterprises, creating innovative and modern products that give them an advantage over the competition. Also, university and internship programs allow the candidates to educate and guide the future employee of the company at a low cost.

To stabilize the process of employee rotation and recruitment in the company due to current and potential future employees, the design-thinking methods (Figure 5.3) are proposed **to describe the user needs, to describe the online recruiting processes, and to look at its current and potential future employees** during the course of the IT Project for the third-year students of bachelor degree Informatics and Econometrics at the University of Economics in Katowice.

Id.	Phases of the recruitment process using the design thinking approach	Description
1	EMPATHIZE = discover	We start with getting to know the nature of the problem (facilitating and improving the process of remote recruitment of new employees to an IT company) through user observation and interviews, surveys, analysis of other companies' solutions (where we are, where we want to be)
2	DEFINE = defining the problem	Based on the collected information, we define the problem
3	IDEATE = creating/generating solutions	We create many possible solutions for the same defined problem
4	PROTOTYPE = develop	We choose the best ideas and build a prototype. We give the selected idea a visual character (in a short time and with little effort)
5	TEST = deliver	We test the solution with users. We check whether the solution is the answer to the problem. We collect feedback, e.g. which needs modification
6	IMLEMENTATION	We are improving solutions

Figure 5.3 Design thinking process.

Source: Own elaboration based on stages of design thinking.

The focus was on getting to know the future user needs of the solution as well as possible; therefore, the stage of empathizing the design-thinking process was continued. One of the design-thinking tools was used, and the following three different personas (Figure 5.4) were created in context of following criteria: name and position, age, place of residence, family, education, lifestyle, goals, values, and frustrations.

Id.	Personas	Criteria Characteristics
1.	Karolina X. - manager of the project team at IT company	a. Age: 35 years old b. Place of residence: Katowice c. Family life: husband d. Education: higher in project management e. Lifestyle: exhausted and stressed, often working late, so there is no time to enlarge the family, which she would like, she is able to save only one evening for her husband a week. f. Goals: to have a better organized workday, stay at work late, spend more time with your husband, start a family g. Values: appreciates family ties, but does not pay enough attention to it due to the sheer volume of work h. Frustrations: she would like to have a well-coordinated team, but browsing CVs and selecting candidates is too much for her, as she has already talked to a few who turned out to be unsuccessful, the long recruitment process takes her time, which she could spend on something else
2.	Tomasz Y. - member of Karolina's design team	a. Age: 40 years old b. Place of residence: Będzin c. Family life: wife, child and dog d. Education: higher in computer science and psychology e. Lifestyle: he has been working at IT company for a year, he has already managed to adapt to the rhythm prevailing in the company, he has less and less time for his family because they have an incomplete project team and they have to work overtime with everything, he spends his free time reading books in the field of psychology and philosophy f. Goals: he would like to stand out from the team and become a manager himself in the future, and at the same time devote as much time as possible to his adolescent daughter g. Values: the family is most important to him, however, he also places great emphasis on personal development h. Frustration: believes that Karolina is unable to find new team members because the company has an underdeveloped recruitment system, unlike other companies that check the candidate's skills before hiring him
3.	Julia Z. -applying	a. Age: 23 years old b. Place of residence: Częstochowa c. Family life: lives with fiancé and cat d. Education: completed bachelor's degree in computer science, during master's studies in project management (extramural) e. Lifestyle: works as an assistant in a company with no development prospects, exercises 4 times a week, spends free time with her fiancé or learning German f. Goals: find a job in which she could develop herself and her career, preferably in a corporation that is of great importance in the market g. Values: focuses on development and self-improvement, would like to start a family in the future, but not in the next few years h. Frustrations: her work bored her, she earns little, and recruiting in companies is a huge challenge for her, because they are often illegible, she does not know whether to submit a CV in Englishor Polish to companies like IT company, she is nervous about the lack of response from companies, to which she sent her CV, and one of such companies is IT company

Figure 5.4 Building a person and identifying their real needs.

Source: Own elaboration based on stages of design thinking.

Functional aspects	a. Entering the system will require logging in using personal email address, b. The colors and appearance of the system will refer to the company's logo, c. Content submitted by the user after approval will not be subject to change, d. The CV file will be inserted in the .pdf format, e. The video file will be inserted in the .mp4 format, f. Application for the position will require a test to check the skills needed for a given position, g. The user will have access to the progress of the recruitment process, h. Direct communication between the company and the applicant will take place via telephone or e-mail address, i. The system will be available to all users interested in working.
Technical aspects	a. It should be a browser system, b. Using the system will only be possible after connecting to the VPN network, c. The system should have a database connected, encrypted using Base64, d. System based on the MySQL database software used by the company, e. Data on the applicant in the database should include his/her name and surname, telephone number, e-mail address, application date, position for which he/she is applying, CV file, video file, completed test.
Financial aspects	a. The budget of the project should be PLN 50,000, b. The budget should include training for staff and a post-implementation help desk.
Organizational aspects	a. System implementation should not take more than 6 months, b. Help desk should be available in the company within 3 months after implementation, c. After approval of the acceptance decision, no changes can be made without the agreement of the parties, d. Progress in the project should be reported on an ongoing basis.

Figure 5.5   Identifying the system requirements due to identifying the personas real needs.

Source: Own elaboration.

Due to the recommendations of personas analysis, the remote recruitment process should be improved by creating a system that would automate this process and open the online functionalities more.

To determine the users' needs that the new system would meet, a analyzes were conducted with an online questionnaires in the group of 25 students of third-year bachelor degree studies of Informatics and Econometrics (2019/2020), which allowed to determine and propose the following (1) functional, (2) technical, (3) financial, and (4) organizational aspects (Figures 10.4 and 10.5).

The conducted analysis, which emphasized design thinking, made it possible to get to know and define the problem of time-consuming and labor-intensive recruitment process, often incomprehensible for applicants.

5.6 Discussion

The chapter presents the selected effects of work results of identifying the part of human resource management system project from individual personas needs described in the IT project – the remote recruitment system. During the IDEATE phase, several ways were invented to solve this problem, including: (1) a mobile application for recruitment, (2) transferring all work to HR employees, or (3) outsourcing the recruitment to an external company. These ideas, however, were verified taking into account the responses of the respondents to (4) the website supporting the recruitment process, which will be used by both – the recruiter and the applicant. The system was divided into five main functions that allow users to fully use it and include the most important issues related to the recruitment process. The above-mentioned functions are: registering the applicant's data, recording the job offers, recording the recruitment files, recording the test results, and managing the users' account. Most of the functions are in three stages, which ensure a quick and easy data flow. In the DT approach, order is important – we always start by defining the needs of people. The solution, result, idea that emerges must be: (1) needed by people (functional aspect), (2) technically, technologically feasible (technical aspect), (3) financially, economically justified (financial aspect), and (4) organized due to users' expectations and needs of the future solution (organizational aspect).

5.7 Conclusions

Design thinking can be applied to various areas of human resource management:

- in designing processes and employee recruitment systems,
- in improving onboarding activities and creating solutions that create an environment conducive to onboarding and training new employees,
- to effectively share knowledge between employees (between employees from different departments, different levels or with different seniority),
- in managing employer-employee relations,
- to improve the efficiency of work in teams,
- in performance management – to evaluate employees or teams in terms of their work input,
- in collecting feedback from candidates or employees,
- collecting experiences and ideas of employees or teams in the workplace and improving their experiences,
- to design or improve the employee development path model.

Beaven K. writes that HR can leverage design thinking via: organizational design, engagement, learning, analytics, HR skills, and digital HR (Beaven, 2019, p. 224).

The tools used in the **empathize** stage of the design thinking can help recruiters create a welcoming environment for new hires. Continuous questioning can help set expectations and identify trouble spots and tasks for the employee to perform in the position. The IDEATE stage is key to creating innovation. HR teams must be willing to abandon conventional approaches and, for example, recruit employees through social media, which is already happening. The combination of the IDEATE and PROTOTYPE phases permits the quick preparation of effective solutions or applications (using, for example, a low-code or no-code platform, with which you can prepare and implement an application in the company even on the same day).

DT is defined as a creative approach to problem solving, which aims to understand the problem and generate an innovative solution. It works perfectly in the implementation of business, social, IT, marketing, and didactic projects. DT is a universal method because it can be used in various areas; it does not matter whether we deal with a local or global problem. The advantage of design thinking is teamwork. "That is social technology at work" (Liedtka, 2018). The key to this approach is cooperation and involvement. The project team should be interdisciplinary, composed of people who specialize in various fields and have different experiences; this diversity will allow the team to view a given problem from many perspectives. The heart of the design-thinking process lies at the intersection of desirability by the user, economic viability, and technical feasibility (Plattner et al., 2011). This method takes into account three key aspects: (1) people's needs, (2) business needs, (3) technical and technological capabilities.

References

Abramek, E., & Sołtysik-Piorunkiewicz, A. (2020). Using the design thinking approach in the project decisions making. *Journal of Decision Systems*. doi: 10.1080/12460125.2020.1848385. Published Online: 03 Dec 2020.

Beaven, K. (2019). Strategic Human Resource Management. An HR professional's Toolkit, KoganPage.

Brenner, W., & Uebernickel, F. (2016). *Design Thinking for Innovation: Research and Practice*. Heidelberg; New York; Dordrecht; London: Springer, Cham.

Brown, T. (2019). *Change by Design: How Design Thinking Transforms Organizations and Inspires Innovation*. New York: Harper Business.

Chatterjee, M. (2020). Use of design thinking in HR. How to use design thinking in human resources. https://www.mygreatlearning.com/blog/use-of-design-thinking-in-hr/, last accessed March 31, 2021.

Hoover, C. (2018) Human-centered design vs. design-thinking: How they're different and how to use them together to create lasting change. Available from: https://blog. movingworlds.org/human-centered-design-vs-design-thinking-how-theyre-different-and-how-to-use-them-together-to-create-lasting-change/, last accessed January 21, 2020.

Kelley, T., & Kelley, D. (2013). *Creative Confidence: Unleashing the Creative Potential Within Us All*. New York: Crown Business.

Kelley, T., & Kelley, D. (2012). Reclaim your creative confidence. HBR. Available from: https://hbr.org/2012/12/reclaim-your-creative-confidence. last accessed January 21, 2020.

Kolb, D.A. (1984). *Experiential Learning: Experience as the Source of Learning and Development*. New Jersey: Prentice-Hall Inc.

Leśniewski, M.A., & Morawska, S. (2012). *Zasoby ludzkie w organizacji*. Warszawa: CeDeWu.

Li, Y. (2016). How to establish a creative atmosphere in tourism and hospitality education in the context of China. *Journal of Hospitality, Leisure, Sports and Tourism Education 18*, 9–20.

Liedtka, J. (2018). Why design thinking works. HBR. Available from: https:// hbr.org/2018/09/why-design-thinking-works, last accessed 2020/06/01.

Liu, C. (2017). Analysis of tourism and hospitality sustainability education with co-competition creativity course planning. *Journal of Hospitality, Leisure, Sports and Tourism Education 21*, 88–100.

Martin, R.L. (2009). *The Design of Business: Why Design Thinking is the Next Competitive Advantage*. McGraw-Hill Professional, Harvard Business Press Books, October 2009.

Plattner, H., Meinel, C.H., & Leifer, L. (Eds.). (2011). *Design Thinking: Understand-Improve-Apply*. Berlin Heidelberg: Springer-Verlag. doi: 10.1007/978-3-642-13757-0.

Schneider, J. (2017). *Understanding Design Thinking, Lean, and Agile*. USA: O'Reilly Media, Inc.

Sołtysik-Piorunkiewicz, A. (2018). *Modele oceny użyteczności i akceptacji mobilnych systemów zarządzania wiedzą o zdrowiu*. Katowice: Uniwersytet Ekonomiczny w Katowicach.

Stanek, S., & Sołtysik-Piorunkiewicz, A. (2011). Analiza porównawcza mind i concept mapperów. W: Wiedza i komunikacja w innowacyjnych organizacjach. Komunikacja elektroniczna, (red.) M. Pańkowska, Uniwersytet Ekonomiczny w Katowicach, Katowice.

Stanek, S., & Sołtysik-Piorunkiewicz, A. (2011). Building creative decision support systems for project management. Mind and concept mapping methodologies. [In] Creativity Support Systems, red. H. Sroka, S. Stanek, Studia Ekonomiczne, No. 88, Uniwersytet Ekonomiczny w Katowicach, Katowice.

Szałkowski, A. (2000). *Wprowadzenie do zarządzania personelem*. Kraków: Wydawnictwo Akademii Ekonomicznej w Krakowie.

UNCERTAINTY AND PRESSURE IN DECISION MAKING

Chapter 6

Increasing the Efficiency of IT Waterfall Projects Control: Modified Earned Value Analysis Combined with Parametric Estimation

Dorota Kuchta

Faculty of Management, Wrocław University of Science and Technology, Wrocław, Poland

Stanisław Stanek

Faculty of Management General Tadeusz Kosciuszko Military University of Land Forces, Wrocław, Poland

Contents

DOI: 10.1201/9781003030966-9

6.1 Introduction

According to the 2015 Chaos Report (https://www.standishgroup.com/sample_research_files/CHAOSReport2015-Final.pdf), over 50% of IT projects were not accomplished within budget. Each such case is usually a financial issue for the organisation implementing the project; it diminishes the organisation's profit and, in extreme cases, may even lead to bankruptcy. It must be emphasized that the same Chaos Reports show that IT projects implemented according to the waterfall model are significantly less successful than the agile ones. Thus, it is important to control cost in waterfall IT projects and to have an efficient warning system; this system would, during project implementation, warn the project manager as early as possible that a budgetary problem is approaching, long before a real problem arises. An early warning would give the project manager time to take necessary measures to avoid the problem or minimise its impact. An analogous approach is required for time management: the same sources indicate that a significant fraction of projects are late, and it is of the utmost importance to attempt to control time during project realisation.

The earned value method (EVA) provides a framework for a warning system for the project realisation phase, in terms of both cost and time. However, the original earned value method (Fleming and Koppelman, 2000) does not guarantee its effectiveness. The formulae used there admit data that are easily accessible but not necessarily informative enough, from the point of view of the project's actual situation in terms of time and cost. Numerous important information is ignored, which might provide an important warning that a significant budgetary and deadline-related problem is approaching. That is why the method should be modified in such a way that significant data is considered. The literature includes some modification proposals that go in this direction, but there is still a need for further improvement of the quality of data used in the EVA framework. The objective of this paper is to propose such an improvement.

The information that is not taken into account in the earned value method is often considered earlier, in the project defining and planning stage. At that time, various estimation methods are used to assess the project's cost and duration. Methods often applied for the IT project estimation are parametric methods, especially the COCOMO models. They use exhaustive sources of information, looking at various project aspects; however, later, in the implementation phase, there is a sudden jump to the control methods (the earned value method), where very few information types are considered. This results in the above-mentioned low performance of IT waterfall projects control. We propose thus to combine the earned value method with the COCOMO method, which belongs to the family of parametric project-estimation methods.

The research methodology is addressed in a literature review on COCOMO methods, in a critical analysis of the EVA method, and in proposing a conceptual model of their combination together, with its initial validation accomplished through a failed case study IT project. The outline of the paper is as follows: in section 6.2, parametric IT estimation methods are reviewed; in section 6.3, the basic earned value method and its existing extensions in terms of information used is described; in section 6.4, the present state of the management of IT waterfall projects is criticised and a new concept proposed; in section 6.5, the case study project is used for the initial validation of the proposed concept. The paper terminates with some conclusions.

6.2 Parametric IT Project Estimation Methods

Several methods (Phillips and Ward, 2010) can be used before the start of an IT project to estimate the effort (e.g. person months), and, consequently, the time needed to accomplish an IT project. Among them, so-called parametric methods can be distinguished, where effort is a function of several parameters.

The best known parametric models for IT projects are known under the common name COCOMO (COnstructive COst MOdel) (Barry Boehm et al., 2000; Cooper, 1992; Dillibabu and Krishnaiah, 2005; Trendowicz and Jeffery, 2014). COCOMO models are statistical regression models. The dependent variable is effort (which can be used in turn to estimate project duration), and it is a function of

a. predicted productivity
b. software size
c. several effort drivers
d. several scale factors

The productivity is usually set to a constant, derived from the literature or practical experience. Software size is measured in terms of thousands of lines of source code. Effort drivers represent characteristics of the software development environment that may have a significant impact on the effort needed. The scale factors influence the degree of diseconomies of scale (e.g. due to growing interpersonal communication).

In the following, we quote one possible list of effort drivers. They are explained in detail in (Trendowicz and Jeffery, 2014), but the principle is that their evaluation is higher on the adopted scale the more they increase the effort needed. For example, the evaluation of "product complexity" will be higher, the more complex the expected project product is. "Documentation match to life-cycle needs" will be evaluated higher, the less the project's documentation is suited to project life-cycle needs. "Platform volatility"' evaluation will be higher, the more complicated the combination of hardware and software needed for the product is. "Required development schedule" will be evaluated higher, the more strict constraints are set on project schedule, etc. Here is the complete list of the effort drivers:

F1. required software reliability
F2. database size
F3. product complexity
F4. developed for reusability
F5. documentation match to life cycle needs
F6. execution time constraint
F7. main storage constraint
F8. platform volatility
F9. analyst capability
F10. programmer capability

F11. personnel continuity

F12. applications experience

F13. platform experience

F14. language and tool experience

F15. use of software tools

F16. multisite development

F17. required development schedule

Literature proposes also a list of scale factors (Trendowicz and Jeffery, 2014). Here is their shortened description:

F18. the extent to which the to-do software is not similar to products developed in already terminated projects;

F19. the degree of obligation to be conformant to preestablished requirements;

F20. degree of risk linked to architecture of the product;

F21. the level of difficulty in synchronising project stakeholders;

F22. the distance of software processes in the organisation to the highest level of capability maturity model (Lacerda and von Wangenheim, 2018).

It is important to underline that some of the above factors, e.g. F8, F9, F10, refer to features of the project team. The project team's importance in calculating effort has been acknowledged to an even higher degree in modifications of COCOMO models. For example, model FECSCE (Kazemifard et al., 2011) considers explicitly communication skills, personality, mood, and interpersonal capabilities of team members as individual effort factors.

The numbers of factors (effort drivers and scale factors) considered in the model used in a given case may vary. Some of the factors F1-F22 can be eliminated if they are insignificant in the given case (Trendowicz and Jeffery, 2014), but also some (Kazemifard et al., 2011) can be added.

It is important to emphasize that the values of some of the above factors (e.g. F1, F2, F22) are fixed for each project, and most certainly will not change during project implementation. However, the value of some of them may change, even drastically (e.g. programmer capability – in case of a change in the project team, mood – in case of difficulties experienced by the team during the project, etc.)

6.3 Basic Information about Earned Value Method

The earned value method (EVA) (Fleming and Koppelman, 2000) is a method that requires a systematic control of projects to update the estimates about total project or activity cost (or resource usage). It must be emphasized that the method is also used to update the estimates about total project or activity duration, but in this aspect, the earned value method is far less reliable because its emphasis lies on the cost control. In the following, the basic form of EVA will be described, limited to the cost control.

Let us define an object O, which may stand for a single project activity, a set of project activities, or a whole project. Let us define:

■ $t_j, j = 1, ..., n$: time units in which project course is expressed (weeks, months...);

■ $S(t_j), j = 1, ..., n$: the starting moments of the periods $t_j, j = 1, ..., n$ (the project starts in the moment $S(t_1)$);

■ $E(t_j)$, $j = 1$, ..., n: the end moments of the periods t_j, $j = 1$, ..., n (the project terminates in the moment $E(t_n)$);

■ T_i, $i = 1$, ..., m: control moments – the moments when cost control according to the EVA method is performed. T_1 can be identified with $S(t_1)$, thus with the project start; here the "cost control" means in fact the initial cost estimation. We assume that for each T_i, $i = 2$, ..., m there exists a $j(i)$ such that $T_i = E(t_{j(i)})$; thus, the control moments are selected among the ends of the time units in which the project course is expressed. All the values of the functions used in the following with the argument T_i are determined in moment T_i and not earlier, when it is known what has actually been done at object O and at what cost up to moment T_i;

■ c_i, $i = 1$, ..., m: unitary cost (or unitary usage of a resource) planned in moment T_i for the course of O after moment T_i. c_1 is the unitary cost (or usage of resources) planned before the project start, c_i, $i = 2$, ..., m are the readjusted unitary costs (the adjustment is made in the control moments T_i, $i = 2$, ..., m);

■ $BAC(T_i)$ (where the abbreviation BAC stands for "Budget at Completion") is the budget assigned officially to O according to the knowledge in moment T_i. $BAC(T_1)$ is the budget assigned to O before the project start. This budget very often remains unchanged until the end (thus, most often, we have $BAC(T_1) = BAC(T_i)$ for $i = 2$, ..., m)). Any change of $BAC(T_i)$ with respect to $BAC(T_{i-1})$ for $i = 2$, ..., m must be authorised by the organization's senior management or be compensated by the symmetric change in the assigned budget in another object. Here we will assume for the sake of simplicity that $BAC(T_1) = BAC(T_i)$ for $i = 2$, ..., m and will be denoted as BAC.

■ $BCWS(T_i)$ (where the abbreviation $BCWS$ stands for "Budgeted Cost of Work Scheduled") is the portion of budget BAC that before the project start was planned to be spent on object O till moment T_i.

■ $BCWP(T_i)$ (where the abbreviation $BCWP$ stands for "Budgeted Cost of Work Performed") is the portion of budget BAC that before the project start was planned to be spent on the actual work accomplished until moment T_i on object O;

■ $ACWP(T_i)$ (where the abbreviation $ACWP$ stands for "Actual Cost of Work Performed") stands for the actual cost (or resource usage) accrued at object O till moment T_i;

■ $EAC(T_i)$ (where the abbreviation EAC stands for "Estimate at Completion") stands for the actual <u>total</u> cost (or resource usage) of object O according to the best knowledge at our disposal in moment T_i. It is thus an estimation or forecast, redone at each control moment. Obviously, we have $BAC(T_1) = EAC(T_1)$. In moments T_i for $i = 2$, ..., m there may be a difference between $BAC(T_i)$ and $EAC(T_i)$. This difference is denoted as $VAC(T_i)$, is defined as $BAC(T_i) - EAC(T_i)$, and stands for the estimation of excess (if positive) or shortage (if negative) of financial means or resource units at the completion of object O according to the best knowledge at our disposal in moment T_i. $VAC(T_i)$, if it is negative, is a warning signal of a shortage which is coming, but may still be influenced, because it has not become a reality yet;

■ $ETC(T_i)$ (where the abbreviation ETC stands for "Estimate to Complete") stands for the estimation of the cost (or resource usage) of the work still (in moment T_i) remaining to be accomplished at object O according to the best knowledge at our disposal in moment T_i.

The main role and objective of the EVA method is to be an early warning system. For values of i as small as possible, the project manager should, in the ideal case, have a fairly accurate estimate

EAC (T_i) of the total project cost. Only then will the project manager have time to undertake certain measures. Thus, it is of primordial importance that *EAC* (T_i) is determined on the basis of a possibly wide knowledge, both of quantitative and qualitative nature, both documented and undocumented (but somehow "felt in the air"). The problem is that the EVA method in its basic form takes into account only documented, easily available quantitative data. And, in fact, even more: it analyses exclusively accounting documents.

Let us present the widely used, basic approach to the determination of *EAC* (T_i) in consecutive control moments T_i for $i = 2, ..., m$. The general formula for *EAC* (T_i) is obvious:

$$EAC(T_i) = ACWP(T_i) + ETC(T_i) \tag{6.1}$$

Of course, the basic problem is the estimation of *ETC* (T_i), which refers entirely to the future (with respect to moment T_i). In the basic version of EVA, it is assumed that *EAC* (T_i) is determined exclusively on the basis of the relation between *BCWP* (T_i) and *ACWP* (T_i). The difference between them is assumed to be transferred to the difference between *BAC* (T_i) and *EAC* (T_i) in respective proportions. Thus, in the basic form of EVA, we have:

$$EAC(T_i) = \frac{ACWP(T_i)}{BCWP(T_i)} \tag{6.2}$$

Formula (6.2) is based on the assumption that the only information we use in control moment T_i to estimate the total cost of O is the past cost of the work already accomplished at O so far and its relation to the planned cost of this work. This is obviously a very restrictive assumption, leaving out important pieces of information, which are often available during project implementation and are of high importance for the estimation of the total project, activity cost, or resource usage. The higher the value of i is, the more we know about the project and its context and the more information can (and should be) used to estimate the cost of the work still remaining to be accomplished at object O. The EVA method does not claim to be able to forecast the total cost of O in control moment T_i with a perfect precision; it does not require the use of advanced forecasting methods, either. However, it should use as much knowledge available in control moment T_i to produce, at a reasonable effort, a value of *EAC* (T_i) that would be as close as possible to reality. *VAC* (T_i) can be a valuable warning or a reassuring signal, helping to make decisions about the project.

For this reason, the EVA method was modified e.g. in (Dałkowski and Kuchta, 1991). The formula (6.1) is used, and it resorts to additional information pieces beyond the ratio $\frac{ACWP(T_i)}{BCWP(T_i)}$ for the estimation of *ETC* (T_i). These information pieces include both documented and quantitative and qualitative or undocumented information. Let us name a few examples of qualitative and undocumented information:

■ rumours about, or confirmed changes in, requirements concerning the work still required to be accomplished on O;

■ rumours about, or confirmed changes in, the unitary price or unitary usage of resources linked to the work still to be accomplished on O;

■ indications or triggers about changes in the technology applied to O.

The idea presented in (Dałkowski and Kuchta, 1991) is that in moment T_i, all relevant information pieces that might (even if they have not been confirmed yet) influence $ETC(T_i)$ should be used.

It must be emphasized that since the paper by Dałkowski and Kuchta (1991) no contributions can be found in the literature improving the quality of the estimation of $ETC(T_i)$ using qualitative or undocumented information. In a recent work (Susilowati and Kurniaji, 2020), the following words can be found: "Estimate to Complete (ETC) is an estimate of the cost of remaining work, assuming that the trend of project performance is the same until the end of the project." This shows that ETC is calculated in the very basic way, using uniquely historical quantitative information. There have been some attempts to increase the quality of the estimation of $ETC(T_i)$, taking into account changes in the schedule (Narbaev and De Marco 2014; Vanhoucke, 2009) and other quantitative information e.g. (Narbaev and De Marco, 2014). Numerous modifications of the EVA method aim at increasing its performance with respect to project duration. Quantitative information is often processed using advanced mathematical forecasting models (e.g. (Batselier and Vanhoucke, 2017), but no soft, unformal information is explicitly considered. There are fuzzy versions of the earned value method e.g. (Moradi et al., 2018), which implicitly cover qualitative, undocumented, soft information, but they do it only an in implicit way. That is why in the following, we will propose how the approach from (Dałkowski and Kuchta, 1991) can be supported by the concept of the COCOMO, improving the quality of the $ETC(T_i)$ estimation, and, in the same way, increasing the efficiency of the earned value method as an early warning system. But before that, we will summarise the current situation in the control of waterfall IT projects in a formal way.

6.4 Critics of the Current Situation in Waterfall IT Projects Control and Proposal of a Modified Approach

In the current situation, we have two stages in the project cost and time management of an IT project implemented according to the waterfall model: cost and time estimation and cost and time control. The two processes are described in the previous sections, but here, we will juxtapose them to propose a modified approach. We are concentrating here on the cost aspect; we will extend it to the duration aspect in the conclusions.

$$BAC(T_1) = \mathcal{F}1\left(\{F_j(T_1)\}_{j=1}^N \right) \tag{6.3}$$

1. In the estimation process, performed before the project start, the total project planned cost, $BAC(T_1)$, is a function of factors: $\{F_j\}_{j=1}^N$, where N stands for the number of factors taken into account in the estimation model used (those mentioned in section 6.2 ($N = 22$) and maybe several other ones). As we stated at the end of section 6.2, the evaluations of some of these factors may change during project implementation; we will treat values $\{F_j\}_{j=1}^N$ as functions of time, where $F_j(t)$ stands for the knowledge concerning possible values of factor F_j after moment t, accessible to the decision maker in moment t. In the estimation process, the knowledge about their values in moment T_1 is taken into account. Thus, $BAC(T_1)$ is a function of $\{F_j(T_1)\}_{j=1}^N$, which will be denoted as:

In the cost control process, in the basic form of the earned value method, used in the everyday praxis of IT project management (Phillips and Ward, 2010), $EAC\,(T_i)$ is calculated in consequent control moment $i = 2,\ldots, n$, according to formulae (6.1) and (6.2). We have

$$BCWP\,(T_i) = \mathcal{F}2_i\!\left(\{F_j\,(T_1)\}_{j=1}^{N}\right) \tag{6.4}$$

Formula (6.4) is a consequence of the fact that $BCWP\,(T_i)$ is the planned cost (depending thus only on $\{F_j\,(T_1)\}_{j=1}^{N}$) for the work that has been accomplished until moment T_i. $ACWP\,(T_i)$ is a hard data item, an accounting figure, from invoices or payrolls. Thus, if we calculate $EAC\,(T_i)$ according to (1) and (2), we have:

$$EAC\,(T_i) = \mathcal{F}3_i\!\left(\{F_j\,(T_1)\}_{j=1}^{N}\right) \tag{6.5}$$

However, formula (6.2) is accurate in rather few situations. As we mentioned in section 6.3, $ETC\,(T_i)$ is a value from the future with respect to T_i and potentially will be determined also by what will happen after moment T_i. Thus, obviously we have in the general form of formula (6.1):

$$ETC\,(T_i) = \mathcal{F}5_i\!\left(\{F_j\,(T_i)\}_{j=1}^{N}\right) \tag{6.6}$$

and thus, actually, we have:

$$EAC\,(T_i) = \mathcal{F}6_i\!\left(\{F_j\,(T_i)\}_{j=1}^{N}\right) \tag{6.7}$$

The discrepancy between (6.5) and (6.7) is the core of the problem. (5) disregards updated information, including changes in the variety of factors in the project and its environment. It is enough to consider the following examples to see that they may lead to high distortion and falsification of the project control results:

■ factor F6: if together with the project advancement, the constraints of the schedule become more and more tough, the initial situation with possibly no rigid constraints will have changed dramatically and require additional resources to fulfill the new requirements
■ factors F9, F10, F11, F14, F21: if there are changes in the composition of the project team or in the attitudes of stakeholders, the initial situation of possibly adequate capabilities and good communication will have changed, requiring new resources to make up for the shortage of capabilities and to solve problems linked to communication.

In short, the situations are as follows:

- in the estimation process, numerous factors are considered, some of which may change later on;
- in the cost control process, the changes of the factors considered in the estimation are disregarded.

If changes in the factors $\{F_j\}_{j=1}^N$ are significant, the project control according to the basic form of the EVA method will be inefficient. Values (1), determined with the use of (2), will deliver no useful information. On the contrary, they may falsely inform the decision makers that the project situation is fairly good, whereas in reality, it will be highly negative. Having such a control system is worse than having no control system at all. This situation will be illustrated with a case study in section 6.5.

That is why we propose not to use formula (6.2), and, while applying formula (6.1), consider factors $\{F_j\}_{j=1}^N$ and their changes in the whole project control process. To minimise the effort needed for project control, we propose to limit this approach to such project activities whose budget is a significant portion of the total project budget (the project manager should set the threshold for the selection of such activities; also groups of activities can be selected). Let us denote the set of such activities as $\mathring{A}$. Then the proposed approach would consist of the following steps:

Step 1. the EVA method (formulae (6.1)) should be applied individually to each selected activity or group of activities from $\mathring{A}$;

Step 2. set $i=2$;

Step 3. in control moment T_i identify considerable (according to experts) changes $\{|F_j(T_i) - F_j(T_{i-1})|\}_{j=1}^N$, $i = 2,...,N$, should be identified (thanks to an extensive and efficient communication system in the project and its environment);

Step 4. the influence of the changes identified in Step 3) on $EAC(T_i)$ of elements of $\mathring{A}$ should be identified;

Step 5. the total of $VAC(T_i)$ for all elements of $\mathring{A}$ should be analysed, added to the total of the $VAC(T_i)$ for the other, miscellaneous activities (where the simplified formula (6.2) will be used) and the conclusion whether the project should be continued in the present form taken;

Step 6. if it is decided to stop the project, then STOP – the project is broken up. Otherwise, decide about corrective measures and continue until the next control moment or the project end. If there is another control moment, set $i = i+1$ and GO TO Step 3; if there is no other control moment, STOP – the project is ended.

The proposed framework allows, in consecutive control moments, to evaluate EAC and thus VAC of the whole project, taking into account all the factors that were considered during the estimation process. This is the only logical approach: EAC is in fact nothing else but a re-estimation of the project cost performed in consecutive control moments, and as such, should be based on the same information. The fact that simplified formulae like (6.2) are used in practice follows uniquely from the need for rapid procedures during project implementation, when project teams are usually busy and want to progress with the project scope, instead of concentrating on control and complex re-estimation issues. However, if the changes in the factors $\{F_j\}_{j=1}^N$ are significant, it is dangerous to ignore them in recalculating a value (i.e. the total expected project cost or time) that was originally derived basis on those factors. In such a case, we risk basing our decision about continuing the project on a completely distorted number VAC (or the equivalent for time management). And this means that we risk continuing with a project doomed to failure or with a project that can be saved, but only uniquely provided that certain measures are undertaken. The above proposal helps us to avoid such situations and to know in time that the project needs profound changes or should instead be dropped because continuing it would not produce a sufficient value to balance the effort needed to conclude the project.

The proposed approach and the need for it will be illustrated (as a post-factum simulation) with a real-world case study.

6.5 Case Study

6.5.1 Characteristics of the Studied Project

The studied project[1] was to lead to the creation of an integrated IT system of the MIS (management information system) type supporting the enterprise management process from the moment of establishing contact with the client, through the execution of the order, to the storage and logistics of the finished products. The system was designed and made based on the CRM (customer relationship management) and MRP II (manufacturing resource planning) standards. It was implemented in a medium-sized printing company that has been operating on the market for over 25 years. The decision to start implementing the system was due to the desire to optimize and automate business processes such as generating commercial offers, accepting and executing orders, making organisational changes, and developing cooperation with demanding contractors.

The scope of the project included customer relationship management, documentation management, order processing, production preparation and planning, production, demand for raw materials and tools, purchasing, sales, and warehouse management. The offer the system supplier presents in the general outline of the solution met expectations in terms of handling the main business processes and was consistent with the recipient's strategic goals, such as:

- improving the customer service process at all stages of cooperation,
- automating the process of technological description of products necessary to perform the calculation and to prepare a commercial offer,
- improving the flow of information between departments, and eliminating errors related to rewriting information,
- centralising and implementing the service of quality processes and control activities,
- optimising production planning and implementation processes,
- improving the storage process and resource management,
- implementing real-time inventory control,

The system should have consisted of the eight modules described below:

6.5.1.1 Preparation of Production

The task of the module was to coordinate the work of technologists, traders, and quality control and supply departments. The module was intended to support all business processes taking place in the company, from handling an inquiry to starting production. It would allow the entry of a detailed description of a product technology, containing information that affects cost or method of implementation of the production process. Based on the technological description, the system should calculate the production costs, using the adopted material price lists, standards, and man-hour rates determined using the information on the costs recorded in the system. In the case of production for industries with specific requirements, the system should allow a quality test plan, depending on the technological description of the product entered into the system. The module should allow the generation of offers, the registration of orders, and controlled product price lists for customers. The configuration of the module should permit the model and control needed to implement any business process – from non-compliance projects, through long-term contracts with recipients, to the implementation of graphic designs.

6.5.1.2 Supply

The module concerns the provision of material coverage for executed orders. It enables the fulfilment of material requirements by reserving available stocks, reserving orders to suppliers, and recalling materials from external warehouses.

6.5.1.3 Production Planning

The production planning module is a tool intended for planners and managers of the production department. By gathering all the necessary information in one place, the system should allow effective planning of material deliveries and creation of production plans, optimizing the use of the company's resources. Validation of planning errors, taking into account technological requirements, resource availability, and expected completion dates, should significantly reduce the risk of losses caused by planning errors.

6.5.1.4 Production Implementation

Software runs on production terminals intended for machine operators. With its help, operators should gain access to the scheduled queue of orders for their workplace, documentation related to the order, and technical data of the order; they should also be able to report noticed errors and indicate the causes of downtime. The module should work without connection to the machines and enable manual registration of lead times and the amount of production performed. The module should also have a built-in quality control function that forces confirmation of the control performance.

6.5.1.5 Warehousing and Trade

The module is responsible for handling the company's warehouses, registration of purchase invoices, payment control, and sales. Users of this module should be able to control the stock levels and carry out receipts, releases, inter-warehouse transfers, and shipments of products to customers. The module should sell products, services, goods, and materials. It should contain information about material reservations for specific orders and to place orders with suppliers. The module should provide support for consignment warehouses of materials and calling materials from suppliers' warehouses. It should also enable full management of the high-bay warehouse, including pallet space occupancy control and reporting on the number of storage operations. In the sales area, the module should enable issuing of all types of sales documents, from advance invoices through debit notes to discount invoices.

6.5.1.6 Quality Analysis and Control

This module is for people managing a company and responsible for controlling and optimizing processes. Its primary task is to support decision making by providing management information. The module should generate multidimensional analyses based on the data collected in the system and make them available to authorised users. The analyses should cover the entire area of the company's activity: production, storage, and sales. Reporting should use the Microsoft SQL Reporting Services technology; the generated reports enable an immediate transition from general to detail; e.g. by controlling the average performance of machines in the last three months, it should be possible to immediately obtain information about the performance recorded on a specific day while executing a selected order.

6.5.1.7 Customer's Portal

This module is available via a browser that would allow printing house customers to have continuous access to orders and a warehouse, directing inquiries regarding a selected product, checking and sending graphic files, and placing orders online. The module should allow the tracking of the order's current status.

6.5.2 Project Outcome

The implementation of an integrated IT system for enterprise management was a failure. The project was not broken up. The initial obligations could not be met. The construction of the system turned out to be too inflexible to allow the supplier to adjust the implemented (promised) functionalities in accordance with the requirements presented by the organisation.

According to the schedule, the project was to be completed within seven months (from March to October). After completion of a given implementation phase, the schedule should have been reviewed and updated (in accordance with the adopted methodology). In practice, updating the schedule consisted of remote meetings, during which the completed tasks were discussed, solutions were presented, and subsequent deadlines were set. However, they concerned both system configuration, training, and tests, were carried out chaotically, and did not refer to the entire project, but to individual system modules.

In the next subsection, selected moments from the project implementation will be described, in which the application of the approach from section 6.4 may have provided a warning and a justification for breaking up – or profoundly changing – the project, instead of continuing it in an unchanged form. Because of this, lots of resources have been lost without producing any added value for the organisation.

6.5.3 Implementation Analysis

The pre-implementation analysis was carried out within two days at the beginning of April (the first meeting of project teams). At the meeting, the supplier conducted an instruction on the preparation of materials necessary for the system configuration. Completed machine configuration sheets, technology templates, and other documents provided by the supplier for completion were delivered in May, as scheduled. The most important documents containing the description of technology, process flow diagrams, lists of raw materials and tools were also handed over to present the supplier with functioning of the company's processes. Thus, in that moment, EAC (and its duration counterpart) will probably be estimated as equal to the original values.

The departure of a key employee from the software supplier, who had the necessary knowledge to introduce changes to the configuration of the warehouse and commercial module and to remove errors, blocked the possibility of their implementation. The supplier was unable to complete the design team to ensure continuity. In that moment, the parameter F10 (programmer capability) has significantly decreased its future value. Changes in the cost of the project should have taken this into account (in the EAC value): an expert in the field had to be sought for and paid additionally, or the project success is in an obvious danger.

There were often communication problems between project participants. Based on observations and correspondence, it was found that the supplier's team was simultaneously involved in a greater number of implementations. This was evidenced by telephone conversations regarding other projects conducted during the visits, or by mistakenly sent correspondence to an employee of a competing company in the industry. The recipient's project team, sending e-mails to the project manager or other employee of the supplier, often received feedback about his absence for several days. Here, the parameter F21 obviously was about to significantly increase its value. Re-estimation of EAC should have been performed, taking the evident, although yet informal, difficulties into account.

According to the assumptions described in the project charter, the business concept description resulting from the pre-implementation analysis and defining the client's needs should be delivered to the system recipient for approval. It is possible that a business analysis of the project was carried out reliably and in accordance with the work methodology. Perhaps the business concept, including a requirements analysis, was developed. However, it was never presented to the recipient, so it is difficult to say whether the information on customer requirements collected by the system provider was complete and well understood. Here, factors F5 and F20 were obviously about to increase their values, which should have been taken into account in the project control; its cost should be re-estimated significantly.

At the beginning of cooperation, exact parameters of the readers (data terminals) owned by the recipient were not checked, which was an obvious mistake. The devices operated on the basis of a different operating system than the prepared application for integration with the IT system, which was not identified during the pre-implementation analysis. The difference did not allow the standard version of the software to be installed on the terminals. Almost two months passed from sending the device to the recipient until finding out that the software could not be installed. An attempt to adapt the application to the device was unsuccessful. Here, parameters F20 and F21 would have provided an early warning if they had had been taken into account in the project control process.

The "struggle" with the system lasted eight months (from its launch to the decision to resign from further implementation). All this time, it was clear that the functionality foreseen in the schedule was not being delivered in the required quality, and the supplier's frequent response to the questions about the possibility of introducing a change was the lack of the configuration possibility to achieve such functionality. Thus, all this time, it was evident that factors F17 and F20 were worsening. An early recognition of this fact in the project control would have led to decisive decisions concerning the project long before the eight-month period had ended.

6.6 Conclusions

This chapter proposes an integration of parametric IT project estimation and earned value method. This integration of two methods, originally used separately in two different stages of the waterfall model, has a high potential of creating a powerful warning system, which in the course of any IT project would deliver, as early as possible, the information about a coming budgetary or deadline problem, before this problem actually happens. Such a system would allow an organization to make early enough decisions or take necessary steps mitigating financial or delay problems in projects; the decisions or steps may include negotiations with the customer, solving internal problems in the team, exchanging selected members of the team or motivating them, delivering emotional or content related support to the team members, negotiations with stakeholders, clarifying misunderstandings etc. Making the decision to stop or completely redesign the project, if its continuation in the present form is highly likely to generate significant losses that would not be balanced by any value added.

Of course, further research is needed to develop detailed indications about how the proposed approach application should look in concrete cases and to verify the idea using real-world case studies. The approach requires, as a *sine qua non* condition, a developed communication system among all the project stakeholders, based on the information on the factors required by the approach, and a high level of acceptance among the stakeholders. The set of factors would have to be defined for each case and each organisation, exactly as it is done in the existing COCOMO models.

Note

1. The project and its implementation is described on the basis of internal documents of an organisation which wants to remain anonymous.

References

Boehm B.C, C.A., Brown, A.W., Chulani, S., Clark, B.K., Horowitz, E., Madachy, R., Reifer, D.J. (2000). *Software Cost Estimation with Cocomo (II)*. Englewood Cliffs, NJ: Prentice-Hall.

Batselier, J., & Vanhoucke M. (2017). Improving project forecast accuracy by integrating earned value management with exponential smoothing and reference class forecasting. *International Journal of Project Management 35*(1), 28–43. http://www.sciencedirect.com/science/article/pii/S0263786316301831.

Cooper, R.E. (1992). "The Complete COCOMO Model: Basic, Intermediate, Detailed, and Incremental Versions for the Original, Enhanced, Ada, and Ada Process Models of COCOMO." In *Cost Estimating and Analysis*.

Dałkowski, T.B., & Kuchta, D. (1991). Classical and modified earned value method in project management (in Polish). *Badania Operacyjne i Decyzje 3/4*, 35–52.

Dillibabu, R., & Krishnaiah, K. (2005). Cost estimation of a software product using COCOMO II.2000 model: A case study. *International Journal of Project Management 23*(4), 297–307. https://www.sciencedirect.com/science/article/pii/S0263786304001024.

Fleming, Q., & Koppelman, J. (2000). *Earned Value Project Management*. Newton Square, PA, United States: Project Management Institute Inc.

Kazemifard, M., Zaeri, A., Ghasem-Aghaee, N., Nematbakhsh, M.A. (2011). Fuzzy emotional COCOMO II software cost estimation (FECSCE) using multi-agent systems. *Applied Soft Computing 11*(2), 2260–2270. http://www.sciencedirect.com/science/article/pii/S1568494610002085.

Lacerda, T.C., & von Wangenheim, C.G. (2018). Systematic literature review of usability capability/maturity models. *Computer Standards & Interfaces 55*, 95–105. https://www.sciencedirect.com/science/article/pii/S0920548916302355.

Moradi, N., Mousavi, S.M., & Vahdani, B. (2018). An interval type-2 fuzzy model for project-earned value analysis under uncertainty. *Journal of Multiple-Valued Logic and Soft Computing 30*(1), 79–103. https://www.scopus.com/inward/record.uri?eid=2-s2.0-85042358530&partnerID=40&md5=b7e49cfc810a67226ad4825617e9b7cf.

Narbaev, T., & De Marco, A.. (2014). An earned schedule-based regression model to improve cost estimate at completion. *International Journal of Project Management 32*(6), 1007–1018. doi: 10.1016/j.ijproman.2013.12.005.

Phillips, J., & Ward, J.A. (2010). IT project management: On track from start to finish. http://www.books24x7.com/marc.asp?bookid=40088.

Susilowati, F., & Kurniaji, W.M. (2020). Effective performance evaluation to estimate cost and time using earned value. In *IOP Conference Series: Materials Science and Engineering.* https://www.scopus.com/inward/record.uri?eid=2-s2.0-85082611507&doi=10.1088%2F1757-899X%2F771%2F1%2F012055&partnerID=40&md5=37492560c8e2085b257d46d1705de0e4.

Trendowicz, A., & Jeffery, R. (2014). Software project effort estimation.

Vanhoucke, M. (2009). *Measuring Time – Improving Project Performance Using Earned Value Management.* Berlin/Heidelberg, Germany: Springer Science + Business Media, LLC.

Chapter 7

An Application of Decision Support Technique for Global Software Project Monitoring and Rescheduling Based on Risk Analysis

Ewa Marchwicka and Tymon Marchwicki

Department of Management Systems and Organizational Development, Wroclaw University of Science and Technology, Wroclaw, Poland

Contents

DOI: 10.1201/9781003030966-10

7.1 Introduction

Risks can result in project failure and can significantly harm companies and their customers (Green, 2016). There are many possible risk sources. Some examples (Green, 2016) are: project location, project environment, project complexity, technology, logistics, communication, human resources. Nowadays, in the age of globalization and technologies that facilitate remote communication, many software companies implement their projects in international teams that are spread all over the world. These types of projects have a specific list of risks (Nicolás et al., 2018) that can be managed. Risk management should be an integral part of project management because every project is exposed to risks (Chapman and Ward, 2003). The PMBoK Guide (Project Management Institute, 2017) in its 11th chapter provides standard guidelines for project risk management and indicates that risk management should be present at each stage of the project (Project Management Institute, 2017). Chapter 11.4.2 of the PMBoK Guide lists basic concepts of quantitative tools and techniques for project risk management, such as simulations, sensitivity analysis, decision trees, and influence diagrams, but without providing details or examples describing how these tools should be used. This paper presents an iterative risk management technique that supports project manager decisions in a global software project. The first version of the technique was presented in (Marchwicka, 2020), which was an extension of the work of (Muriana and Vizzini, 2017), with a nondeterminism that reflects the true nature of risks. The technique has been further developed, and the current version presented in this paper includes a new risk-ranking approach (based on principal component analysis), which is used to assess the level of risk for subsequent project stages. Moreover, the ranking uses a different set of measures. The technique has the following important features: is iterative (i.e. it is based on a project control step, called work progress status, abbreviated as WPS), data-centeric (i.e. the more data is collected, the more accurate the risk estimations should be), and nondeterministic (i.e. it is based on simulations). In addition, it allows controlling the level of project risks at different stages of the project, as well as controlling the overall level of risk. This technique allows project rescheduling at the end of each WPS in response to updated project information.

The motivation for this work is to provide a complete description of a quantitative risk management technique for practitioners to support their decisions. The technique is described in full detail, with examples, and should be ready for implementation, based on the description given. As mentioned above, the PMBoK Guide (Project Management Institute, 2017) does not provide any examples of practical application of the quantitative tools it mentions. Moreover, the literature study shows that not many examples of papers are available to present risk management techniques in detail. The above facts about risk management are confirmed by the observations made on the case described in this paper. It was observed that the project manager made an initial qualitative risk assessment, but subsequently, this knowledge could not be quantified.

The paper is organized as follows: Section 7.2 describes literature related to decision support systems for risk management, as well as literature related to iterative risk management and risk management in the context of global software projects. Section 7.3 presents a concise description of the new technique (including the new risk-ranking method), but with the required amount of detail to enable implementation of the technique. Section 7.4 describes a use case setting that illustrates the technique. Section 7.5 presents the calculations performed and the results obtained. Section 7.6 provides a summary.

7.2 Related Literature

7.2.1 Decision Support Systems for Risk Management

Decision support systems (DSS) in risk management are already widely discussed. The first proposals identified in this literature review date back to year 2010. Some decision support systems consider only selected risks (e.g., scope change risk, novelty risk, etc.), while others deal with project risks in general. In the second group, many project risk management frameworks have been proposed. Regarding only selected risks, (Shirazi et al., 2017) described project scope change risk and launched a fuzzy analytical hierarchy process for scope change management. (Marmier et al., 2013) provide a tool for strategic decision making about the continuous consideration of novelty in the project, which helps the project manager choose the best way to improve the project success rate while controlling the risk level. The decision support system considered in (Relich, 2010) supports the selection of alternative projects, by estimating critical tasks for several alternatives. It uses both intelligent techniques and traditional statistical techniques. In terms of general risk management in the context of decision support systems, one can mention the work of (Fang and Marle, 2012), which proposes a framework responsible for the identification, assessment, and analysis of risk networks. This framework models risk interactions and risk chain effect and uses a simulation-based approach. It also supports risk mitigation and project management (PM) actions in response to risk. The same group of researchers (Fang et al., 2012) proposes a topological analysis method that is based on network theory, which attempts to identify the risk structure by searching for interrelated risks that may affect a large engineering project. The research presented in (Aslam et al., 2017) describes an automated decision support system that is responsible for assessing risks and deciding on control strategies. It takes into account a knowledge base that is represented in the form of rules. Another complex risk management framework is presented in (Marques et al., 2010), where a multi-dimensional project performance-measurement system is proposed, which is based on an extended version of Project Management Iron Triangle. It has a built-in data aggregation tool to deal with large amounts of data. (Hossain et al., 2016) formulate a multi-objective linear programming model that can simultaneously minimize total project cost, completion time, and crashing cost. This model also uses the concepts of direct and indirect costs. As a result, the authors build a framework to measure the satisfaction level of the decision maker using fuzzy goals, fuzzy cost coefficients, and an analytical hierarchy process. This framework allows the selection of the desired trade-off solution at different risk levels.

7.2.2 Iterative Risk Management

Most of the iterative methods and techniques available in the literature to support project risk monitoring use earned value management (EVM). EVM concepts appear in methods, techniques, and frameworks. (Bonato et al., 2019) integrate and apply EVM with Monte Carlo simulation for project cost monitoring. (Elwany and Elscharkavy, 2016) focus on a technique to improve current project management knowledge by identifying the effect(s) of integrating EVM with risk management, discussing its impact on accurately predicting future project performance, and describing how this leads to project success. A case study (Elwany and Elscharkavy, 2016) also examines the use of EVM based on the distribution of financial and schedule risk and the effect of EVM on project performance. Interestingly, according to (Tereso et al., 2018), the concepts of EVM and risk management are usually considered separately in project management literature, but they should be considered together. For this reason, they describe their framework to integrate these two concepts. (KhodaBandehLou et al., 2016) have similar observations about EVM and risk management and suggest a method to integrate these two concepts that maximizes project performance. In (Babar et al., 2016), an integration model of risk performance index (RPI), cost performance index (CPI), and schedule performance index (SPI) is presented; this model extends the standard EVM model and provides a better estimate of the EAC measure (estimate at completion). A graphical framework that integrates the concepts of EVM and risk management is proposed in (Acebes et al., 2013). This framework uses a Monte Carlo simulation approach and proposes a simple output of the method in the form of five possible project states. Moreover, the authors performed a sensitivity analysis on their method. The article of (Acebes et al., 2014) is another method that shows the advantages of integrating EVM and risk management in a single methodology. (Hayashi et al., 2019) propose a quantitative risk management method that is based on EVM and logistic regression analysis. (Muriana and Vizzini, 2017) combine EVM, risk management, and project controlling into an adaptive risk analysis and mitigation technique in which preventive actions are taken to reduce the negative impact of risk. To do so, they use all three measures of the project management triangle. Unlike many risk management methods and techniques, their technique is deterministic.

7.2.3 Risk Management in Global Software Projects

Research on risk management in the context of global software projects dates back to 2009. In their work, (Hossain et al., 2009) conduct a systematic literature review and propose a conceptual framework for risk management. This framework is based on the list of risks, grouped in several classes, that have been identified for global software projects. Another work on risk classification for global software projects is presented in (Nicolás et al., 2018). Similarly, an exploratory analysis is conducted in (Shrivastava and Rathod, 2017) to identify and categorize risk factors associated with global software development projects. The risk factors are also ranked. The authors in (Akbar et al., 2020) present the list of 20 challenges through a questionnaire survey, but many of the challenges the authors identify can be considered as risks, and the list partially overlaps with the lists presented in (Hossain et al., 2009), (Shrivastava and Rathod, 2017), and (Nicolás et al., 2018). The authors of (Arumugam et al., 2018) propose an agile-based risk identification and mitigation framework for global software projects. However, both the identification part of the framework and the mitigation part are described at a high level without providing much detail. Similarly, a socio-technical model for global software projects is presented in (Bider et al., 2018), which is designed to facilitate risk identification and mitigation. There is a lot of discussion about risk, but no details of risk management are actually provided, and the main focus is on modeling a global software project in terms of various types of distances, including geographic, time-related, and cultural distances. In (Rafeek et al., 2019), the authors perform systematic literature review related to risk mitigation for global software development.

7.2.4 Risk Management Literature Summary

From the list of literature items presented above, only the work by the authors (Muriana and Vizzini, 2017) presents a technique that is fully described step by step in the form of an algorithm and can be directly implemented, based on the description given. The other works give some general concepts or frameworks that provide too little information to be implemented.

7.2.5 Principal Component Analysis (PCA) Context

The developed technique uses principal component analysis (PCA) as a ranking approach. Principal component analysis is widely used in many engineering applications, and it is well established in statistical analysis. There are many references in the literature that present the idea of PCA and its general applications. Examples include (Berrar et al., 2003; Daultrey, 1976). Regarding PCA in the context of ranking, several positions can also be found: (Petroni and Braglia, 2000; Kardiyen and Örkcü, 2006; Sezhian et al., 2011).

7.3 Decision Support Technique

7.3.1 Research Methods

The three main research methods that were used to develop the technique described in this paper are: literature review, simulation, and observation. The method itself was developed using in-depth literature review research. The literature review identified gaps in the base technique (Muriana and Vizzini, 2017) and explored options for extending the technique. The first version of the extended technique (Marchwicka, 2020) was designed using simulations. Real-world project data was collected using observations (one of the co-authors was part of the project team), and then the technique was adjusted by analyzing the results of applying it to a real-world project, resulting in a version of the technique presented in this paper.

7.3.2 Application Area

The technique presented here is specific to global software projects, and it should be applied in such a context because of two simple features inherent in it:

1. the specific list of risks that are related to global software projects,
2. the fact that project activities are represented as high-level activities that are assigned to various geographically dispersed project sub-teams (rather than to individuals).

The list of risks has already been presented in (Marchwicka, 2020) and will not be duplicated here. The individual risks that have been identified and are described in this paper, based on the list presented in (Marchwicka, 2020), are: immature technology, technology that has not been used in prior projects, processes that are not well-defined, difficulty of extracting relevant information from stakeholders, highly complex tasks being automated, large number of links to other systems required, and corporate politics with negative effect on task (data protection issues). These risks are managed using the technique described in this paper by including them in the risk register (presented further in the subsection "Overview of the Technique") and by estimating the impact they have on duration, cost, and scope (presented further in "Calculating WPS Measure" subsection). Regarding the activities assigned to different sub-teams, this assumption simplifies the dependencies between activities: most of the activities performed at the team level are independent of the activities of other teams. In the current version of the technique, no other features are taken into account that would make the method specific to global software projects. This means that by changing the list of risks and weakening the assumptions about activities, the technique can possibly be applied to other types of projects.

7.3.3 Basic Features of the Technique

The technique described in this paper is an adjusted and developed version of a technique that was described in (Marchwicka, 2020). The greatest difference, comparing to the article mentioned, is in the risk-ranking approach. The new ranking uses a different set of measures and is based on the principal component analysis statistical method, often abbreviated as PCA. The most important features of the technique are presented in Table 7.1.

7.3.4 Updated Elements of the Technique

The first version of the technique that was presented in (Marchwicka, 2020) was designed based on the work of (Muriana and Vizzini, 2017), and it used the same measures and rankings that the authors proposed. Either way, the (Muriana and Vizzini, 2017) technique is deterministic and

Table 7.1 Most important features of the technique

Feature	Description
Iterative	It takes advantage of project control step (referred to as WPS).
Risk-based	It considers risks from the PM Iron Triangle: time, cost, and scope. Risk correlations are also considered (new ranking method developed). Ranking is used to build a risk profile on the WPS level.
History-based	It takes advantage from the history of risks (referred to as the risk register) that already appeared.
Forecast-based	It takes advantage from risk estimations that may appear in the future (provided by team).
Non-deterministic	Nondeterminism is provided by Monte Carlo simulations.
Adaptive	Risks that have appeared in WPS are used to update activities. Rescheduling is possible and recommended.

assumes that risks are "hidden" in project activities. To quantify risks, the amount of work performed, the actual work performed, the amount of residual man days, and the number of quality requirements are quantified. At the same time, the technique developed in this paper includes simulations of materialized risks, so it also allows easy direct measurement of the quantity of risks. For this reason, a new set of measures that directly reflects the amount of risk is proposed. What remains unchanged is that the measures are calculated in a similar way as in (Muriana and Vizzini, 2017), based on the intersections of WPS and activities. The new measures are presented in detail later (section "Stage 5 – Calculating WPS Measures on Activities"). Another updated element of the technique, compared to (Marchwicka, 2020), is the new ranking method. To illustrate the differences, a simplified example of artificial data for two dimensions is shown below. The example (Figure 7.1) shows that the original ranking method proposed in (Muriana and Vizzini, 2017) can produce similar results to the PCA ranking presented here, which should justify staying with the original ranking method. Either way, the PCA ranking is more flexible, and when it does not use factor weights, it can produce more desirable results.

The covariance matrix for this data set and w_x and w_y weighting factors from (Muriana and Vizzini, 2017) are presented in Figure 7.2.

The normalized rankings for the various ranking methods are shown below in Table 7.2. For PCA, the following vector measure was used: $\|(x,y)\| = x + y$ (Table 7.2).

7.3.5 Overview of the Technique

The overview of the technique is presented in Figure 7.3. It consists of nine main stages that are described below in more detail.

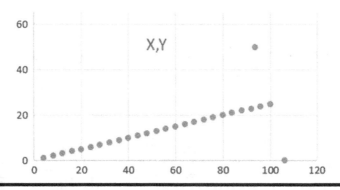

Figure 7.1 Two-dimensional artificial data set (*X*, *Y*), where *Y* = 1...25 and *X* = 4*Y*. Additionally, two data points were added to this data set: point (*93.75, 50*), here on the top right, and point (*106.25, 0*), here on bottom right.

X	Y		
967.1074	229.0064	wx	0.780013 wx = [cov(x,x) + cov(x,y)] / [cov(x,x) + cov(x,y) + cov(y,x) + cov(y,y)]
229.0064	108.3333	wy	0.219987 wy = [cov(x,y) + cov(y,y)] / [cov(x,x) + cov(x,y) + cov(y,x) + cov(y,y)]

Figure 7.2 Covariance matrix for the given data set and the weighting factors from (Muriana and Vizzini, 2017).

Table 7.2 Normalized rankings for different ranking methods

Selected points	Original ranking #1	PCA ranking with actors weights #2 (λ1 = 1024.36, λ2 = 51.08)	PCA ranking without factor weights #3 (λ1 = 1024.36, λ2 = 51.08)
(X,Y) = (93.75, 50)	1.00	1.00	1.00
(X,Y) = (100, 25)	0.99	0.98	0.79
(X,Y) = (106.25, 0)	0.98	0.97	0.59
(X,Y) = (4, 1)	0.00	0.00	0.00

All nine stages are performed iteratively in each control step, called work progress status (WPS). A WPS is defined in days and partitions project schedule to smaller pieces (Muriana and Vizzini, 2017). The risk level is measured separately for each WPS, which creates a risk ranking profile of the project and allows the project manager to take actions at the most endangered project stages and balance risks between them. Actions are made by rescheduling, after which a new ranking profile can be calculated and compared with the original one. The method also allows to calculate the optimistic, pessimistic, and average project duration, cost, and scope. Table 7.3 briefly describes the nine steps. Then a detailed description of nonobvious stages that require some calculations is presented.

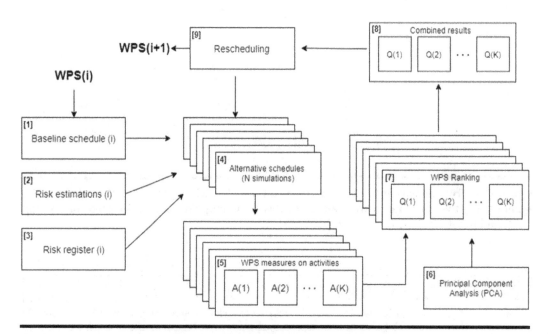

Figure 7.3 Overview of the technique depicted in nine main steps.

Table 7.3 Stages of the technique

No.	Stage	Description
1	Use baseline schedule	Input the schedule that is currently planned.
2	Update risk estimations	Update the list of identified risks with estimations. Estimated maximum values for duration increase, cost increase, scope increase when given risk appears and estimated probability (low/medium/high), together with the list of activities that can be affected. Not all the risk components (duration, cost, scope) need to be assigned. Some components can be empty and will not be considered in simulations.
3	Use risk register	Apply full history of materialized risks (also from other projects) with their actual duration increase, cost increase, and scope increase. After risks have been found to materialize for the activity, the activity is updated (duration, cost, scope) and the associated activity is removed from the list of risk-associated activities.
4	Generate alternative schedules (N simulations)	Generate simulations according to risk estimations and risk register. A triangular distribution can be used with the following parameters ($a < b < c$): $a = 0$, $b = mean$(risk register historical values) or $b = c/2$ when no history is available, $c = max$\{risk estimation, max \{risk register historical values\}\}. Simulations are cut and top $(1 - R_*)N$ extreme values are removed, where $R_* \in \{0, 1\}$ is a given risk level that is accepted. Schedules that are built for the simulations can be calculated, for example, using ASAP approach.
5	Calculate WPS measures on activities	Each alternative schedule is partitioned into WPS structure. For each of the WPS, a list of WPS-related activities is determined and three risk measures (normalized duration risk measure, normalized cost risk measure, and normalized scope risk measure) are calculated. This step produces three vectors of measures.
6	Apply Principal Component Analysis (PCA)	Principal component analysis is performed on the three vectors calculated in step no. 5, and the new space is determined (referred to as eigen space). The new space has three dimensions, ranked by its eigen values.
7	Obtain WPS ranking	Each vector from step no. 5 is represented in the new space, which reflects the greatest variance of risks and creates risks ranking.

(Continued)

Table 7.3 (Continued)   Stages of the technique

No.	Stage	Description
8	Combine results	WPS rankings for each simulation are combined and average ranking for each WPS is calculated. Here also, pessimistic, optimistic, and expected values for project total duration, total cost, and total scope are obtained.
9	Perform rescheduling	Project can now be rescheduled, and a new ranking can be obtained for this new schedule. It can be compared with the initial ranking. What is more, pessimistic, optimistic, and expected values for the project's total duration, total cost, and total scope can be compared.

7.3.6 Stage 4 – Generating Alternative Schedules

Because most programming languages usually offer only a uniform-distribution number generator, we provide here a pseudo-code (Figure 7.4) that can be used for obtaining triangular distribution numbers. This number is based on calculating the inverse-cumulative function, which is a standard approach used in computer simulations (Stein and Keblis, 2009).

In the method being described, all simulations representing alternative schedules are generated according to the ASAP approach. The ASAP algorithm is relatively easy to be implemented and does not introduce high computational complexity.

7.3.7 Stage 5 – Calculating WPS Measures on Activities

This stage is based on determining a measure of how much risk is estimated for each WPS. Only activities intersecting given WPS steps are considered. There might be four types of intersections: there are activities that start before WPS starts and are planned to be finished after WPS ends (Figure 7.5, top). For these activities, the intersection length equals WPS length. There are also activities that are planned to entirely fall into WPS (Figure 7.5, middle). For them, the intersection length equals the activity length. There are also activities that are planned to be finished in the WPS (Figure 7.5, bottom left). For them, the intersection length equals activity end minus WPS start. The last type are activities that are planned to be started in the WPS but are planned

```
FUNCTION TriangularNumber (low, med, high)

    U = UniformNumber()
    F = (med - low) / (high - low)

    IF (U <= F)
        RETURN low + SQRT(U * (med - low) * (high - low))
    ELSE
        RETURN high - SQRT((1 - U) * (high - low) * (high - med))
```

Figure 7.4   Pseudo-code for generating numbers from triangular distributions, assuming that uniform number generator is available (used in step 4).

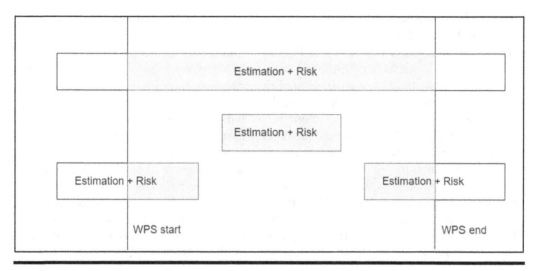

Figure 7.5 **Four types of intersections used for calculating risk-related WPS measures for each simulated schedule (used in step 5).**

to be finished later (Figure 7.5, bottom right). For them, the intersection length equals WPS end minus activity start. For all the activities considered, the end time is a sum of estimated duration and estimated duration risk.

The WPS risk measure is determined as a sum of risk measures for all the activities that intersect WPS. The activity risk measure for WPS is determined as a product of two ratios: ratio of intersection length to the total length and ratio of estimated time/cost/scope risk to the total duration/cost/scope. The equations are summarized in the Table 7.4.

The above WPS measures are calculated on each simulation and on each WPS. In this meaning, we have $N^*|WPS|^*3$ measures to be calculated, where N is the number of simulations and $|WPS|$ is the number of WPS steps. Three is the number of risk components (time, cost, scope).

7.3.8 Stage 6 – Principal Component Analysis

Principal component analysis (PCA) is used here to change the data representation and have the risk space with new dimensions that are ordered from the greatest variance to the lower variance.

Table 7.4 **Equations used for determining WPS risk measures on each simulation. Activities is denoted as $a \in A$**

WPS Measure	Equation
Time risk	$\sum_{a \in A} \dfrac{intesection\ length}{time\ estimation + time\ risk} \cdot \dfrac{time\ risk}{time\ estimation + time\ risk}$
Cost risk	$\sum_{a \in A} \dfrac{intesection\ length}{time\ estimation + time\ risk} \cdot \dfrac{cost\ risk}{cost\ estimation + cost\ risk}$
Scope risk	$\sum_{a \in A} \dfrac{intesection\ length}{time\ estimation + time\ risk} \cdot \dfrac{scope\ risk}{scope\ estimation + scope\ risk}$

This provides a good ranking for the new risk dimensions. Additionally, it reduces the correlation between project risk data (initially represented in time-risk dimension, cost-risk dimension, and scope-risk dimensions). The first step of PCA is to normalize data vectors. The inputs are the three vectors of time risks, cost risks, and scope risks with data points corresponding to subsequent WPS steps. In PCA, the vectors are first normalized. In our case, the normalization is already "hidden" in the measures that are used. The measures express how much risk of given type is in all the activities. Because the total number of project requirements equals the sum of requirements for all activities and the total project cost equals sum of costs for all activities, it means that measures for costs and requirements are expressed in the same units. The only difference is for the duration measure. Total project duration equals the length of its critical path and is not a sum of durations for all activities. For this reason, we need to normalize the vector of time risks by multiplying it by special coefficient. This coefficient is calculated as the duration of the critical path (measured in calendar days, together with Saturdays and Sundays) to the sum of durations of all activities. Thanks to this coefficient, we get the time-risk measure expressed in the same units as the cost- and scope-risk measures. The time normalization coefficient c_{time} is presented in (7.1).

$$c_{time} = \frac{Duration\,(project\;\;critical\;\;path)}{\sum_{a \in A} Duration\,(a)} \tag{7.1}$$

After the vectors are normalized, the next step is to subtract the vector means from vector values. In case of using PCA for ranking, as considered in this paper, this step would produce inappropriate results, i.e. the negative values. The idea of ranking is to measure how far from point (0, 0, 0) the results are, not how far from the "middle" data point they are. PCA without mean subtraction will only rotate the reference space to the directions of greatest variance, without changing the (0, 0, 0) reference point. That is why the mean subtraction step is omitted. The next step is to compute a covariance matrix between vectors. In this case, the covariance matrix will be a 3 × 3 matrix with the components that are listed in Table 7.5.

For the covariance matrix, eigen values and eigen vectors are computed. Eigen values rank the new dimensions, and eigen vectors allow to represent the risk data in the new space.

7.3.9 Stage 7 – WPS Ranking

The ranking is obtained by first multiplying each three-dimensional data point by each of the three-dimensional vectors (which produces a three-dimensional vector) and then taking the measure of this vector (e.g. vector's norm). For example, if eigen space is defined by three vectors

Table 7.5 Covariance matrix used for PCA

	Time risk (t)	Cost risk (c)	Scope risk (s)
Time risk (t)	Cov(t,t)	Cov(t,s)	Cov(t,s)
Cost risk (c)	Cov(c,t)	Cov(c,c)	Cov(c,s)
Scope risk (s)	Cov(s,t)	Cov(s,c)	Cov(s,s)

[1, 0, 0], [0, 1, 0], and [0, 0, 1], and we try to obtain ranking for data point (1, 2, 3), then the resulted ranking will be calculated as in (7.2).

$$rank\,(1,\,2,\,3) = \|(1{\cdot}1 + 0{\cdot}2 + 0{\cdot}3,\, 0{\cdot}1 + 1{\cdot}2 + 0{\cdot}3,\, 0{\cdot}1 + 0{\cdot}2 + 1{\cdot}3)\| = =\|(1,\,2,\,3)\|$$
$$= \sqrt{1 + 4 + 9} = \sqrt{14} \tag{7.2}$$

The vector has not changed because the eigen space is the original space of the data-point vector. Such a space will be generated if two risk components are always zero and one risk component is non-zero. This is practically impossible for the real project data, as long as we use not only experts' risk estimations (which can prefer only one type of risks), but we also track the values from the materialized risks, which usually update more than one risk component. Using PCA as a ranking method allows us to use different measures for resulted vectors. The Euclidean norm from (2.2) can be replaced with other measures.

7.4 Use Case Setting

7.4.1 Research Design

As mentioned in the "Research Methods" subsection, the initial version of the technique was developed based on an in-depth literature review and based on simulations (Marchwicka, 2020). In parallel, data for the technique was collected at the same time. The selected project was a real-world global software project that was carried out by three different teams geographically distributed in two different locations. Project selection was straightforward because one of the co-authors of this paper was a member of the project team. The technique was tested post-factum and applied to data already collected, after the project was completed. During testing on real data, the first version of the technique that was implemented in (Marchwicka, 2020) was revised. The adjustments included a new set of risk-related measures introduced and a new ranking approach. The technique is iterative, but it was only tested in two iterations: the first iteration was a projected project plan using the knowledge that was available at the beginning of the project. The second iteration was an updated project plan based on updated risk information and information about risks that had materialized.

7.4.2 Researched Project Characteristics

The basic characteristics of the project that was selected are presented in the table below (Table 7.6). Because of data-protection concerns, sensitive data (like project name, locations, industry, scope, and realization reference time) are not given, although they are known to the authors.

7.4.3 Data Collection

Overview of data collection that was needed to test the technique developed in this paper is presented below in Table 7.7.

Table 7.6 Basic characteristics of the project selected for the research

Characteristic	Value	Comments
Project type	Global software project	–
Number of countries	2	–
Number of sub-teams	3	Two teams placed in the same location in one country. Third team located in a different country.
Number of team members	2 + 2 + 2 + 1	Each sub-team consisting of two persons, one project manager.
Number of project stages	4	–
Stages with data collected	1	First stage only
Time estimated for the project (all four stages)	~9 months	Initial estimation (before project started)
Time estimated for the first stage of the project	~2.5 months	Initial estimation (before project started)

7.4.4 *Additional Assumptions*

It is worth mentioning that several assumptions were made that simplify the calculations presented in this paper and the use of the technique in general. Some data (such as cost of activities) has only been estimated (this information was not available to the authors). The duration of the activities is estimated in days. The scope of the activity is estimated in the number of functional or technical requirements estimated for the activity. The cost of the activity is estimated in the size of the team performing the activity. It was assumed that a workday costs 200$, which means that the estimated cost of an activity is equal to 200$ times the number of people performing the activity (team size) times the number of days estimated for the activity. This cost was set to illustrate the example, but to use the technique, it does not matter how expensive the cost of a workday is. It could be set to 1000$ as well, because in the end, the activity cost is calculated as the unit cost times the number of resources needed. All that matters is that the risk of an increase in activity cost is measured in the same units. Since the information about how many additional resources were needed after the risk was materialized, the cost risk can be quantified by comparing the final number of resources needed with the initial number of resources planned for the activity times the unit cost (here set to 200$, as an illustration). Another assumption is that this technique uses a scale of days to represent time, and these are relative values of the number of days from the project start date. The next assumption is that the risk estimates are given as absolute values (e.g. the occurrence of a risk caused a ten-day delay in the project, one resource had to be added for ten days, and the number of functional requirements increased by two, etc.). The last important assumption is that the risk values simulated in the project are also always rounded to whole numbers.

Table 7.7 Data collection overview

Artifact	Data source	Collection time range	Collection frequency	Comments
Preliminary project plan	Project Manager	Project start	One-time	Only data from first stage were collected
Preliminary risks list	Project Manager	Project start	One-time	Risks with qualitative assessment (consequences: low, medium, high)
Updated project plan	Project Manager	1st stage deadline	One-time	Updated plan to complete the first stage
List of risks that have materialized (additional time, resources, scope change)	Observation	From project start to the end of the first stage (a few months)	Every-day basis	Collected by the co-author of the paper who was a member of the project team; the exact time of data collection was not given, as this would indicate the final length of the first stage, which is sensitive information
Qualitative risk assessment at the start of the project	Own elaboration	Post-factum	One-time	Evaluated based on the initial list of risks and its qualitative assessment, and the assumptions that the PM made at the beginning of the project
Qualitative risk estimation when deadline was reached	Own elaboration	Post-factum	One-time	Evaluated based on information about risks that materialized (e.g. how much additional time was needed, how many additional resources were required, how scope changed)

7.5 Results

As already noted in the subsection on research design, the results of the technique will be presented in three steps. In the first step, the initial schedule is the input for the technique, and alternative schedules are generated based on the initial risk information (known at the beginning of the project). In the second step, time is moved forward to the date that was initially estimated as the end date of the first stage of the project, and the schedule is updated according to the new project conditions (change in time/cost/scope estimations). In the third step, the updated schedule is the input to the technique, new risk estimates are provided, a history of risks that have materialized is presented, and new simulations are launched. The results are compared with the simulations available at the beginning of the project.

7.5.1 Step 1 – Simulations Based on Data Available When Starting Project

The initial project schedule (without risks considered) is presented in Figure 7.6. The work in project has been organized in three different teams: Front-end team (responsible for developing the user interface), back-end team (responsible for developing core back-end functionalities), and testing team (responsible for testing the solution and verifying the provided acceptance criteria).

The division at the top of the Figure 7.6 represents division into two-week sprints, which also reflects a suitable partitioning into project control steps (WPS). The total time planned for the milestone is then 10 weeks. The initial plan for the first stage of the project contains five high-level stages (activities A, B, C, D, E). Three horizontal lines represent three teams that are working on the project. Front-end works are on the top. Tests are in the middle. Back-end works are on the bottom. The first stage of front-end works is environment preparation (A). The second stage is front-end development (B). The third stage is front-end–back-end integration (C). Arrows represent the sequence of planned works. Front-end development (B) is possible as soon as

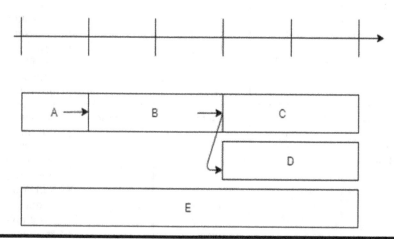

Figure 7.6 Initial project schedule (first milestone). Legend: The letters represent activities. Arrows represent relationships between activities. The rows where the activities are placed represent the breakdown into sub-teams. The scale at the top represents the WPS breakdown (here in biweekly steps).

Table 7.8 Project activities for the first milestone and their estimations

Activity Symbol	Description	Estimation (duration [days], cost [resources], scope [functional / technical requirements])	Predecessors
A	Environment preparation (2 trainings + 3 IT tools)	(10, 2, 5)	–
B	UI development (10 screens)	(20, 2, 10)	A
C	Integration (~10 back-end API calls)	(20, 2, 10)	B
D	Testing (20 test scenarios)	(20, 2, 20)	B
E	Backend development (23 functional requirements)	(50, 2, 23)	–

preparation works (A) are finished. Integration works (C) are possible as soon as development (B) is finished. Back-end works (E) are realized independently from other works. Because it is the front end that needs to integrate the back-end changes (not the opposite), the back end is not waiting for the front end. Tests (D) are also waiting for the initially integrated work of the front-end development team (B). More activity details are given in Table 7.8. It is also worth mentioning that although initially some project risks were assumed for the project, they were not included in estimations, and the initial schedule was developed in its very optimistic version.

Below, in Table 7.9, the risk estimations used for simulations are presented. Besides risks, project activities from Table 7.8 are also used as an input to simulations.

Simulation results are presented in Table 7.10.

7.5.2 Step 2 – Updated Project Schedule When Deadline was Reached

After the deadline was reached, the schedule was different than the schedule at the beginning of the project. We present the updated schedule in Figure 7.7.

The changes are: Environment preparation (activity A) has taken 40 days (instead of 10, as initially planned) because risk **R3** (processes that are not well defined) and risk **R7** (corporate politics) have been materialized, and they both increased the total duration by 30 days. Estimated time needed for testing (activity D) has been doubled because risk **R5** (highly complex task being automated) has been materialized, and it increased the duration by 20 days. Starting activity D needed to be moved forward by 30 days because it was waiting for the activity B (integration) to be finished. Back-end development (activity E) increased in estimations because risk **R6** (large number of links to other systems) has been materialized and it increased the duration by 25 days. New activities were added: activity F (UI new functional requirements), activity G (integrating new requirements), and activity H (back-end new functional requirements). Table 7.11 presents updated list of activities.

Table 7.9 Risks forecasted during project planning

Risk	Estimation (duration, cost, scope, probability)	Activities that can be affected
R1: Immature technology	(5, 0, 0, LOW)	B, C
R2: Technology that has not been used in prior projects	(5, 0, 0, LOW)	B, C
R3: Processes that are not well defined	(10, 0, 0, LOW)	B, C
R4: Difficulty of extracting relevant information from stakeholders	(10, 0, 0, MED)	B, C, D, E
R5: Highly complex task being automated	(10, 0, 0, MED)	D
R6: Large number of links to other systems required	(10, 0, 0, MED)	E
R7: Corporate politics with negative effect on task (data-protection issues)	(5, 0, 0, MED)	A

The list of risks list did not change, but the risks' probabilities have been increased (Table 7.12). What is more, the activities for which risks have been materialized are deleted from the list of activities that can be affected.

A list of risks that have materialized with their actual time/cost/scope increase is shown in Table 7.13 below.

7.5.3 Step 3 – Simulations when Deadline was Reached

New simulations were generated based on the updated project data. The results are presented in Table 7.14.

7.5.4 Discussion

The technique was applied to one project and its first milestone only. This is because only this data was available and collected. However, this relatively small amount of data makes the example simpler and more illustrative. This first milestone was initially estimated as much shorter than it later turned out because many risks materialized during milestone realization, while none of the risks were included in the baseline schedule. Simulations, which the technique is based on, show that schedules with risks included and without them can be very different. According to the available project data from the latest moment of time (depicted in Table 7.14), the expected duration can almost double (140 calendar days without considering risks and expected 234 calendar days if risk information is included). This shows how important it is to consider risks when planning a project. What is more, the differences between the baseline project schedule, when no risks have been considered, and the schedule calculated in the second iteration of the technique,

Table 7.10 Simulation results for project planning data

Input schedule
Days = 50, Calendar Days = 70, Cost = 48000, Scope = 68
WPS count: 5
Schedule without risks:
A [0;10] (10,4000,5)
B [10;30] (20,8000,10)
C [30;50] (20,8000,10)
D [30;50] (20,8000,20)
E [0;50] (50,20000,23)
Output ranking
Min Days = 59, Min Calendar Days = 83, Min Cost = 48000, Min Scope = 68
Mean Days = 67, Mean Calendar Days = 94, Mean Cost = 48000, Mean Scope = 68
Max Days = 75, Max Calendar Days = 105, Max Cost = 48000, Max Scope = 68
Sample alternative schedule:
A [0;13] (10,4000,5)
B [13;44] (20,8000,10)
C [44;68] (20,8000,10)
D [44;64] (20,8000,20)
E [0;50] (50,20000,23)
Mean ranking for WPS steps:
(6.93,7.24,5.97,8.23,9.86,9.32,4.96,0.55)

Legend: In square brackets, the activity start day and activity end day are given. In parentheses, activity estimations without risks are given. "Days" states for project length in working days. "Calendar Days" states for project length is calendar days (including Saturdays and Sundays). "Cost" states for activity/project cost in dollars. "Scope" states for project scope measured in number of requirements. "WPS count" states for total number of WPS steps calculated. "Sample alternative schedule" states for the first schedule that was simulated using the technique. "Mean ranking for WPS steps" states for final WPS ranking measures that reflect the forecasted amount of risk in each WPS step (non-normalized values are given).

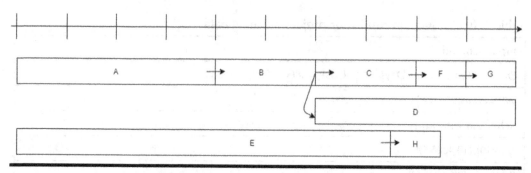

Figure 7.7 New schedule when deadline was reached. Legend: The letters represent activities. Arrows represent relationships between activities. The rows where the activities are placed represent the breakdown into sub-teams. The scale at the top represents the WPS breakdown (here in biweekly steps).

Table 7.11 Updated list of activities when deadline was reached

Activity Symbol	Description	Estimation (duration [days], cost [resources], scope [functional / technical requirements])	Predecessors
A	Environment preparation (2 trainings + 3 IT tools)	(**10 + 30**, 2, 5)	–
B	UI development (10 screens)	(20, 2, 10)	A
C	Integration (~10 back-end API calls)	(20, 2, 10)	B
D	Testing (20 test scenarios)	(**20 + 20**, 2, 20)	B
E	Backend development (23 functional requirements)	(**50 + 25**, 2, 23)	–
F	UI new functional requirements	(10, 2, 5)	C
G	Integrating new requirements	(10, 2, 5)	F
H	Back-end new functional requirements	(10, 2, 5)	E

Table 7.12 Updated list of activities that can be affected and risk probabilities

Risk	Estimation (duration, cost, scope, probability)	Activities that can be affected
R1: Immature technology	(5, 0, 0, HIGH)	B, C, F, G
R2: Technology that has not been used in prior projects	(5, 0, 0, HIGH)	B, C, F, G
R3: Processes that are not well defined	(10, 0, 0, HIGH)	A, B, C, F, G
R4: Difficulty of extracting relevant information from stakeholders	(10, 0, 0, HIGH)	B, C, D, E, F, G, H
R5: Highly complex task being automated	(10, 0, 0, HIGH)	D
R6: Large number of links to other systems required	(10, 0, 0, HIGH)	E
R7: Corporate politics with negative effect on task (data protection)	(5, 0, 0, HIGH)	A

Table 7.13 List of materialized risks

Risk	Actual values (duration increase, cost increase, scope extension)
R3: Processes that are not well defined	(15, 10, 0)
R5: Highly complex task being automated	(20, 0, 0)
R6: Large number of links to other systems required	(25, 0, 0)
R7: Corporate politics with negative effect on task (data protection)	(15, 5, 0)

including risks, are even more visible. The initial project schedule assumed 70 calendar days (Table 7.10), and the mean expected time, including both updated project data and risks simulations, is more than three times longer (and equals 234 days shown in Table 7.14). Because all project-related information is sensitive, the final date of finishing the first stage of the project is not given here (although it is known to the authors). The presented technique allows to easily modify project data and then compare different schedules obtained after rescheduling. A very important part of the technique is building a risk profile that allows the identification of the stages of the project that are characterized by the highest risk scores and allows a balancing of the measures in the form of rescheduling. The inputs required for the technique are list of risks, risk estimations (probabilities and quantification), and project schedule (activities). The outputs are an updated project schedule that includes risk estimations (pessimistic, optimistic, and expected

Table 7.14 Simulations of the project just after planned deadline was reached

Input schedule
Days = 100, Calendar Days = 140, Cost = 90000, Scope = 83
WPS count: 10
Schedule without risks:
A [0;40] (40,16000,5)
B [40;60] (20,8000,10)
C [60;80] (20,8000,10)
D [60;100] (40,16000,20)
E [0;75] (75,30000,23)
F [80;90] (10,4000,5)
G [90;100] (10,4000,5)
H [75;85] (10,4000,5)
Output ranking
Min Days = 149, Min Calendar Days = 209, Min Cost = 90400, Min Scope = 83
Mean Days = 167, Mean Calendar Days = 234, Mean Cost = 94264, Mean Scope = 83
Max Days = 184, Max Calendar Days = 258, Max Cost = 97400, Max Scope = 83
Sample alternative schedule:
A [0;40] (40,16000,5)
B [40;79] (20,8000, 10)
C [79;119] (20,8000, 10)
D [79;123] (40,16000, 20)
E [0;80] (75,30000, 23)
F [119;138] (10,4000, 5)
G [138;168] (10,4000, 5)
H [80;96] (10,4000, 5)
Mean ranking for WPS steps: (0.24,0.24,0.24,0.24,4.61,4.61,4.7,5.93,10.32,8.02,5.82,7.35,8.46,8.49,8.44,7.38,4.76,1.97,0.16)

Legend: In square brackets, the activity start day and activity end day are given. In parentheses, activity estimations without risks are given. "Days" states for project length in working days. "Calendar Days" states the project length in calendar days (including Saturdays and Sundays). "Cost" states for activity/project cost in dollars. "Scope" states for project scope measured in number of requirements. "WPS count" states for total number of WPS steps calculated. "Sample alternative schedule" states for the first schedule that was simulated using the technique. "Mean ranking for WPS steps" states for final WPS ranking measures that reflect the forecasted amount of risk in each WPS step (non-normalized values are given).

variants), as well as a risk profile that includes risk rankings. These outputs can be used to monitor project risks and allow risk-aware rescheduling. The input activities are high-level project stages (representing a certain set of functionalities to be implemented), which are assigned to entire teams, not to individuals. This property corresponds to the high-level view of the project that best matches the view expected by the project manager of a global IT project with geographically dispersed teams. Teams work on tasks that should, for the most part, be independent of the tasks of other teams. In this sense, the decision support system constructed in this way is specially crafted for project managers and frees them from having to know too many details of the project implementation. While the technique described supports project manager decisions and allows the easy monitoring of project risks in global software projects, it also requires some effort to prepare input data for the technique. The input data may affect the quality of the technique. For example, when risks are incorrectly quantified and listed, the desired results of the technique may be of poor quality. At the same time, the advantage of this technique is that it is based on historical data. This means that individual risk estimates are supported by risks that have been recorded in the risk register, which should improve the quality of the risk estimates when large amounts of historical data are available. Another advantage of the technique is that it allows to easily replace or extend the set of measures and ranking methods. The described technique uses PCA as a ranking approach that can be further adjusted for the best possible results. The set of measures selected includes three basic risk components, namely: time risk, cost risk, and scope risk, but they can also be modified or extended.

7.6 Summary

This chapter presents the application of the decision support technique for global software projects. A post-factum project data was used to describe the technique. The numerical example shows how this technique applies to real-world global software projects. A custom computer simulation was used to perform the required calculations. This work updates previous research (Marchwicka, 2020), with different risk measures developed and a new ranking method based on principal component analysis. It also complements the previous technique by a numerical example that shows how to use the technique, which may be of interest to practitioners. This technique can be used to estimate the total duration, cost, and scope of a project. Another important feature of the method is the ability to monitor the level of risks by building a risk profile for project control steps, called WPS steps. This makes rescheduling much easier as activities can be rescheduled to a point of time with less risk and allows to easily compare alternative schedules before deciding to reschedule. As mentioned in the introduction, PMBoK Guide (Project Management Institute, 2017) does not provide examples of the practical use of the quantitative tools mentioned therein. In particular, it does not show how to apply quantitative risk management techniques to risk monitoring in the context of global software projects. This chapter, as the authors believe, fills this gap. The chapter presents the developed version of the technique, which was implemented and applied to the real-world project data. The given description should be sufficient to implement the technique in the selected programming language. This technique is designed to support the decisions of global software project managers, based on risk information, and enables easy risk monitoring and rescheduling.

References

Acebes, F., Pajares J., Galan, J.M., & Lopez-Paredes, A. (2014). A new approach for project control under uncertainty: Going back to the basics. *International Journal of Project Management 32*(3), 423–434. doi: 10.1016/j.ijproman.2013.08.003

Acebes, F., Pajares, J., Galan, J.M., & Lopez-Paredes, A. (2013). Beyond earned value management: A graphical framework for integrated cost. Schedule and risk monitoring. *Procedia – Social and Behavioral Sciences 74*, 181–189. doi: 10.1016/j.sbspro.2013.03.027

Akbar, M.A., Alsand, A., Mahmood, S., & Alothaim, A. (2020). Prioritization-based taxonomy of global software development challenges: A FAHP based analysis, digital object identifier. *Applied Soft Computing 95*, 1–15. doi: 10.1016/j.asoc.2020.106557

Arumugam, S., Kameswaran, S., & Kaliamourth, B. (2018). Risk assessment framework: ADRIM process model for global software development, towards extensible and adaptable methods in computing. In *Towards Extensible and Adaptable Methods in Computing* (pp. 3–12). Singapore: Springer. doi: 10.1007/978-981-13-2348-5_1

Aslam, A., Ahmad, N., Saba, T., & Almazyad, A.S. (2017). Decision support system for risk assessment and management strategies in distributed software development. *IEEE Access 5*, 20349–20373. doi: 10.11 09/ACCESS.2017.2757605

Babar, S., Thaheem, M.J., & Ayub, B. (2016). Estimated cost at completion: Integrating risk into earned value management. *Journal of Construction Engineering and Management 143*(3), 1–12. doi: 10.1061/ (ASCE)CO.1943-7862.0001245

Berrar, D.P., Dubitzky, W., & Granzow, M. (2003). Singular value decomposition and principal component analysis. In D.P. Berrar, W. Dubitzky & M. Granzow (Eds.). *A Practical Approach to Microarray Data Analysis* (pp. 91–109). Norwell, MA, USA: Kluwer Academic Publishers. doi: 10.1007/0-306-47815-3_5.

Bider, I., Otto, H., & Willysson S. (2018). Using a socio-technical model of a global software development project for facilitating risk management and improving the project structure. *Complex Systems Informatics and Modeling Quarterly (CSIMQ) 86*(15), 1–23. doi: 10.7250/csimq.2018-15.01

Bonato, F., Aparecido de Albuquerque, A., & Santana da Paixão, M.A. (2019). An application of earned value management (EVM) with Monte Carlo simulation in engineering project management. *Gestao & Producao 26*(3), 1–15. doi: 10.1590/0104-530x4641-19

Chapman, C., & Ward, S. (2003). *Project Risk Management*. Chichester: John Wiley & Sons Ltd.

Daultrey, S. (1976). *Principal Components Analysis*. Norwich: Geo Abstracts Ltd.

Elwany, M., & Elscharkavy, A. (2016). Impact of integrating earned value management and risk management on the success in oil, gas and petrochemicals engineering procurement and construction EPC projects. *International Journal of Advanced Scientific Research and Management 1*(9), 75–88.

Fang, C.H., & Marle, F. (2012). A simulation-based risk network model for decision support in project risk management. *Decision Support Systems 52*, 635–644.

Fang, Ch., Marle, F., & Zio E. (2012). Network theory-based analysis of risk interactions in large engineering projects. *Reliability Engineering and System Safety 106*, 1–12. doi: 10.1016/j.ress.2012 .04.005

Green, P.E.J. (2016). *Enterprise Risk Management: A Common Framework for the Entire Organization, Butterworth-Heinemann*. Oxford: Elsevier.

Hayashi, A., Kataoka, N., Kino, Y., & Aoyama, M. (2019). Quantitative risk management method using logistic regression analysis. *International Journal of Informatics Society 11*(1), 3–11.

Hossain, E., Babar, M., Paik, H., & Verner J. (2009). Risk identification and mitigation processes for using scrum in global software development: A conceptual framework. *16th Asia-Pacific Software Engineering Conference 3*, 457–464. doi: 10.1109/APSEC.2009.56

Hossain, S., Mahmud, S., & Hossain, M. (2016). Fuzzy multi-objective linear programming for project management decision under uncertain environment with AHP based weighted average method. *Journal of Optimization in Industrial Engineering 20*, 53–60. doi: 10.22094/joie.2016.250

Kardiyen, F., & Örkcü, H.H. (2006). The comparison of principal component analysis and data envelopment analysis in ranking of decision making units. *G.U. Journal of Science 19*(2), 127–133.

KhodaBandehLou, A., Parvishi, A., Taghifam, R., Lotfi, M., & Taleei, A. (2016). Integrating earned value management with risk management to control the time-cost of the project *IIOABJ 7*(4), 114–119.

Marchwicka, E. (2020). A technique for supporting decision process of global software project monitoring and rescheduling based on risk analysis. *Journal of Decision Systems*, 1–15. doi: 10.1080/12460125 .2020.1790825

Marmier, F., Gourc, D., & Laarz, F. (2013). A risk oriented model to assess strategic decisions in new product development projects. *Decision Support Systems 56*, 74–82. doi: 10.1016/j.dss.2013.05.002

Marques, G., Gourc, D., & Lauras, M. (2010). Multi-criteria performance analysis for decision making in project management. *International Journal of Project Management 29*, 1057–1069. doi: 10.1016/ j.ijproman.2010.10.002

Muriana, C., & Vizzini, G. (2017). Project risk management: A deterministic quantitative technique for assessment and mitigation. *International Journal of Project Management 35*, 320–340. doi: 10.1016/ j.ijproman.2017.01.010

Nicolás, J., Carrillo de Gea, J.M., Nicolas, B., & Fernandez-Aleman, J.M. (2018). On the risks and safeguards for requirements engineering in global software development: Systematic literature review and quantitative assessment. *IEEE Access 99*, 1–31.

Petroni, A., & Braglia, M. (2000). Vendor selection using principal component analysis. *Journal of Supply Chain Management 36*, 63–69. doi: 10.1111/j.1745-493X.2000.tb00078.x

Project Management Institute (2017). *A Guide to the Project Management Body of Knowledge (PMBoK Guide)*. 6th edn. Newton Square, Pennsylvania: Project Management Institute.

Rafeek, M.A., Arbain, A.F., & Sudarmilah, E. (2019). Risk mitigation techniques in Agile development processes. *International Journal of Supply Chain Management 8*(2), 1123–1129.

Relich, M. (2010). A decision support system for alternative project choice based on fuzzy neural networks. *Management and Production Engineering Review 1*(4), 46–54.

Sezhian, M.V., Muralidharan, C., Nambirajan, T., & Deshmukh, S.G. (2011). Ranking of a public sector passenger bus transport company using principal component analysis: A case study. *Management Research and Practice 3*(1), 62–71.

Shirazi, F., Kazemipoor, H., & Tavakkoli-Moghaddam, R. (2017). Fuzzy decision analysis for project scope change management. *Decision Science Letters 6*, 395–406. doi: 10.5267/j.dsl.2017.1.003

Shrivastava, S.V., & Rathod, U. (2017). A risk management framework for distributed agile projects. *Information and Software Technology 85*, 1–15. doi: 10.1016/j.infsof.2016.12.005

Stein, W.E., & Keblis M.F. (2009). A new method to simulate the triangular distribution. *Mathematical and Computer Modelling 49*, 1143–1147. doi: 10.1016/j.mcm.2008.06.013

Tereso A., Ribeiro P., & Cardoso M. (2018). An automated framework for the integration between EVM and risk management. *Journal of Information Systems Engineering & Management 3*(1), 1–13. doi: 10.2 0897/jisem.201803

Chapter 8

Type-2 Fuzzy Numbers in Models of Project Time Affected by Risk

Barbara Gładysz

Department of Operations Research and Business Intelligence, Faculty of Management, Wroclaw University of Science and Technology, Wrocław, Poland

Contents

8.1 Introduction

There are many views on how to measure project success. A common assumption is that project success has quantitative dimensions: time, cost, and scope (the golden triangle rule). However, apart from these three dimensions, it is also important to measure the success of the project in terms of the team, manager, or organisation implementing the project, as well as in terms of the customer. Extremely important as well is the dimension of satisfaction of the project owner and user: whether the project has met their expectations. Project success cannot be measured only by quantitative criteria; it is a subjective evaluation of particular project stakeholders (Bartis and Mitev, 2008).

A serious problem that may occur in project management is keeping the project deadline. On the basis of the conducted research, it can be concluded that the deadline is not kept in most cases. According to Standish Group Report (2014) only 16.2% project software are completed on

DOI: 10.1201/9781003030966-11

time and budget. The average extension of the original time is over 200%. The longer time of execution leads to an increase in the project costs. In the construction industry, 75% of the projects are delayed (Senouci et al., 2016) and in public procurement, it is 72% and its average delay is about 44% (Urgilés et al., 2019). The consequences of the extension of the projects in all these and other areas are significant social, human, and financial costs. The reasons for not keeping the deadline may result from an improper project management process (including the lack of experience of the project manager, as well as the lack of knowledge of both the project manager and the team in the scope of project management techniques), communication problems among the project stakeholders, the lack of trust and kindness among the members of the project team, and their significant rotation (Frączkowski et al., 2019, Frączkowski and Gładysz, 2019, Kuchta et al., 2017).

Another significant factor that influences project duration is unplanned outages during its execution. A typical example of an outage is a situation in medical healthcare where the lack of personnel, as well as poor organisation of patient service, contributes to long queues of patients waiting for planned medical procedures (Palvannan and Teow, 2012). The Covid 2019 pandemic makes the situation even more serious (Baas et al., 2021). Santibáñez et al. (2021) studied this situation in the British Columbia Cancer Agency's ambulatory care unit. In this facility, patient waiting time is about 36% of the total patient time in the facility. Effective room utilisation is about 50%. This workflow results in significant opportunity costs (inefficient use of system capacity), as well as a significantly longer waiting queue for patients; this translates into a lack of patient trust in the healthcare system. Moreover, each medical procedure is a respective case. It is not possible to standardise most procedures due to their character, which additionally impedes the medical procedures scheduling.

A crucial element in project scheduling is a proper determination of the deadlines for particular project tasks. The factors such as resources availability or risks that may affect the time of the project execution, and thus threaten the deadline, must be considered at the moment of constructing the schedule. This results in uncertainty about the timing of a project's final design being rated by 87% of managers as high, very high, or total.

In the 20th century, traditional waterfall methodology was used in project management. At the beginning of the 21st century, a new project management methodology called Agile was proposed (Agile Manifesto 2001). There are many variations of this Agile methodology (Scrum, Kanban, Lean, Extreme Programming). According to The State of Scrum Report (2015) Scrum is the most popular project management practice. Some 42% of respondents declared that they use exclusive Scrum in project management, and 42% use Scrum in combination with other techniques. Project members say that Scrum improves their teams' quality of work life (87%) and improves the practice (81%).

In the Scrum methodology, each team member is involved in the time estimation process. There are various estimation methods used in Scrum projects, including i.e.: Planning Poker, T-Shirt Sizes, Relative Mass Valuation, Bucket System or Dot Voting.

Here we will present the rules of Planning Poker. The logic of the game is simple and has many advantages. The game of poker is based on the wisdom of crowds. It allows you to leverage the collective intelligence of the entire development team. Planning Poker leads to better task duration estimates because at its core is the assumption that the duration of project tasks is estimated based on the opinions of a group of experts representing different disciplines. Each expert independently estimates the duration of individual tasks. What is important in this game is that the experts estimate the task duration independently and present it to the manager at the same time. Playing Planning Poker is a kind of escape from formal meetings and everyday duties;

therefore, Planning Poker makes the work of the development team more effective and enjoyable, as emphasised by The Scrum Guide. In Planning Poker, everyone has a chance to speak, there is a chance for the project team to discuss, and averaging the individual evaluations leads to better estimation of task duration. It is important to emphasise that proper estimation of individual task duration (taking into account the availability of resources and specific risks that may affect the task duration) of a project allows to build a schedule that is easier to meet.

Mike Cohn (2007) proposed to use of Goldratt (2016) method for task duration estimation and time buffer in Agile methodology. In this method, task duration is estimated according to the critical-chain technique, which in it is assumption when estimating task duration takes into account the so-called "student syndrome" by introducing time buffers into the schedule. In classical project scheduling, the CPM (critical path method) method waterfall technique assumes that task times are deterministic, meaning that tasks can be completed in a strictly defined time. However, as Goldratt pointed out, in reality, such an assumption is impossible to keep, primarily because projects are unique endeavors and thus the duration of individual tasks cannot be accurately predicted. In addition, the psychological predisposition of people causes them to estimate a longer deadline for the task to be more confident that they will complete the task in the given time. There is one more element of the so-called "student syndrome," namely, that human nature inclines people to perform tasks at the last minute. It was based on these observations that Goldratt suggested incorporating time buffers into the project schedule. He suggested that when constructing a project schedule, the median ME of the time estimates given by the experts should be taken as the time to complete a given task. In this way, extreme time evaluations are eliminated. Time buffer is estimated on the basis of two parameters: the median ME, 0.9 percentile $Q_{0.9}$ and buffer = $(Q_{0.9} - ME)/2$

Suppose now that three experts evaluate the task completion time giving the following values of task completion times 5, 6, 7 days. According to the assumptions above, the planned task realisation time equal to ME = 6 days and buffer time is equal to $(Q_{0.9})$ –ME)/2 = (6.8 − 6)/2 = 3 hours 12 minutes.

In the classical PERT (Malcolm et al., 1959), based on the same task duration evaluations, the task duration would be assumed to have beta probability distribution (beta(x,4,4,5,7)) with expected value $E = \frac{t_{opt} + 4m + t_{pes}}{6}$ = 6 days, percentile $Q_{0.9}$ = 6.7 days, buffer time is equal to 2 hours 48 minutes.

If we now assume, following Hahn (2008), that the time of a task performed under stable conditions has beta distribution beta(x,4,4,5,7), and further assume that the time of task performance under risk conditions is a mixture of beta and uniform distribution Unif (5,7), then task time distribution will have the form $F(x) = (1 − w) * Beta(x, 4, 4, 5, 7)) + w * (x − 5)/2$, where w ∈ [0,1]) is the uncertainty index. If we assume that the uncertainty index w = 0.5, then the scheduled time of the task equals ME = 6 days, $Q_{0.9}$ = 6.65 days and time buffer is equal to 2 hours and 36 minutes.

The project task time estimation methods presented above are probabilistic methods. We will now present another methodology for estimating task time in the form of a fuzzy number. Suppose that the same experts are asked to evaluate the possibility (on a scale from 0 to 1) of completing the task in 4, 5, 6, 7 days. The time assessments given by the experts are shown in Table 8.1. Based on these assessments, we estimate the membership function of type-2 fuzzy number by taking the minimum and maximum time given by the experts, respectively, as the lower and upper possibility of performing the task in a given time, see Figure 8.1 and Table 8.1. For example, the possibility that we accomplish the task in 6 days takes values from 0.7 to 1. If we

Table 8.1 Experts'time estimations

Duration	Expert 1	Expert 2	Expert 3	Lower possibility (min)	Upper possibility (max)	Average possibility	Average normalise possibility
4	0.1	0.3	0.2	0.1	0.3	0.20	0.23
5	0.2	0.7	0.6	0.2	0.7	0.50	0.58
6	0.7	1	0.9	0.7	1	0.87	1
7	1	0.8	0.6	0.6	1	0.80	0.92

average and normalise the possibility of performing the task in a given time, we obtain the time characteristics of the task in the form of normalised type -1 fuzzy number, Figure 8.2. In this case, we can say that the most possible task duration is 6 days. The details of determining the expected value and time buffers of tasks for fuzzy task time evaluations are given in the paragraph 8.2.

In literature, there are many methods for scheduling projects under risk. There are proposed probabilistic models, fuzzy models, and hybrid (fuzzy – probabilistic) models. The first proposed method of project scheduling in nondeterministic conditions is PERT (program evaluation and review technique). In the classical PERT, it is assumed that the duration of a task has a beta distribution. PERT has been subjected to numerous modifications (Abdelkader, 2004; Grubbs, 1962; Hahn, 2008; Kamburowski, 1997). In the literature, in addition to probabilistic models, there are also models proposed for the time analysis of projects in which the times of activities are a mixture of distributions of random variables and fuzzy variables (Gładysz, 2017). There is also a wide representation of a stream of models in which the times of activities are type-1 fuzzy numbers (Pour et al., 2011; Shankar et al., 2010; Gładysz et al., 2014). Along with probabilistic models and fuzzy methods, in which the times of activities are type-1 fuzzy numbers, project

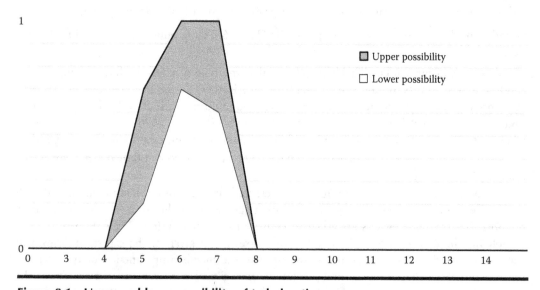

Figure 8.1 Upper and lower possibility of task duration.

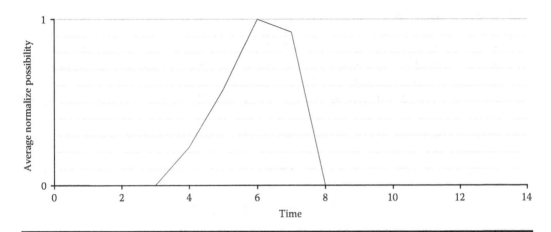

Figure 8.2   Average possibility of task duration.

critical time analysis methods are also proposed, in which the times of activities are type-2 fuzzy numbers. Anusuya and Balasowandari (2017) define the critical time and the critical path using various distance metrics. Dorfeshan et al. (2018) and Dorfeshan and Mousavi (2019) propose a multicriteria method of the critical path which, in addition to the time factor, also takes into account the cost, risk, quality, and security of the project. They apply the arithmetic proposed in the work by Hu et al. (2013). To determine the optimal solution, they use the MULTIMOORA, MOOSRA, and TOOPS methods. The problem of the risk of delay of project activities start times is considered and related, especially to the construction sector (Gładysz and Kuchta, 2020; Gładysz et al., 2021). Helen and Sumathi (2014), for the time analysis of a project, propose the time-cost trade-off model. Klaus-Rosińska et al. (2019) consider a research project planning problem based on SCRUM. To assign activities to particular project teams in particular project sprints, they apply the knapsack algorithm.

In this paper, we propose a new fuzzy PERT algorithm for a project affected by risk. We assume that the task times are type-2 fuzzy numbers and that the expected critical time is an interval number. A novelty of the proposed method involves the analysis of the critical time of the project, which is based on the interval expected value of the type-2 fuzzy number. The proposed method is useful in situations where we do not know the probability distributions of the task durations of the project that is being implemented in conditions of risk. In such situations, experts can extrapolate activity duration using fuzzy theory. Type-2 fuzzy numbers are especially useful in situations when experts differ in their opinions on the shape of the membership function or when the shape of the membership function depends on the conditions in which the project is implemented.

The outline of the chapter is as follows. In the next paragraph, we will present the basis of fuzzy sets theory. In paragraph 8.3, we will present the method of project time analysis affected by risk. In paragraph 8.4, we will present an example of project scheduling in the construction industry. Paragraph 8.5 covers a case study of a surgery in a hospital's operating theatre. The paper terminates with some conclusions and research perspectives.

8.2 Basic Notions

An interval number is a closed interval $\overline{A} = [\underline{a}, \overline{a}] = \{x \in \mathfrak{R}: \underline{a} \leq x \leq \overline{a}\}$. Values $\underline{a} = -\infty$ and $\overline{a} = +\infty$ are allowed. The interval number is the unknown realisation $x \in [\underline{a}, \overline{a}]$ of number $\overline{A}$, which may take values from the interval $[\underline{a}, \overline{a}]$.

Let $\overline{A} = [\underline{a}, \overline{a}]$ and $\overline{B} = [\underline{b}, \overline{b}]$ be two interval numbers. The sum and maximum of $\overline{A}$ and $\overline{B}$

are defined respectively as

$$\overline{A} + \overline{B} = [\underline{a} + \underline{b}, \overline{a} + \overline{b}] \tag{8.1}$$

$$\max(\overline{A}, \overline{B}) = [\max(\underline{a}, \underline{b}), \max(\overline{a}, \overline{b})] \tag{8.2}$$

The degree to which the number $\overline{A}$ is greater or equal to the number $\overline{B}$ is defined as follows:

$$degree\,(\overline{A} \geq \overline{B}) = |\{x: x \in \overline{A} \ \ and \ \ \vee \ y \ \epsilon\,\overline{B}, \ \ x \geq y\}|/|\overline{A}| \tag{8.3}$$

In 1965, Zadeh proposed his concept of possibility theory (Zadeh, 1965). We will present the basic notions of this theory. First, we will present the concept of a fuzzy number (type-1 fuzzy number). Let $\widetilde{X}$ be a single valued variable whose value is not precisely known. The membership for $\widetilde{X}$ is a normal, quasi concave and upper semi-continuous function $\mu_X: R \rightarrow [0, 1]$ – see (Dubois and Prade, 1988; Zadeh, 1978). The value $\mu_X(x)$ for $x \in \mathcal{R}$ denotes the possibility of the event that the fuzzy variable $\widetilde{X}$ takes the value of x. We denote this as follows: $\mu(x) = Pos(\widetilde{X} = x)$. For a given fuzzy number $\widetilde{X}$ and a given λ, the λ-level is defined to be the closed interval $[\widetilde{X}]_\lambda = \{x: \mu(x) \geq \lambda\} = [\underline{x}(\lambda), \overline{x}(\lambda)]$.

An interval-valued type-1 fuzzy number $\widetilde{X}$ is called an $L - R$ fuzzy number if its membership function takes the form of (Dubois and Prade, 1978):

$$\mu_X(x) = \begin{cases} L\left(\dfrac{\underline{m}-x}{\alpha}\right) & for \quad x < \underline{m} \\ \mu_m & for \quad \underline{m} \leq x \leq \overline{m} \\ R\left(\dfrac{x-\overline{m}}{\beta}\right) & for \quad x > \overline{m} \end{cases} \tag{8.4}$$

where: $L(x), R(x)$ – continuous nonincreasing functions $x; \alpha, \beta > 0$.

Functions $L(x), R(x)$ are called the shape functions of a fuzzy number. The most commonly used shape functions are: $\max\{0, 1 - x^p\}$ and $\exp(-x^p)$, $x \in [0, +\infty)$, $p \geq 1$. An interval-valued fuzzy number for which $L(x) = R(x) = \max\{0, 1 - x^p\}$ and $p = 1$ is called a trapezoid fuzzy number, which we denote as $(\underline{x}, \underline{m}, \overline{m}, \overline{x})$. A trapezoid fuzzy number for which $\underline{m} = \overline{m} = m$ is called a triangular fuzzy number, which we denote as $(\underline{x}, m, \overline{x})$.

A type-2 fuzzy set (T2FS) $\widetilde{A} \in \mathcal{F}_2(X)$ is an ordered pair $\widetilde{A} = \{(x, u), J_x, f_x(u)/x \in X; u \in J_x \subseteq [0, 1]\}$, where $\widetilde{A}$ represents uncertainty around the word A, J_x is the primary membership function of x, u is the domain of uncertainty, and $\mathcal{F}_2(X)$ is a class of type-2 fuzzy sets (Mendel, 2001):

$$\widetilde{A} : X \rightarrow [0, 1]$$
$$\widetilde{A} = \int_{x \in X} \int_{u \in J_x} 1/(x, u), \quad J_{x \in [0,1]} \tag{8.5}$$

An interval type-2 fuzzy number is a simplification of a T2FS. Its secondary membership function is assumed to be 1:

$$\widetilde{A} = \int_{x \in X} \int_{u \in J_x} 1/(x, u) = \int_{x \in X} \left[\int_{u \in J_x} 1/u \right] /x, \tag{8.6}$$

where x, u are primary and secondary variables, and $f_x(u)/u = 1$ is the secondary membership function.

The footprint of uncertainty of the interval type-2 fuzzy number $\widetilde{A}$ is bound by two functions: an upper membership function UMF and lower membership function LMF. When the upper and the lower membership functions are interval trapezoid membership functions, the fuzzy number is called a trapezoid type-2 fuzzy number. For the trapezoid interval type-2 fuzzy number we will use the following notion $\widetilde{X} = \left(\left(\underline{x}^U, \underline{m}^U, \overline{m}^U, \overline{x}^U; \mu_m^U \right) \left(\underline{x}^L, \underline{m}^L, \overline{m}^L, \overline{x}^L; \mu_m^L \right) \right)$. When $\underline{m}^U = \overline{m}^U$ and $\underline{m}^L = \overline{m}^L$, this number is a triangular type-2 fuzzy number. In the case when the primary and membership function are the same (equal to each other), the type-2 fuzzy number is a type-1 fuzzy number.

We will use fuzzy arithmetic based on Zadeh's extension principle (Zadeh, 1965) of $\mu_Z(z) = \sup_{z=f(x_1, \ldots, x_n)} \min\{\mu_{X_1}(x_1), \ldots, \mu_{X_n}(x_n)\}$, which is extended to type-2 fuzzy numbers (Dinagar and Anabalagan, 2012):

$$\mu_Z(z) = \left(\left(\sup_{z=f(x_1, \ldots, x_n)} \min\left\{\mu_{X_1}^U(x_1), \ldots, \mu_{X_n}^U(x_n)\right\} \right) \left(\sup_{z=f(x_1, \ldots, x_n)} \min\left\{\mu_{X_1}^L(x_1), \ldots, \mu_{X_n}^L(x_n)\right\} \right) \right) \tag{8.7}$$

The interval possibility that the realisation of type-2 fuzzy number $\widetilde{X}$ will be greater or equal to the realisation of type-2 fuzzy number $\widetilde{Y}$ is equal to (Gładysz et al., 2021):

$$\overline{Pos(\widetilde{X} \geq \widetilde{Y})} = \left[\sup_{x \geq y} \left(\min\left(\mu_X^L(x), \mu_Y^L(y) \right) \right), \quad \sup_{x \geq y} \left(\min\left(\mu_X^U(x), \mu_Y^U(y) \right) \right) \right] \tag{8.8}$$

The interval expected value of the type-2 fuzzy variable is (Gładysz et al., 2021):

$$\overline{E(\widetilde{X})} = \left[\min\left\{ \int_0^1 \frac{1}{2}(\underline{x}^L(\lambda) + \overline{x}^L(\lambda))\,d\lambda , \int_0^1 \frac{1}{2}(\underline{x}^U(\lambda) + \overline{x}^U(\lambda))\,d\lambda \right\}, \right.$$
$$\left. \max\left\{ \int_0^1 \frac{1}{2}(\underline{x}^L(\lambda) + \overline{x}^L(\lambda))\,d\lambda , \int_0^1 \frac{1}{2}(\underline{x}^U(\lambda) + \overline{x}^U(\lambda))\,d\lambda \right\} \right] \tag{8.9}$$

8.3 Analysis of the Duration of a Project

Let a project be represented as an acyclic network $G\,(N,\,A,\,\widetilde{T}\,)$, where $N = \{1, \dots, n\}$ is the set of nodes (events), $A \subset N \times N$ is the set of arcs (tasks, activities), and $\widetilde{T}\colon A \to F^+$ – a function representing the fuzzy durations of these tasks. Let us denote the fuzzy duration of task $(i,\,j) \in A$ as $\widetilde{T}_{ij}$. Let the durations of these tasks be type-2 fuzzy numbers. The exact form of these fuzzy durations is chosen on the basis of expert opinions. For each task $(i,\,j) \in A$, the experts determine the optimistic duration t_{ij}^{opt}, the most possible duration m_{ij}, and the pessimistic one t_{ij}^{pes} for stable (normal, most typical, scenarios where no risks materialise) conditions (circumstances) for the realisation of a project. Following this, the experts determine a list of risks $R = \{R_1, \dots, R_K\}$, which may cause the prolongation of tasks beyond the assumed pessimistic duration t_{ij}^{pes}. The experts also judge which risks may influence the duration of individual tasks ($Z_{ijk} = 1$ if the k-th risk influences the duration of task $(i,\,j)$, $Z_{ijk} = 0$ otherwise). The experts also give the amount of time Δt_{ijk}, by which the duration of task $(i,\,j)$ will be increased as a consequence of the occurrence of the k-th risk. If the k-th risk does not influence the duration of task $(i,\,j)$, we have $\Delta t_{ijk} = 0$. Let us assume that the duration of task $(i,\,j)$ is an interval trapezoid type-2 fuzzy number in the following form:

$$\widetilde{T}_{ij} = \left(\left(t_{ij}^{opt},\, m_{ij},\, t_{ij}^{pes};\, 1 \right) \left(t_{ij}^{opt},\, m_{ij},\, \left(1 + \sum_{k=1}^{K} \Delta t_{ijk}{\cdot}Z_{ijk} \right) t_{ij}^{pes};\, 1 \right) \right) \qquad (8.10)$$

We will now present a critical time-analysis algorithm (Gładysz, 2020).

Algorithm 1

Step 1. Number the nodes of network $i \in N$ ascendingly, starting with the initial node: $i = 1,\ 2,\ \dots, n$.

Step 2. Using equation (9.9) to find the interval expected value of task duration $\overline{E\,(\widetilde{T}_{ji})}$ for $(i,\,j) \in A$

Step 3. Set $E\,(\widetilde{T}_1) = 0$.

Step 4. For $i = 2, \dots, n$:

  find the expected value of the earliest time of $i \in N$.
  $$E\,(\widetilde{T}_i) = \max_{(j,\,i)\in P_i} \{E\,(\widetilde{T}_i) + E\,(\widetilde{T}_{ji})\}$$

  where P_i – the set of predecessors of i.

Step 5. Find the interval expected value of critical time $\overline{E\,(\widetilde{T}^{crit})} = \overline{E\,(\widetilde{T}_n)}$. The proposed method can be used in situations when we do not know the probability distributions of the task durations of the project that is being implemented in conditions of risk. In such situations, we can use the knowledge of experts to assess the project task durations and extrapolate task durations as fuzzy numbers. However, experts may disagree or may have different opinions. Type-2 fuzzy numbers have been proposed for modelling such situations. They apply in cases when experts differ in assessing the shape of the membership function, as well as when the shape of the membership function depends on the conditions of the project. Such a situation occurs, e.g. when we analyse the duration of a project carried out under risk conditions. The method can be used to analyse the sensitivity of the impact of individual risk categories on the critical time of the project, as well as on the critical time of individual project stages. This analysis can be carried out for various scenarios involving the impact of risk on the project. For this purpose, experts should determine (based on Formula (8.10)) the fuzzy duration of tasks, with the assumption of $Z_{ijk} = 1$ for the risk categories adopted in a given scenario $\{R_k\} \subset \{R_1, .., R_K\}$ and tasks $\{(i, j)\} \subset A$, which will be affected by these risks. The results of this analysis can be used by the project manager in the project management process to prevent against the risks that have the greatest impact on the critical time of the project. However, conducting such an analysis requires multi-variant analysis, especially when many risk categories affect the project. Therefore, the obtained results can be helpful at the stage of making a decision about starting a project, as well as in the risk management process during its implementation.

8.4 Example

Let us consider the project "Construction of a Sales and Service Center" – see Skorupka (2011). This project is composed of 18 tasks. Experts have listed risks that may influence the completion time of the project: computational errors in the design (R_1), errors in the bill of quantities (R_2), imprecise formulations in the contract (R_3), incorrect fieldwork (R_4), technological changes (R_5), equipment breakdowns (R_6), delays in the delivery of materials (R_7), construction disaster or accident (R_8), low quality of the work on site (R_9), low quality of materials (R_{10}), and disadvantageous weather (R_{11}). Experts also estimated the durations of tasks. Those estimations are presented in Table 8.2. Durations of tasks are modelled as type-2 fuzzy numbers. Figure 8.3 presents the membership functions of duration of the task Ground floor works (stage 1).

We can see that possible delays prolong the possible task duration with respect to the situation when risks materialises. There is a grey surface in Figure 8.1, showing the difference in possibility of realisation of given duration of Ground floor works in the case of risks materialisation.

Using Algorithm 1, we founded the expected value of critical time. It is equal to $\overline{E\,(\widetilde{\widetilde{T}}^{crit})} = [187,\ 199.3]$. In this there are two possible critical paths. One critical path is composed of the following tasks: preparation work (P), ground work (G), fundaments (stage1) (F1), ground floor (stage 1) (GF1), 1st floor (stage 1) (FF1), 2nd floor (stage 1) (SF1), 3rd floor (stage 1) (TF1), and roof above the 3rd floor (R), with the expected time $\overline{E\,(\widetilde{T}_{Path1})} = [187,\ 199.3]$. In the second path with the expected time $\overline{E\,(\widetilde{T}_{Path2})} = [186,\ 198.3]$, there is the task "drainage on the roof above the 3rd floor (Dhr)" instead of the task "roof above the 3rd floor (R)." The rest of the tasks are the same in both paths. Gantt chart for critical activities is presented in Figure 8.4.

Let's now find the degrees of criticality of the Paths 1 and Paths 2. According to equation (8.3), we obtain:

Table 8.2 Time characteristics (in days) of the tasks in a project and the risks influencing individual tasks

Name of task	Symbol	Predecessors	Risks	Duration	Expected duration
Preparation work	P	–	11	((9,10,11.24;1) (9,10,11;1))	[10, 10.8]
Ground work	G	P	1,4,6,8,9,10,11	((14,15,19.51;1) (14,15,16;1))	[15, 16.6]
Fundaments (stage 1)	F1	G	1,3,4,6,7,8,9,10,11	((19,20,27.04;1) (19,20,21;1))	[20, 22.6]
Fundaments (stage 2)	F2	F1		((7,9, 13.94;1) (7,9,11;1))	[9, 11.2]
Ground floor (stage 1)	GF1	F1	1,2,3,5,7,8,9,10,11	((28,30,41;1) (28,30,32;1))	[30, 33.6]
Lift shaft (stage 1)	L1	F1	1,2,3,5,7,8,9,10	((16,17,22.94;1) (16,17,18;1))	[17, 19]
Ground floor (stage 2)	GF2	F2, GF1		((9,11, 16.92;1) (9,11,13;1))	[11, 13.5]
1st floor (stage 1)	FF1	F2, GF1		((21,23,31.78;1) (21,23,25;1))	[23, 26.2]
Lift shaft (stage 2)	L2	F2, GF1		((16,17,22.94;1) (16,17,18;1))	[17, 19]
1st floor (stage 2)	FF2	GF2, FF1, L1		((14,16,23.01;1) (14,16,18;1))	[16, 18.8]
2nd floor (stage 1)	SF1	GF2, FF1, L1		((29,30,39.34;1) (29,30,31;1))	[30, 32.8]
Lift shaft (stage 3)	L3	GF2, FF1, L1		((18,19,25.48;1) (18,19,20;1))	[19, 21.1]
2nd floor (stage 2)	SF2	FF2, SF1L2		((14,16, 23.1;1) (14,16,18;1))	[16, 18.8]
3rd floor (stage 1)	TF1	FF2, SF1L2		((38,40,53.52;1) (38,40,42;1))	[40, 44.4]
Lift shaft (stage 4)	L4	FF2, SF1L2		((16,17,22.94;1) (16,17,18;1))	[17, 19]
3rd floor (stage 2)	TF2	SF2,TF1, L3		((4,6, 10.19;1) (4,6,8;1))	[6, 8.1]
Drainage on the roof above the 3rd floor	DhR	TF2, L4	2,5,7,8,9,10,11	((11,12,14.08;1) (11,12,13;1))	[12, 13]
Roof above the 3rd floor	R	SF2, TF1, L3	5,7,11	((18,19,23.43;1) (18,19,20;1))	[19, 20.6]

Source: Gładysz (2020).

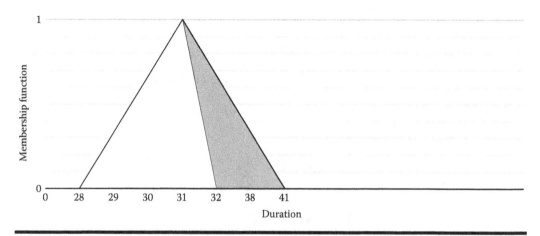

Figure 8.3   Fuzzy duration of Ground floor works (1 stage).

- Path 1 is critical to the degree $(E\,(\overline{\widetilde{T}_{Path1}}) \geq E\,(\overline{\widetilde{T}_{Path2}})) = 1$
- Path 2 is critical to the degree $(E\,(\widetilde{T}_{Path2}) \geq E\,(\widetilde{T}_{Path1})) = 0.92$

Let us assume that our required project duration is 192 days. The question is how to guarantee that the expected value of the project duration is not greater. According to equation (8.3), the degree of not keeping the desired deadline of 192 days is equal to 0.59: degree $\overline{(E\,(\widetilde{T}^{crit})} > =192) = 0.59$.

Using equation 8.7, we can find the membership functions of critical time: lower membership function:

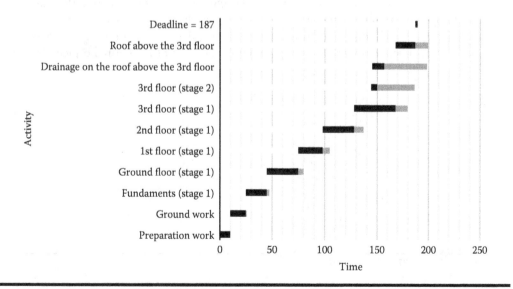

Figure 8.4   Gantt chart for critical activities. Scheduling: for stable conditions (black colour), possible lateness in the case when risks materialise (grey colour).

$$\mu^{L}_{\widetilde{T}^{crit}}(t) = \begin{cases} 1 - \frac{187-t}{187-176} & for \quad t \in [176, \ 187] \\ 1 - \frac{t-187}{198-187} & for \quad t \in [187, \ 192.5] \\ 1 - \frac{t-186}{199-186}) & for \quad t \in [192.5, \ 199] \end{cases} \quad (8.11)$$

upper membership function:

$$\mu^{U}_{\widetilde{T}^{crit}}(t) = \begin{cases} 1 - \frac{187-t}{187-176} & for \quad t \in [176, \ 187] \\ 1 - \frac{t-187}{247.3-187} & for \quad t \in [187, \ 202.2] \\ 1 - \frac{t-186}{248.1-186}) & for \quad t \in [202.2, \ 248.1] \end{cases} \quad (8.12)$$

The membership function of critical time of the project is presented in Figure 8.5.

Let us now determine the possibility of exceeding the directive deadline of 192 days. Based on Formulas (8.8), (8.11) and (8.12), we obtain $\overline{Pos(\widetilde{T}^{crit} \geq 192)} = [0.54, 0.9]$. Therefore, the analysed risks have a significant impact on the possibility of not completing the project within the planned timeframe. If the project is implemented in the stable conditions where no risk $R_1, ..,R_{11}$ materialises, then the possibility of exceeding the directive deadline is equal to 0.54. However, in a situation where it is possible that all risk categories $R_1, ..,R_{11}$ will materialise, then the possibility of exceeding the directive deadline increases to 0.9.

8.5 Case Study

In this paragraph, we will present an example of the application of the proposed Algorithm 1 for the time analysis of planning operations in an operating block in hospital in Poland. The operating theatre is a specific organisational unit of a hospital, the structure of which is very complex and, at the same time, dependent on many aspects of the work of the entire hospital. The main

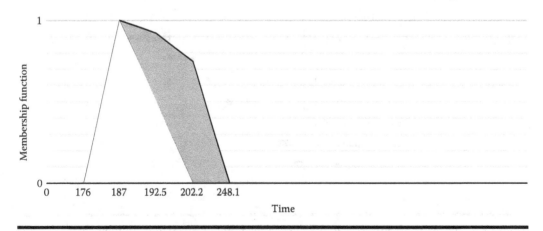

Figure 8.5 Fuzzy critical time of the project of constructing a shopping mall.

problem of the ward of the hospital being researched was unpunctual execution of medical procedures. In this hospital, the work in the operating theatre is scheduled one day ahead. The daily surgery schedule is determined on the basis of the number of patients waiting in the queue and on the expert knowledge of the person in charge of composing the schedule. The surgery schedule includes a one-day list of procedures for the following day, including their order of execution and the number of the operating theatres assigned to a given procedure. Nonetheless, it does not include the estimated time of the procedure because that is very difficult to determine. The person in charge of composing the schedule consults the experts (operators) to estimate the time of execution of a given procedure and to predict the number of procedures to be carried out this day.

The process of operation comprises many activities that can be divided into three groups: pre-operating activities, the operation itself, and post-operating activities. If a scheduled procedure is not carried out in the designated time, it has a negative impact on the whole work of the hospital. A patient who is supposed to be returned to the ward after surgery is rescheduled, which results in the postponement of other procedures and the drastic extending of the queue of patients. It negatively impacts both patients and the performance of the hospital; what is more, the patients fail to trust the medical healthcare system. This situation also generates more financial costs for the hospital connected with a repeated hospitalisation and the image losses. The person in charge of composing the schedule must really precisely assign the operating theatre to the kind of procedure and estimate the time of the operation. The information about the duration of particular procedures is vital to reliably prepare the surgery schedule for the following day. Incorrectly selected operations may lead to overtime in the work of the operating theatre staff. This is an economically undesirable situation for the hospital.

As it has been concluded from the initial analysis of the situation in the operating block, the duration of the procedure in a particular operating theatre was an even more vital factor influencing the timeline of the whole operating block. The duration of particular activities included in the whole process of the operation was to be determined. This process was addressed as one operation, together with its pre-operating and post-operating activities. The description of all activities is presented in Table 8.2. These activities are so-called procedural activities that are described in the working procedures that are operative in the operating block of a given hospital. These activities are obligatory to perform, and their performance is strictly determined. In order to analyse the performance of the processes of operation, the observation of the medical personnel's work was carried out.

The structure of the network of activities of a process occurring in selected operating theatre is presented Table 8.2. For each activity $(i, j) \in \mathscr{A}$, the experts determined the optimistic duration t_{ij}^{opt}, the most possible duration t_{ij} and the pessimistic one t_{ij}^{pes} for stable (normal, most typical, scenarios) conditions (circumstances) for the realisation of a project. It needs to be emphasised that when experts estimate shapes of membership functions, experts should take into account availability of the personnel which is, among others, the condition for timely realisation of particular stages of the project. Based on that data we estimate the type-1 triangular fuzzy membership function of durations of those activities (Table 8.3).

During research, it turned out that the activities, which are not procedural activities, have the influence on the duration of the whole process of operation. The description of these activities, together with their connection with the corresponding procedural activity, was included in Table 8.4.

Table 8.3 Network's structure and activities' durations

Activity	Predecessor	Description of activities	Duration [min]	Expected duration
A	--------	Taking over the patient to the operating ward by operating room nurses and taking him to the waiting room	(2, 3, 3, 6)	3.5
B	A	Preparing the patient by the anaesthesiologist team	(9, 10, 10, 25)	13.5
C	A	Preparing the patient by the nurse in the preparatory room	(6, 7, 7, 19)	9.75
D	---------	Preparing the operating room by operating room nurses	(5, 7, 7, 18)	9.25
E	---------	Preparing instruments in the operating room by the operating room nurse	(6, 7, 7, 38)	14.5
F	B, C, D	Taking in the patient to the operating room (time between the patient's readiness in the waiting room and taking the patient to the operating room)	(2, 2, 2, 7)	3.25
G	E, F	Anaesthesia	(4, 5, 5, 24)	9.5
H	G	Performing the surgery (duration is counted from cutting the patient until suturing)	(54, 95, 95, 375)	154.75
I	H	Filling in documentation by the anaesthesiologist	(5, 7, 7, 17)	9.0
J	G	Filling in documentation by the operating room nurse	(6, 8, 8, 12)	8.5
K	H	Postoperative activities with the patient performed in the operating room	(4, 5, 5, 44)	14.5
L	K	Taking the patient to the recovery room	(2, 2, 2, 17)	5.75
M	K	Postoperative activities performed by operating room nurses in the operating room	(5, 5, 5, 31)	11.5
N	H	Preparing instruments for sterilisation by operating room nurses	(4, 5, 5, 26)	10.0
O	I, J, L, M, N	Cleaning of the operating room by the cleaning personnel	(6, 7, 7, 35)	13.75

Source: Own elaboration on the base: Gładysz et al. (2021).

Table 8.4 Description and pessimistic time of "non-productive" activities

Activity	Description of the "waiting" time of activity	Employee performing the activity	Pessimistic delay [min.]	Interval expected delay [min.]
A	Patient waiting to be taken in the waiting room reason: e.g. lack of patient's documents	Operating room nurses	21	[5.25, 10.5]
B	Waiting for the first anaesthesiologist reason: occurs only before the first surgery as anaesthetists have the morning briefing at 7:30 am	The anaesthesiologist team	42	[10.5, 21]
F	'Prepared' patient's waiting to be taken in the operating room (time between completion of anaesthetic preparation and taking the patient in the operating room), change of surgeries in the daily plan, related with e.g. change of instruments reason: e.g. unprepared room, unprepared instruments, no instructions	Operating room nurses	25	[6.25, 12.5]
H	Waiting for the operator reason: e.g. the operator is in the ward, fills in documentation	Operator	46	[11.5, 23]
O	Waiting for the cleaning service reason: e.g. cleaning rooms as they are located, not according to priorities	Cleaning service	18	[4.5, 9]

Source: Own elaboration on the base Gładysz et al. (2021).

The experts also judge which activities could start later because of poor organisational reasons and determine the pessimistic possible delay τ_{ij} in the starting time of the activity (i, j). Then, for each activity $(i, j) \in \{A, B, F, H, O\}$, we propose to modify the project network according to the following procedure: replace arc (i, j) with two arcs (i, i') and (i', j) such that the length of

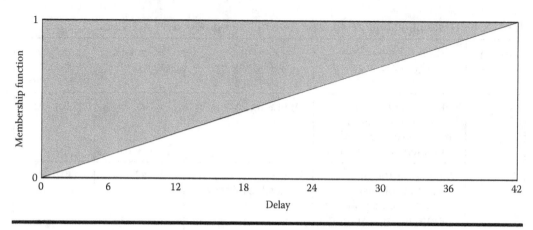

Figure 8.6 Fuzzy delay in starting activity A - Patient waiting to be taken in the waiting room.

arc (i, i') is equal to $\widetilde{T}_{ij} = ((0, \ 0, \ \tau_{ij}, \ \tau_{ij}; \ 1) \ (0, \ \tau_{ij}, \ \tau_{ij}, \ \tau_{ij}; \ 1))$ and the length of arc $(i', \ j)$ is equal to $\widetilde{T}_{ij} = \left(\left(t_{ij}^{opt}, \ m_{ij}, \ m_{ij}, \ t_{ij}^{pes}; \ 1 \right) \left(t_{ij}^{opt}, \ m_{ij}, \ m_{ij}, \ t_{ij}^{pes}; \ 1 \right) \right)$. Arc $(i, \ i')$ represents the possible delay in the starting time of the activity, arc $(i', \ j)$ the activity duration. For example, Figure 8.6 presents possibility of delay in starting the activity A- Patient waiting to be taken in the waiting room (possible reason: lack of patient's documents).

Applying Algorithm 1 to the project from Table 8.2 (without taking the risks influencing the starting times of individual activities into account), we obtain the project duration as equal to triangular type-1 fuzzy number (86,132,132,547). Figure 8.7 presents membership function of this critical time. The project will take, most possibly (in delays in project activities starting times are not taken into account), about 132 minutes; however, all the values between 86 and 547 minutes are to some extent possible. The critical path consists of activities: A (Taking over the patient to the operating ward by operating room nurses and taking him to the waiting room), B (Preparing the patient by the anaesthesiologist team), F (Taking in the patient to the operating

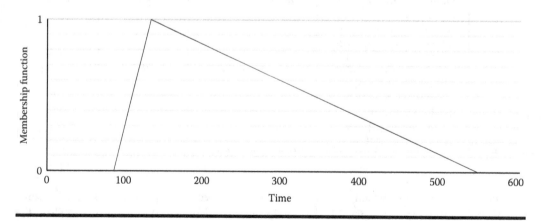

Figure 8.7 Fuzzy critical time of a surgery in the case when each activity starts on time.

room), G (Anaesthesia), H (Performing the surgery), K (Postoperative activities with the patient performed in the operating room), M (Postoperative activities performed by operating room nurses in the operating room), and O (Cleaning of the operating room by the cleaning personnel). The expected value of critical time is equal to 224.25 minutes. (about 3 hours and 25 minutes.).

Let's now do analysis of the influence of the delays in starting of activities on the project duration. Let's apply the Algorithm 1 to the project with modified arcs. The result we obtain for the project duration is equal to ((86, 132, 132,547;1) (86, 132, 247, 662;1)), see Figure 8.8. In this case the critical paths is the same, consists of the activities A, B, F, G, H, K, M and O.

We can see that possible delays prolong the most possible project duration with respect to the situation when its influence on the starting activities times was not considered. There is a grey surface in Figure 8.6, showing the difference in opinion among the experts: according to the more optimistic experts, project durations close to 132 minutes are highly possible, even when considering a delay in activities and its influence of project activity starting times; other experts estimate their possibility lower. In this case, the interval expected value of critical time is equal to [224.25, 281.75] minutes. ([3 hours and 25 minutes, 4 hours and 42 minutes]).

We can see that there is the great difference (1 hour and 17 minutes) between expected critical times when project activities start on time and when the delays in starting activities are possible.

As the hospital experts emphasise, to minimalize the duration of delays should be a priority; however, its total elimination is not possible due to the hospital's and the state's financial policy. As a result of the described herein analysis of delays in the given hospital, some corrections have been introduced and their aim is to minimize the delays. The most important improvements cover the work of anaesthesiologists and cleaning services. Namely, the anaesthesiologists who assist at the first procedure on the given day have been exempted from the participation in the morning briefing. Moreover, it has been pointed out that the operating theatres that are planned to be used for procedures on the given day must be prepared first. The implementation of these alterations has improved the performance of procedures and minimized the number of un-executed procedures to 16%. It must be emphasized that the proposed solutions did not require

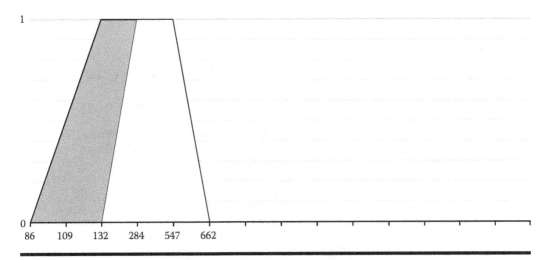

Figure 8.8 Fuzzy critical time of a surgery in the case when delays in starting activities are possible.

any additional financial means; they only required the work reorganisation and the improvement of the already existing procedures.

8.6 Conclusions

In this chapter, we proposed a new fuzzy PERT algorithm for a project affected by risk. We assume that task durations are type-2 fuzzy numbers and that the expected critical time is an interval number. The parameters of the lower and upper membership functions of these durations are determined by experts: the lower membership function corresponds to the duration of the task in stable conditions, with no risks materialising, and the upper membership function corresponds to the duration of a task in the case that a risk does occur. The proposal was applied to a real-world construction project. The case study for operating theatre in hospital in Poland was presented.

The proposed method is useful in situations where we do not know the probability distributions of the task durations of the project that is being implemented in conditions of risk. In such situations, experts can extrapolate activity duration using the fuzzy-number theory. Type-2 fuzzy numbers are especially useful in situations when experts differ in their opinions on the shape of the membership function or when the shape of the membership function depends on the conditions in which the project is implemented.

In the next stage of research, we plan to extend the proposed method with an analysis of the variance of the critical time of the project.

Acknowledgement

This research was supported by the National Science Centre (Poland), under Grant 394311, 2017/27/B/HS4/01881: "Selected methods supporting project management, taking into consideration various stakeholder groups and using type-2 fuzzy numbers".

References

Abdelkader, Y.H. (2004). Evaluating project completion times when activity times are Weibull distribution. *European Journal of Operational Research 157*, 704–715.

Anusuya, V., & Balasowandari, P. (2017). Critical path with various distances of type-2 fuzzy numbers. *International of Fuzzy Mathematical Archive 13*(1), 1–7.

Baas, S., Dijkstra S., Braaksma, A., van Rooij, P., Snijders, F.J., Tiemessen, L., & Boucherie, R.J. (2021) Real-time forecasting of COVID-19 bed occupancy in wards and Intensive Care Units. *Health Care Management Science 24*, 402–419. doi: 10.1007/s10729-021-09553-5.

Bartis, E., & Mitev, N. (2008). A multiple narrative approach to information systems failure: A successful system that failed. *European Journal of Information Systems 17*, 112–124.

Cohn, M. (2007). Mountain goat software: Don't average during planning poker. https://www.mountaingoatsoftware.com/blog/dont-average-during-planning-poker, accessed May 2021.

Dinagar, D.S., & Anabalagan, A.A. (2012, March). A new type -2 fuzzy number arithmetic using extension principle. in *Proceedings of the 1st International Conference on Advances in Engineering, Science and Management (ICAESM '12)*, 113–118, Nagapattinam, Tamil Nadu, India.

Dorfeshan, Y., & Mousavi, S.M. (2019). A new interval type-2 fuzzy decision method with an extended relative preference relation and entropy to project critical path selection. *International Journal of Fuzzy Systems Applications 8*(1), 19–47.

Dorfeshan, Y., Mousavi, S.M., Mohagheghi, V., & Vahdani, B. (2018). Selecting project-critical path by a new interval type-2 fuzzy decision methodology based on MULTIMOORA, MOOSRA and TPOP methods. *Computers & Industrial Engineering 120*, 160–178.

Dubois, D., & Prade H. (1978). Operations on fuzzy numbers. *International Journal of Systems Science 9*(6), 613–626.

Dubois, D., & Prade, H. (1988). *Possibility Theory: An Approach to Computerized Processing of Uncertainty.* New York: Plenum Press.

Frączkowski, K., & Gładysz, B. (2019) Stakeholder impact on the success and risk af failure of ICT project in Poland. In: Intelligent Information and Database Systems: 11th Asian Conference, ACIIDS 2019, Yogyakarta, Indonesia, April 8-11, 2019: proceedings. Pt. 1 / eds. Ngoc Thanh Nguyen [et.al.] Cham: Springer, (Lecture Notes in Computer Science. Lecture Notes in Artificial Intelligence, ISSN 0302-9743; vol. 11431), 530–540

Frączkowski, K., Gładysz, B., Mazur H., & Prałat E. (2019) Behavioural aspects of communication in the management process of IT projects. In: Information Systems Architecture and Technology: Proceedings of 39th International Conference on Information Systems Architecture and Technology, ISAT 2018. Pt. 3 / eds. Zofia Wilimowska, Leszek Borzemski, Jerzy Świątek. Cham: Springer, cop. s. (Advances in Intelligent Systems and Computing, ISSN 2194-5357; vol. 854), 335–347.

Gładysz, B. (2017). Fuzzy – probabilistic PERT. *Annals of Operations Research 258*(2), 437–452.

Gładysz, B. (2020). Type-2 fuzzy numbers in models of the duration of a project affected by risk. *Journal of Decision Systems 8*, 19-47.

Gładysz, B., & Kuchta, D. (2020) Project delay as a consequence of project activities start times delays – fuzzy approach. In: *Proceedings of the 35th International Business Information Management Association Conference (IBIMA): 1-2 April 2020, Seville, Spain* / ed. Khalid S. Soliman. [King of Prussia, PA]: International Business Information Management Association, 16749–16760.

Gładysz, B., Kuchta, D., Skorupka D., & Duchaczek A. (2014, September). Fuzzy analysis of project duration in situations of risk. *Proceedings International Conference on Numerical Analysis and Applied Mathematics*, art. 600003, *1648*, 1–4, Rhodes, Greece.

Gładysz, B., Skowrońska-Szmer, A., & Nowak, W. (2021, June). The use of type-2 fuzzy sets to assess delays in the implementation of the daily operation plan for the operating theatre. In *International Conference on Computational Science* (pp. 486–499). Cham: Springer.

Goldratt, E.M. (1997). *Critical Chain: A Business Novel.* Great Barrington, MA: North River Press.

Grubbs, F.E. (1962). Attempts to validate PERT statistics or "Picking on PERT". *Operations Research 10*, 912–915.

Hahn, E. (2008). Mixture densities for project management activity times: A robust approach to PERT. *European Journal of Operational Research 210*, 450–459.

Helen, R., & Sumathi, R. (2014). Time-cost trade-off problem using type-2 trapezoidal fuzzy numbers. *International Journal of Mathematical Trends and Technology 10*, 51–59. doi: 10.14445/22315373/IJMTT-V10P510.

Hu, J., Zhang, Y., Chen, X., & Liu, Y. (2013) Multi-criteria decision making method based on possibility degree of interval type-2 fuzzy number. *Knowledge-Based Systems 43*, 21–29.

Kamburowski, J. (1997). New validations of PERT times. *Omega-International Journal of Management Science 25*(3), 323–328.

Klaus-Rosińska, A., Schneider, J., & Bulla, V. (2019). Research project panning based on SCRUM framework and type-2 fuzzy numbers. Research project planning based on SCRUM framework and type-2 fuzzy numbers. In: *Information Systems Architecture and Technology: Proceedings of 39th International Conference on Information Systems Architecture and Technology, ISAT 2018.* Springer, 2019, AISC, *854*, 381–391.

Kuchta, D., Gładysz B., Skowron, D., & Betta J. (2017). R&D projects in science sector. *R & D Management 47*(1), 88–110.

Malcolm, D.G., Roseboom, C.E., Clark, C.E., & Fazar, I. (1959). Application of a technique for research and development program evaluation. *Operations Research 7*, 646–649.

Manifesto for Agile Software Development (2001). http://agilemanifesto.org

Mendel, J. (2001). *Uncertain Rule-Based Fuzzy Systems: Introduction and New Directions*. Cham: Pearson Education, Inc. Springer. doi: 10.1007/978-3-319-51370-6

Palvannan, R.K., & Teow, K.L. (2012) Queueing for healthcare. *Journal of Medical Systems 36*(2), 541–547. doi: 10.1007/s10916-010-9499-7

Pour, N.S., Kheranmand, M., Fallah, M., & Zeynali, S. (2011). A new method for critical path method with fuzzy processing time. *Management Sciences Letters 1*, 347–354.

Santibáñez, P.S., Chow, V.S., French, J., Puterman, M.L., & Tyldesley, S. (2009). Reducing patient wait times and improving resource utilization at British Columbia Cancer Agency's ambulatory care unit through simulation. *Health Care Management Science 12*(4), 392–407.

Senouci, A., Ismail, A., & Eldin, N. (2016). Time delay and cost overrun in Qatari public construction projects. *Procedia Engineering 164*, 368–375.

Shankar, N.R., Sireesha, V., & Rao, B.B. (2010). An analytical method for finding critical path in a fuzzy project network. *International Journal of Contemporary Mathematical Sciences 5*(20), 953–962.

Skorupka, D. (2011). A method of identification and assessment of risk of construction projects. WAT, Wrocław (in Polish).

The Standish Group Report. (2014) Chaos. https://www.projectsmart.co.uk/white-papers/chaos-report.pdf (available 04.05.2021).

The 2015 State of Scrum Report. (2015). How the world is successfully applying the most popular Agile approach to projects. *Scrum Alliance* 10–10.

Urgilés, P., Claver, J., & Sebastián M.A. (2019). Methods for quantitative risks analysis of cost and deadline overruns in complex projects. *Procedia Manufacturing 41*, 658–665.

Zadeh, L.A. (1965). Fuzzy sets. *Information and Control 8*, 338–353.

Zadeh, L.A. (1978). Fuzzy sets as a basis of theory of possibility. *Fuzzy Sets and Systems 1*, 3–28.

SOFTWARE APPLIED TO DECISION MAKING IN ORGANISATIONS

Chapter 9

Socialising Decision Enactment: Living Provenance in Decision Support

Patrick Humphreys

London School of Economics and Political Science, London, United Kingdom

Contents

DOI: 10.1201/9781003030966-13

9.1 Introduction: Transaction Provenance as a Basis for Supporting Decision Enactment

This chapter focuses on innovative and creative ways of socialising decision enactment once a decision maker has committed to a choice. It identifies novel opportunities for handling this socialisation in a generative way by distributing the decision enactment elements throughout a multisided transaction network where participants on all sides collaborate and transact; the full decision commitment is enacted in such a way that each of its elements exhibits good provenance, with the details worked out bottom-up by the individual transactors.

In effect, this process extends individualised perspective inherent in the traditional, individualised perspective on support for decision enactment, socialising this perspective in theory and practice in a way that enables the effective development of a new generation of decision support systems offering transaction provenance decision support platforms.

A case study ("PROFLOURI") is presented, throughout this chapter, that explores the process by which the enactment of a complex decision to *implement the Flouri ecosystem* was constructed according to this socialised model for decision enactment. The case study describes and evaluates how the implementation of this ecosystem was supported in practice by WRT Technologies Limited's SIlubi.io multisided trading and provenance-building platform.

9.2 Experiencing the Need to Socialise Decision Enactment

The conventional, individualised perspective on decision enactment requires that the decision maker commits to a course of action that will be implemented in reality by him/her or those under his/her command and control (Humphreys, 2021; Pomerol and Adam, 2008).

This requirement has its roots in the "scientific management" idea that the organisation is something to be *acted upon* or to be transformed by management, whose own practice in attempting to do so is somehow split off from the human practice of those in the organisation who maintain these structures and processes through their own productive activities (Guillen, 1994).

This idea has also promoted management centrism in decision making and enactment. Thus, *management* makes decisions, *management* gains support for these decisions, and *management* transforms the organisation (Merkle, 1980). This model perpetuates the view that successful management within organisations is dependent on both those who 'make' the decisions and those who secure their implementation having the power to enforce them within a control hierarchy.

Vari, Vecsenyi and Paprika (1986) describe how, in analysing decision making in bureaucratic organisations, most of the decision maker's motivations could be traced to the desire for controlling (through understanding and influencing) the three phases of the decision-making process, i.e. gaining or maintaining control over:

■ the planning of the decision (problem structuring, analysing, and proposal formulating);
■ the choice process; and,
■ the implementation of the decision.

From the decision maker's point of view, when immersed in this paradigm, the central possessor of the power to make the decision and get it implemented is himself or herself, i.e. the decision maker is the 'decision owner' (Checkland, 1981). Moreover, the power to do so should be analysed in descending form, through the levels of middle management below the decision maker in the management control hierarchy, to those whose actual practices within the organisational work system are to be acted upon.

Hence, once the decision maker (individual or corporate) has committed to enact a decision, he or she then has to take complete control over his or her immediate actions resulting from the commitment. In this case, there is little, or no, chance for sharing with others the responsibility for implementing the decision, and thus, socialising its enactment.

Larichev (1984) called this kind of decision making 'holistic decision making', pointing out that, in contrast, there are many contexts where the holistic approach is inappropriate because:

■ the decision maker has not enough expertise or information for constructing, exploring, estimating, and constructing potential solutions on his own in planning the implementation of the decision, and
■ where the action plan to be adopted requires that a variety of other parties act in accord with the prescriptions of the decision taken.

In such contexts, decision makers who, when faced with the need to enact their decisions, adopt the conventional individualised perspective, requiring that they take command of, and control, the decision implementation process top down; they are usually left "adrift in a sea of uncertainty" (Humphreys and Berkeley, 1995).

One can escape from this conundrum by underpinning the enactment process with a socialised, rather than an individualised, model of decision enactment where the decision maker's perspective changes from focusing on the need to command and control, to the possibility of arranging facilitation and support. Thus, participants are engaged at all levels (Humphreys and Jones, 2006), and share the responsibly for decision enactment.

In this respect, Pomerol and Adam (2008) point out that

> Decision support systems should primarily be geared as models for action, but action in an organization is a cascade at intertwined sub-actions and consequently DSS design must accommodate human reasoning at a variety of levels, from the strategic level to the lowest level of granularity of action decided by managers.

In actualising this model for decision enactment support, the decision maker may well be able to locate the implementation of the decision in a socialised ecosystem where the participants in the ecosystem can take collective and collaborative responsibility for the set of transactions between agents in the ecosystem to create and provide the resources and activities needed for successful implementation of the chosen course of action (Adner, 2017).

Here, the enactment of the decision is threaded through a network of linked transactions whereby each of the participants on all sides in the ecosystem will deliver, as "transacting agents," a part of the required resources and/or activities in areas where they have particular competency and efficacy; thus, the course of action is ensured to achieve well at all levels, that is, in a way that, collectively, minimises implementation failure risk as described by Berkeley et al. (1991).

This process is enhanced in ecosystems powered by a *transaction-provenance decision support platform* that is able to facilitate this socialised enactment process between participants on all sides. Parker et al. (2016) explain how such platforms achieve this:

> The platform provides an open, participative infrastructure for this interaction and sets governance conditions for them. The platform's overarching purpose is to consummate matches among users and facilitate transaction of goods, services or social currency, thereby enabling value creation for all participants

A transaction-provenance decision platform also provides features that support exploration authentication and improvement of the provenance of the agents and entities involved in these transactions, thereby enhancing collective decision enactment. (Humphreys, 2021)

The PROFLOURI case example that is explored in sections 9.10 to 9.12 of this chapter explores the process by which the complex decision *to implement the Flouri ecosystem* is enacted, constructed according to the socialised mode of decision enactment identified above. This ecosystem is supported by WRT Technologies Limited's Silubi.io multisided trading and provenance-building platform.

Sections 9.4 and 9.5 of this chapter provide details of Raw Coffee Company's decision and the issues involved in socialising its enactment. Section 6 describes how the participants at all levels in the socialised enactment process are actively involved bottom-up in this process, and how they all benefit and create value collectively through this process.

Sections 9.6 through 9.9 of the chapter provide details of the features provided by Silubi.io, serving to generate a climate of transparency and trust between the ecosystem's participants so that everyone on all sides can see, and explore, how the initial decision, to which Raw Coffee Company was committed, was successfully and collectively implemented bottom-up by all sides in the Flouri ecosystem.

9.3 The Context for the Enactment of the Flouri Decision

Raw Coffee Company, located in Dubai, is a coffee bean purchasing, roasting, and international retail distribution company that buys coffee beans directly from suppliers in Latin America (Colombia, Peru, Guatemala and Nicaragua) and Africa (Ethiopia, Rwanda, Burundi). These suppliers are predominantly cooperatives formed by coffee growers to process and market the individual coffee growers' production of green coffee beans. Raw Coffee Company aims to build direct transactions and good relations with the individual coffee growers based on mutual trust and transparency, cutting out intermediary traders and avoiding the coffee commodity trading market.

Many of the cooperatives now trading with Raw Coffee Company were previously established, according to the international Fairtrade model (FLO), whereby the "Fairtrade premium" that reached the cooperative was effective in strengthening the participation of the individual coffee growers in their cooperative's governance, innovative actions, and social and community development programmes.

However, emerging problems with the underlying Fairtrade financial and trading model (Haight, 2011) have led to the cooperatives currently selling a part of their coffee via Fairtrade to seek partnerships with direct buyers, usually coffee roasters and sellers into consumer markets (coffee bars and restaurants in North America, Europe and Asia). This is particularly the case when cooperatives trade high-quality "single origin" micro-lot coffees outside of the Fairtrade buyer community.

Raw Coffee Company's mission statement (published on their website at raw-coffeecompany.org) is:

> We source premium green beans from around the world and have selected the niche specialty market looking for quality and sustainability. It's really important to us that our beans are ethically sourced and the farmers and their families growing our coffee are treated fairly and can make a sustainable living. We deal directly with our farmers and the processing partners and buy fresh beans each year.[1]

The Raw Coffee Company has not joined the Fairtrade network and does not act as a Fairtrade buyer. However, Raw Coffee Company does appreciate the way that Fairtrade's FLO system has helped the growers' collectives to improve the livelihoods of their members by means of their own bottom-up efforts.

In this respect, Enelow (2012) has identified five separate capabilities that are enhanced by participation in the FLO system:

1. The opportunity to organise cooperatively and democratically.
2. The opportunity to learn new production techniques that conserve the environment and increase yields.
3. The increased social interaction across communities, which Robert Putnam would call "bridging social capital."
4. Increased access to market information and low-cost credit.
5. Increase in self-esteem, or what political philosopher John Rawls called the "social bases of self-respect."

However, as Enelow (2012) comments, "one could argue that these capabilities or functioning stem from the growers' participation in the cooperative, rather than the FLO."

These achievements by the coffee growers' collectives are consonant with Raw Coffee Company's motivation and aims, and Raw Coffee Company would like to develop a direct coffee transaction system linking growers' collectives, roasters, distributors, and individual retailers (coffee bars and restaurants) worldwide. This direct transaction system would "cut out the middlemen" (coffee commodity market traders, etc.) and would incorporate innovative ways of providing support for development opportunities initiated by the collectives in the ecosystem.

However, Raw Coffee Company would not want to adopt the financial trade model developed by Fairtrade, which was based on paying growers a minimum price (set at the minimum price which Fairtrade believed was sufficient to enable them to survive financially) if the market price dropped below this level. But otherwise, the Fairtrade buyers would pay the market price for commodity coffee.

Retailers of coffee carrying the Fairtrade logo are required to include a Fairtrade premium in the price for which they sell this coffee. The assumption here is that the Fairtrade logo improves the provenance of the coffee in the eyes of potential consumers who would thus be happy to pay the higher price, including the premium that would then benefit the coffee growers' association that originally produced this coffee.

Fairtrade's FLO decides centrally on the rules about how this premium can be spent in the coffee growers' communities (e.g. on schemes for providing educational opportunities for growers' family members, help in paying healthcare expenses, etc.).

Instead, Raw Coffee Company would like to operate a transaction system where the co-operatives with which it trades find ways to improve and demonstrate the provenance of the single-origin producer-branded coffees that they grow and which Raw Coffee Company roasts and distributes; these could then be sold as top-quality coffee, with good provenance that can be investigated and authenticated by the intending consumers themselves. These consumers would then be happy to pay the higher price for this coffee because it marks their association with this good provenance and their active participation in maintaining it through purchasing the particular Flouri single origin micro-lot coffee.

Raw Coffee Company imports the coffee beans that it purchases in Latin America and Africa to Dubai, where it roasts them; it brands the roasted coffee by means of packaging that identifies its "single origin micro-lot" (generally specified as the locality in which the supplying cooperative is located). It currently sells the majority of its roasted coffee to small businesses, usually coffee bars and restaurants in Saudi Arabia and the Emirates, with whom Raw Coffee Company has close long-term relationships.

9.4 The Flouri Decision

Raw Coffee Company made the decision to expand its retail markets for its branded coffee. The company made a start in this direction by selling their roasted coffee to individual retail customers worldwide directly via their website in single-origin branded packaging. Their long-term aim was to develop close relations with individual retailers (coffee bars and restaurants) in many countries. They also wanted to support the individual growers of these "single-origin micro-lot coffees" who could produce high-quality coffee through marketing it under the name of the actual grower and the locality from where it originated.

Raw Coffee Company realised that enactment of this decision could not be achieved effectively by Raw Coffee Company acting, or trying to control the enactment process, on its own. So, the company formed a partnership with World Reserve Global Ltd, incorporated as Flouri Limited, wherein the partners, working together, could effectively socialise the enactment process by forming the Flouri safe direct-trading and provenance-building ecosystem wherein all sides identified above would participate in a climate of mutual trust and transparency. The Flouri ecosystem would be supported by WRT Technologies' SIlubi.io multisided trading and provenance-building platform[2] described in Section 9.6, below (see also Humphreys, 2021 and Hill et al., 2020).

Flouri would also create and implement a Living Provenance certification and assurance scheme: demonstrating and publicising the good provenance of the single-origin coffee from the producer in a way that would engage and convince consumers that it is well worthwhile to pay a premium for this particular coffee.

These actions should increase both Flouri's single-origin micro-lot coffee sales and the amount of the profit on each sale, generating substantial income that could enhance the profits of the Flouri partners. They also provide funding for innovation and social and economic developments innovated bottom-up by the coffee growers' cooperatives participating in Flouri.

9.5 How All Sides Benefit from Participation in Flouri

The multisided groups participating in the joint enactment of Raw Coffee company' decision within the Flouri ecosystem are: the individual coffee growers, local coffee growers' cooperatives, Raw Coffee Company (the Flouri network hub), shipping agents, Flouri coffee retailers (coffee bars, for instance), and their customers.

Each side benefits from participation in Flouri as follows:

9.5.1 Individual Coffee Growers

Benefits include:

■ Implementing a safe transitive medium of exchange, managed by Silubi.io, between accredited participants in the Flouri ecosystem would benefit growers, who are usually situated in rural locations where there are no banks and where they must engage with transportation facilities of uncertain provenance in transacting their products.
■ Flouri's growers gain the ability to demonstrate innovative living provenance for their products and themselves, through making audiovisual stories and showing and talking about their innovations in this respect. These are published on the Silubi.io platform, where they inform Flouri coffee consumers about the living provenance of the single-origin micro-lot coffee for which they grew the beans

9.5.2 Local Coffee Growers' Cooperatives

Benefits include:

■ Facilitation of their innovation of local development projects bottom-up
■ Actualization of projects benefiting the community funded by the "Living Provenance" premium (contributed by retail customers world-wide)
■ Enables the cooperative to demonstrate transparency regarding their payments to their own farmers/growers.

9.5.3 The Flouri Hub: Raw Coffee Company in Dubai

Benefits include:

■ Better assurance of product source and quality
■ Better ability to plan and adjust for yield fluctuations

- Direct access to growers/cooperative
- Benefit from increase in coffee sales and price levels resulting from Living Provenance certification and assurance
- Confidence in ethical marketing statements (through access to Flouri Living Provenance certification and assurance scheme)
- Creation of a sense of community in its customer base resulting from the Living Provenance certification

9.5.4 Shipping Agents Located in Ports in Peru and Colombia

- Ability to work with coffee growers' collectives so they can export their beans directly to the Flouri hub in Dubai
- Increase in supply-chain efficiency: coordinate transport chain from growers, to export port, to the Flouri hub in Dubai
- Prove that food-grade transport standards are met
- *Flouri coffee retailers and their customers*

Benefits include:

- Better assurance of product source and quality
- Confidence in ethical marketing statements (through access to Flouri Living Provenance certification and assurance scheme)
- Direct access to growers/cooperatives in the Flouri ecosystem

9.6 The Silubi.io Multisided Trading, Provenance Building and Authentication Platform Supporting Flouri

The multisided trading, provenance building, and authentication platform supporting the Flouri ecosystem is SIlubi.io developed by WRT Technologies. The initial version of Silubi.io has been operational since 2020 (Humphreys, 2021).[3]

In ecosystems supported by the SIlubi.io platform, all participants are permissioned and accredited within a system founded on universal transparency and trust, wherein they engage in collaborative transacting where all sides benefit. In such ecosystems, essential provenance data is socially generated, focusing on transaction construction, authentication, and exploration. This makes a strong contrast with crypto-currency platforms that operate within non-permissioned ecosystems founded on individualisation, anonymity, and subversion of trust, promoting greed and speculation (Casey and Vigna, 2018; He et al., 2016; Lyons and Courcelas, 2019).

Silubi.io offers its users two principal views on its features on their dashboard. Users can switch between views at any time, in line with their current perspective on their trading and provenance-building activities. These are the transaction-management view and the provenance-building and authentication view. Each view places in the foreground the services pertinent to the user's current perspective.

However, all SIlubi.io's features can be accessed within any view, through a navigation process that matches user's changes in perspective and capitalises on the synergies and complementarities between the functions that are thus dynamically accessed[4]: The features that initially occupy the foreground within each view are as follows:

i. *Features foregrounded within the provenance-building and authentication view:*

- Agent and entity profile management;
- Tapestry access (historical provenance database);
- Provenance search;
- Living Provenance audio-visual story extraction and presentation;
- Provenance analytics (interrogation and visualisation).

Provenance chains for the entities and agents involved in the transaction are established in this view and woven as threads in the provenance tapestry, and made visible so that everyone in the accredited community can access them, ensuring good provenance. The features accessed in this view also provide help in detecting and resolving provenance problems.

ii. *Features foregrounded within the Multisided Transaction Management view*

- Collaborative contract construction;
- Provenance-backed Smart Transitive Token (payment unit and economic coin);
- Verification and validation (system and commentary);
- Transacted entity "track and trace" system.

By means of these features, each transaction contract is within this view and implemented by Silubi.io's transaction-management services through all its stages, from proposal to completion.

At the technical level, these multisided platforms integrate the World Wide Web Consortium's provenance ontology (PROV-O) for the representation of transaction data (Moreau and Groth, 2013) and distributed-ledger technology (Rauchs et al., 2018) to provide a comprehensive transaction-processing system that explores, assesses, and validates the provenance of all the entities transacted in accord with the W3C's Provenance standard and stores the verified transaction records transparently and immutably in a permissioned blockchain (Lyons and Courcelas, 2019), guaranteeing transparency, accessibility, and verification throughout the ecosystem.

9.7 Transactions in the Flouri Ecosystem Supported by SIlubi.io

In the Flouri ecosystem, participants come together as agents because they want to trade something. They play an active role in forming and implementing transactions. The entities that they transact with include: services, products, rights, licences, and ownership. In Silubi.io both private (closed) and public (open) transactions are conducted within the same integrated transaction-management system and transaction records entered in the same unified transaction-provenance tapestry. This greatly strengthens SIlubi.io's provenance search capacity, as described in Section 9.8 of this chapter.

9.7.1 Transferring Ownership of Goods in the Private Domain

There are four major variants of this reciprocal exchange process involved in trading goods in the private domain. These are barter, buy/sell, gift, transfer of rights (e.g. title to ownership or another legal rights document), as shown in Figure 9.1.

As SIlubi.io's transaction-management services operate within a multisided trading platform that is not merely a payment-processing platform, it will not accept the construction of a transaction that does not have a reciprocal component. Absence of reciprocity raises a question about the good provenance of the entity transacted and of the transactors, leaving open the possibility of theft, or diversion. Even in the case of a gift, some reciprocity is required (e.g., an acknowledgement of receipt such as a thank-you letter) to ensure that the transacted entity is not an unsolicited "gift," and the recipient accepts responsibility for it (as new owner or keeper).

Within the Flouri ecosystem, a typical *barter* transaction would be affected between individual coffee growers as a kind of labour sharing between their households, known in Peru as choba-choba (Enelow, 2012); inter-household mutual aid is provided through bartering the labour needed in planting or harvesting crops at a particular time with a share in the products thereby grown and/or a commitment to exchange labour from the other household.

Buy/sell is the usual form of transaction in the Flouri ecosystem for coffee bean entities between growers, their cooperatives, and Raw Coffee Company in the case of green coffee beans, and for roasted coffee products, between Raw Coffee Company and the retailers (coffee bars, restaurants, and bespoke coffee outlets) participating in Flouri's worldwide.

An example of a "transfer of rights" transaction in the Flouri ecosystem is affected when Raw Coffee Company sends contractual documentation for Flouri's Living Provenance certification and assurance scheme to a coffee growers' cooperative. This documentation confirms the rights the collective has on how they will use the Flouri premium earned through sale of their coffee. In return, the collective sends documentation specifying the innovative projects that they intend to implement bottom-up, within the specified rights framework, to benefit the community.

An example of a *gift* transaction is the first transaction made by a coffee collective joining the Flouri ecosystem to market its coffee beans. The collective initially sends, as a gift, a free sample of its coffee beans to Raw Coffee Company. Sometimes only a small amount of coffee will be hulled, polished, and sent as a sample. (Most roasters need only 200 grams of coffee beans to roast to assess the coffee's quality and characteristics.) The roasted coffee sample is then "cupped" (tested

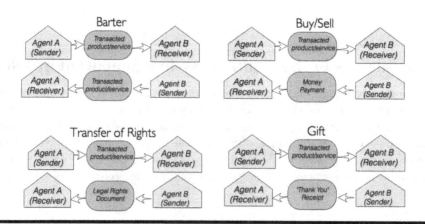

Figure 9.1 Types of transaction pairs for public goods.

for quality and taste). Raw Coffee Company then acknowledges the gift sample, reports on the "cupping" evaluation and starts negotiating a contract with the sending collective to buy a proportion of its annual coffee crop.

9.7.2 Transferring Privately Owned Goods into Public Ownership

At their time of creation, all goods are entities located in their creator's private domain, but the agent who created them, or their current owner, can transfer them into common ownership by depositing them in a repository or archive that holds and shares entities marked as goods located in the public domain (examples of such repositories are Internet Archive, YouTube, and Vimeo).

In the Flouri ecosystem, this kind of transfer is effected for the audiovisual stories demonstrating Living Provenance created, produced, and published by the coffee growers participating in the collective, working together in participatory video groups according to the SaRA model (Humphreys et al., 2001). An example of how this is supported within the PROFLOURI case study is given in Section 9.12, below.

When depositing an entity in an archive, the depositing agent may specify the terms of its Creative Commons use licence (usually CC-BY)[5] that ensures that users will keep this entity in the public domain and that the provenance of each entity involved can be clearly established. Lessig (2008) describes this process as "using private rights to create public goods."

Goods deposited in the public domain can exist as multiple copies, open to borrowing or copying (or in the case of digital video, streaming) via an *access entity copy request,* made via SIlubi.io. There should be no charge for access, but the specification of the accessor's borrowing and sharing rights should also be included in the transaction. Figure 9.2 gives the details of the deposit entity and access request transactions involved.

9.8 Modelling and Structuring Provenance with the Aid of Silubi.io

The process of investigating provenance and creating transaction-provenance records, with the aid of SIlubi.io's multisided transaction-authentication platform, builds on the World Wide Web Consortium's *Provenance Ontology,* PROV-O (Moreau and Groth, 2013) where *provenance* is defined as "a record that describes the people, institutions, entities, and activities involved in producing, influencing or delivering a piece of data or a thing, which can be used to form assessments about its quality, reliability or trustworthiness." PROV-O is a set of recommended standards that define a data model, serializations, and definitions to support the interchange of

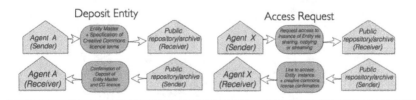

Figure 9.2 Deposit and access transaction pairs for public goods.

provenance information on the Web. The starting point of PROV-O is a small set of classes and properties that can be used to create simple, initial provenance descriptions.

In PROV-O, provenance is established through representing and exploring all entities, agents, and activities that have been influential through involvement and interactions in the historical provenance chain. The starting point of PROV-O is a small set of classes and properties that can be used to create provenance descriptions, thus:

- A *prov: Entity* is a physical, digital, conceptual, or other kind of thing with some fixed aspects; entities may be real or imaginary.
- A *prov: Activity* is something that occurs over a period of time and acts upon or with entities; it may include consuming, processing, transforming, modifying, relocating, using, or generating entities.
- A *prov: Agent* is something that bears some form of responsibility for an activity taking place, for the existence of an entity, or for another agent's activity.

The three primary classes relate to one another and to themselves using the properties shown in the entity-relationship diagram in Figure 9.3, where PROV-O classes and properties descriptions are specialised and extended as PROV-WRT, as employed within the Silubi.io context.

Since agents (transactors) and entities (the objects that they transact) are described with unique, transparent ("real-life") identifiers, we can use SIlubi.io's provenance-building and authentication feature to establish and explore the immutable audit trail of ownership and location of any particular entity transacted within the ecosystem as it changes over time through its history. In doing so, we establish the provenance chain for the entity as it accords with the general definition of provenance given above.

The semantic information represented in PROV-WRT pertinent to each pair of transactions in a trade handled by Silubi.io's blockchain transaction management platform is structured within the transaction record schema as instances of the provenance attributes characterising descriptions of: "*when*" (transaction start and end dates); "*who*" (agents acting in sender and receiver roles in

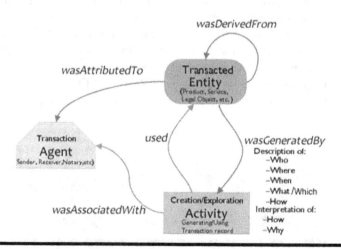

Figure 9.3 PROV-WRT framework, specialised for transaction provenance schema.

the transaction); "*where*" (named location or latitude and longitude coordinates for sender, receiver and entity transacted); "*what/which*" (transacted entities) and "*how*" (trade type).

In addition, interpretive data regarding "how" and "why" is referenced in the blockchain transaction record, but it is actually stored in the blockchain data store. These interpretive data are not immutable because, for instance, notaries, investigators, etc., may want to add comments subsequently: relating to the (historical) provenance of the particular transaction as new information on "how" and "why" is discovered after the transaction has been made.

However, all comments of this type in the blockchain data store will contain the unique blockchain identifier of the transaction to which they apply. They will be time stamped at the date when they were made and be "signed off" by the unique identifier of the permissioned agent who authored the comment. This would usually be a contemporary expert (notary, historian, etc.). Thus, on-chain there is trusted record of hashes of these documents stored off-chain. These documents containing interpretive data are not immutable because, for instance, access-permissioned "expert" agents (provenance analysts, investigators, etc.) may want to add a comment relating to the provenance of the particular transaction as new information on "how" and "why" is discovered.

SIlubi.io's provenance authentication view enables us to establish and explore the historical provenance of an entity involved in any particular transaction of interest transaction right back to its first transaction in which it was involved, marking that entity's "creation." This constitutes the *historical provenance chain* for that entity.

Within the Flouri ecosystem, this enables us to trace the historical provenance of the Flouri single-origin branded coffee used to make a cup of Flouri-branded single-origin coffee, sold to a particular customer in a restaurant participating in the Living Provenance certification scheme back to the coffee's creation.

The historic provenance exploration path stretches from the consumer, and the coffee bar or restaurant where the coffee branded as "Flouri single origin" was purchased, through the circumstances of its roasting (where, when, by whom) to the actual transportation path to the roaster from the producing collective (CAC Pangoa) in Peru, for the actual batch of raw coffee beans (in a 69 kg. sack) and to the actual transaction between CAC Pangoa by which these beans were sourced from the actual grower in Pangoa.

In a similar way, we can establish and explore the historical provenance chain for any agent, acting in sender and/or receiver roles, from the most recent transaction in which they played a role, right back to their earliest transaction within a Silubi.io platform-supported ecosystem. Moreover, these entity-provenance and agent-provenance chains interact at every transaction in their establishment. Thus, one can trace and explore, in any way one wishes, provenance threads (paths through the provenance terrain) involving both persons (agents) and objects (entities) of interest to us. In SIlubi.io's Provenance Tapestry, these threads are woven together (intersecting at transaction nodes) to make the complete provenance net representation (Yang et al., 2018), that forms the core structure that underpins the investigation, validation, and establishment of provenance within Silubi.io.

9.9 Living Provenance

Uniquely, Living Provenance combines historical provenance exploration, addressing the past authenticated through verified and validated transaction records stored publicly and immutably in a blockchain, and anticipated provenance, addressing the future and open to conjecture on how the provenance of an agent or entity may be anticipated and improved.[6]

Fundamentally, historical provenance search, as described above, is anchored in the past, exploring through, and beyond, agent and entity provenance threads in the Provenance Tapestry containing henceforth immutable transaction records, and authenticating the information about "what actually happened" that is found there.

In this way, we improve our understanding of the provenance of agents and entities that were the focus of our search explorations. However, in this historical context, there is no opportunity for anticipating and improving the actual provenance of these entities and agents, or of the transactions in which they were involved. This would involve the creation of "fake news," something that is explicitly guarded against in the provenance search process described above.

Then, for further rich investigation of provenance issues relating to, and anchored on, a particular transaction discovered to be of interest to the explorer, the search may be continued through the material in the blockchain data store that is referenced in the transaction record at this location in the provenance tapestry.

This material includes:

- A *Profile* for each agent and entity referenced in the transaction record
- *Stories* expressed as interpretive material in various kinds of media including: *stories* regarding "how" and "why" for any particular transaction;
- *Stories* relating to the particular entities and agents engaged in the transaction and *stories* relating to the enactment of the transaction in the first place and its consequences.
- *PROV-O relationship patterns*, structuring selected, significant elements of the stories in relation to each other. These are modeled by means of relationship patterns, constructed according to PROV-O specifications, structuring details of a relationship between PROV-O objects (agents, entities, activities) referenced in a story.

9.10 PROFLOURI: A Study of the Flouri "Proof of Value" Use Case

Flouri would like to implement an ecosystem, supported by the SIlubi.io multisided trading and provenance-building platform, linking in all the growers that Raw Coffee Company does business with in Latin America and Africa.

However, the Flouri partners considered it wise to initiate the rollout of this implementation with a "Proof of Value" use case, covering all the features identified above, but initially limited to the context of a single-coffee growers' collective, which had already established a good track record in direct trading and provenance-building activities and which was keen to collaborate in actualising Flouri. This was the Cooperativa Agraria Cafetalera de Pangoa (CAC Pangoa) located in the Junín region of Peru.

Thus, the PROFLOURI research and development project that would implement and evaluate this use case was commissioned from Real-time (real-time.org.uk) an established and successful participatory media charity in the UK, with an international reputation for media and community development projects.[7]

The PROFLOURI case study is designed to investigate, demonstrate, and evaluate the way that the Flouri ecosystem is developed in Peru, and Colombia, supported by Silubi.io trading and provenance-building platform. It will assess SIlubi.io's attractiveness to users (via audiovisual testimony in their own words) in the context of the Flouri ecosystem incorporating four coffee growers' cooperatives in Peru and Colombia, with an initial focus on the Cooperativa Agraria Cafetalera Pangoa in Peru, as described in this chapter.

9.10.1 The Context for PROFLOURI: CAC Pangoa Coffee Growers Collective

Just east of the Andes mountain range in Central America is the Cooperativa Agraria Cafetalera Pangoa. CAC Pangoa was founded in 1977 by 50 farmers from the town of San Martín de Pangoa.

In the early 1980s, CAC Pangoa grew to almost 1,700 members, and the future looked very promising. With an internal agreement to set aside 3% of each sale of coffee beans for internal investment, members were able to build much of the infrastructure that is still in use today.

However, the 1980s ushered in the turbulent time commonly known as "the period of terrorism," which lasted 20 years. The militant group, Shining Path, swept through what had been a remarkably peaceful area of Peru, killing thousands of innocent people and waging a tremendously effective campaign of fear. As a result, Pangoa lost hundreds of farmers who fled to cities to escape the violence. Since then, it has slowly regained membership and today has nearly 700 member farmers.

Esperanza Dionoso Castillo, the architect of this recovery, and now general manager of CAC Pangoa, explains how this rebuilding was achieved:

> The legacy of the Sendero era was that no one trusted anybody any more. Afterwards we began gaining back trust little by little through good communication with the cooperative members, many assemblies, making sure all businesses transparent and always explaining everything about the business.[8]

In 1998, young people from the Pangoa growers' families formed a club called "Sonkari" within the SaRA project.[9] The club started initiatives aimed at regenerating the community in a climate of trust, transparency, and innovation. They also made audiovisual stories that they shared and discussed with the other SaRA Groups throughout Peru (see Humphreys et al., 2001, for details).

These stories focused on, and brought alive the provenance of:

■ "My community";
■ Economic activities generated by the SaRA club's young entrepreneurs in the locality;
■ Innovative research and development, benefiting the community.[10]

In 2001, CAC Pangoa received FLO Fairtrade certification and quickly established two programs that continue to serve members today, the Education Fund and the Health Services Fund. CAC Pangoa then encouraged its members to switch to organic products through a formal training program and documentation practices in accordance with international organic standards. In 2002, Pangoa received its first organic certification. This led to innovative activities enhancing certified organic group growing being planned and executed bottom-up by the growers in the collective.

For example, in 2009, building on the research and development of innovative organic soil fertilisation technique initiated by the Sonkari club in 1999, CAC Pangoa started production of organic fertiliser incorporating mountain micro-organisms, together with a training programme for its growers on how to use it fertilising the land-enabled crop diversification: CAC Pangoa could now cultivate coffee on newly fertile land at high altitudes, and the original lower altitude land transferred to cocoa growing and honey production, using choba-choba work practices.[11]

Since 2010, CAC Pangoa promoted local ecotourism projects in the Pangoa community to supplement family income, coupled with tours of the collective's coffee, cocoa, and honey-producing facilities and the development of local markets for the sale of roasted coffee.

In 2017, CAC Pangoa built a coffee lab, roaster, and cafeteria on their premises to ensure, not only that members can rate the quality of their coffee, but also that locals can enjoy it. These facilities enabled CAC Pangoa to initiate a local training programme for "baristas" as well as classes on "coffee cupping."

9.10.2 Current Position of CAC Pangoa in Regard to PROFLOURI

Membership of Fairtrade, and its style of management of the FLO premium funds received from its Fairtrade coffee sales, enabled the Pangoa collective to activate successfully all five "capabilities" identified by Enelow (2012) (see above) though the activities identified above. However, it is important to know that, while Fairtrade was an enabler for the collective's development, CAC Pangoa is not bound to the FLO model in is motivation and operation.

At present, although a minority of CAC Pangoa's production is sold as Fairtrade, CAC Pangoa prefers to sell the majority of its coffee beans to roasters abroad, not marketed as "Fairtrade," since selling to "Fairtrade" buyers does not produce as good returns, or help much to improve its provenance as a producer of single-origin high-quality coffee. CAC Pangoa would welcome a better direct trading arrangement with an international roaster and distributor of the single origin coffee.

9.11 Ensuring Safe and Secure Transportation and Payment for Transacted Goods

When using Silubi.io to conduct a trade, the actual transactions are made and recorded in virtual space, the physical distance between sender and receiver is immaterial. When the goods transferred in a transaction are in digital form, they can be transferred electronically: they do not have to be transported physically from sender to receiver (examples of such goods within the Flouri ecosystem are documents relating to Living Provenance certification procedures, coffee roasters' reports, digitised media containing audiovisual stories). But when the goods transferred exist in physical form, they still need to be moved from place to place. Within the Flouri ecosystem, a typical example is the transfer of coffee beans from growers' cooperatives in rural locations in, for example, Latin America to Raw Coffee Company in Dubai.

For an example in the PROFLOURI case study, CAC Pangoa (the sender of the beans) takes responsibility for arranging transportation by road to the port of Lima by a commercial truck operator. At this point, the receiver of the transported beans (Raw Coffee Company) takes over responsibility for the beans' safe transportation by ship, in a registered cold-storage reefer (when required), onward to Dubai. Details of the transportation (name of ship, route, and schedule) are arranged by a shipping agent in the port of Lima. Through participation in the Flouri ecosystem, the shipping agent gains support from SIlubi.io's "entity track and trace" feature. Raw Coffee Company implements the goods-in-transit insurance process, starting with the invoice for the goods being transported created by CAC Pangoa and the shipping documents produced by the port agent.

Increasingly, the movement of coffee beans throughout the Flouri ecosystem will be via distribution networks with local transfer intermediary agents, as exemplified in the PROFLOURI case. It is useful to be able to investigate a transfer and distribution network's provenance. An investigation is particularly useful when transfers of high-value goods are involved. Here, a transaction package can be arranged that incorporates separate, linked transactions with the agents responsible for transporting the goods. These transactions with shippig agentsare recorded in the provenance tapestry; this record protects the transfer of the coffee beans against leakage or substitution of goods while in transit.

In general, the provision, through the use of Silubi.io, of a unique, publicly shared record for all transactions effecting the movement and transfer of ownership of goods will effectively guard against leakage and fakery.

9.11.1 Advantages of Employing a Smart Transitive Token (Provenance Backed Economic Coin) as the Payment Unit within SIlubi.io

Within ecosystems supported by Silubi.io, the risks associated with leakage of currency needed to finance transactions are mitigated when SIlubi.io employs the Silubi, a smart provenance-backed transitive token as the unit of account, store of value, and medium of exchange in its transactions (thus positioning Silubi as a next-generation, provenance-backed coin). No fiat or cryptocurrency, with the associated risk of loss of real value, is deployed. Silubi constitutes a *provenance-backed coin*, because it is founded on the aggregated value of every transaction ever made in Silubi.io supported ecosystems; thus, the Silubi coin is guaranteed to hold its value safely.

Silubi is transitive because each instance of the Silubi smart transitive token is tied to a particular transaction while that transaction is being made. As such, it is nonfungible. However, the value an agent gains by sending goods in a transaction in exchange for payment in Silubi, as a result of that transaction, remains available for productive reinvestment through further transactions conducted within the ecosystem supported by SIlubi.io; it is also exchangeable with fiat currency, at a rate agreed with the central bank issuing that fiat. In this case Silubi, is fungible and able to promote real economic growth on all sides within the ecosystem

9.12 Pilot Implementation within PROFLOURI of a Living Provenance Certification and Assurance Scheme

The Flouri partners realised that their "Living Provenance" certification and assurance scheme would need to be multisided; it could not be implemented solely on the initiative and from the perspective of an individual decision-making organisation. It would need the active involvement of participants in Flouri on all sides, creating, demonstrating, investigating, and appreciating communication media that would be shared throughout the Flouri ecosystem, building living provenance for all parties.

Thus, the PROFLOURI case study involves a pilot implementation where coffee growers create their own audiovisual stories, demonstrating their contribution to the provenance of the single-origin coffee referenced in the QR code on its retail packaging to the coffee retailers' customers who scan this QR code with their mobile phones.

The unique selling point that underpins this relation-building effort is that these customers would find that the branded bespoke single-origin micro-lot coffee products, sourced within the Flouri ecosystem, offered a unique attraction to them. The customers are able, through scanning the QR code with the aid of Silubi.io, to explore, authenticate, and participate in the "Living Provenance" of the Flouri single-origin coffee offered to them.

This serves to build the coffee growers' own provenance regarding their part in promoting innovation and well-being in their wider community. Moreover, the provenance-building process is now extended to include the participation of the purchasers of coffee, varying the Living Provenance certification stamp worldwide.

The characteristics of this provenance-building system, end to end, are as follows:

> *At the Retail end:* The Living Provenance QR Code on the retail packaging or a cup of Flouri single-origin micro-lot coffee is scanned by a retail customer interested in exploring the particular coffee's provenance on his or her mobile phone.

This makes a direct link to a url, at which is specified: Coffee product entity profile / Individual grower agent profile / producing cooperative agent profile

By accessing the specified profile, one can explore the following:

> *Within the individual coffee growers' profiles*: audiovisual stories that they had made about their family community resulting from and enabled by income from participation in the Flouri network.

Within the coffee grower collective's profile: audiovisual stories made about bottom-up initiatives resulting from/ enabled by how the Flouri premium paid to the collective were used.

Within the single origin coffee product's profile: Audiovisual stories made by growers and the producing collective, about how the particular coffee was conceived and grown.

Within Raw Coffee Company's profile: Audiovisual stories about how the particular coffee was branded, roasted, packaged, and any awards it won, and about the Flouri Living Provenance and assurance scheme in action.

9.13 Support Provided by the PROFLOURI Expertise and Innovation Promotion App

Participants on all sides in the Flouri ecosystem are supported in this creative process by means of the PROFLOURI Expertise and Innovation Promotion App, which enables them to make their creative activities and offerings (products, services) much more visible and attractive in both the real and the virtual worlds. This app provides techniques to promote innovative creations, in each case, "with attribution" under Creative Commons licence, and for letting others know what one has available for sharing and transaction; this is done through establishing a virtual gallery or media channel on a public resource like an Internet archive or a Vimeo.

In the PROFLOURI case study, the audiovisual stories created by Flouri participants on all sides are uploaded to the PROFLOURI media collection in a Vimeo Pro archive, which also is freely accessible by the Living Provenance certification and assurance system.

The Expertise and Innovation Promotion App supports its users in making and sharing, as public goods, media products about their own innovative creations, the process by which they were created, and the expertise about this process available in the local context. It also provides audiovisual composition support on making, editing, and communicating techniques that enable participants to create media products that, unlike the video blogs that are common in social media, remain informative, attractive, and useful through time and mark innovation milestones.

9.14 Conclusion

The Pangoa case study is still in progress, with some fieldwork delays due to Covid-19 lockdown restrictions during 2020–21, but it is now proceeding according to plan. So, it is not yet possible to assess the impact of the Flouri Living Provenance audiovisual story generator (making and sharing audiovisual stories: uploading them to the PROFLOURI Collection on Vimeo as a key component of the Flouri Living Provenance certification and assurance scheme) or consumer's evaluations of their own access to the Living Provenance of Flouri single-origin coffee.

However, we are already able to identify aspects of the socialised, multisided enactment of Raw Coffee Company's ambitious decision in 2020 that it would not have been possible to carry out on an individualised, top-down basis in building and implementing the Flouri ecosystem.

These enactment elements include:

- An efficient, multisided direct trading system in which the individual coffee growers, their associations (coffee bean producer cooperatives), and the Raw Coffee Company would participate and benefit bottom-up.
- A Living Provenance certification and assurance scheme actualising methods for improving, demonstrating, and publicising the good provenance of the single-origin coffee from the producer.

The key thread holding this socialisation process together is the multisided implementation of Living Provenance. This process is achieved successfully through the collaboration of all parties concerned in the end-to-end process for building and appreciating the Living Provenance of the single-originmicro-lot coffee prducts that carry its QR code.

In general, the PROFLOURI case study has already demonstrated that Living Provenance is a rich and powerful concept, powerful for building an integrated mutual recognition, trust and well-being ecosystem, whose active participants construct and enact. So, while the PROFLOURI case study continues to establish the Flouri "proof of value" use case, this chapter concludes by integrating the diverse components of Living Provenance into a single, comprehensive schema.

9.14.1 Three Layers of Living Provenance Supporting Decision Enactment

The three layers in Living Provenance whose functions are detailed below are (Figure 9.4):

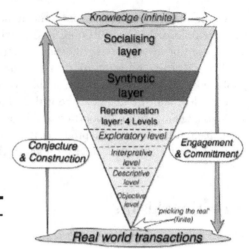

Figure 9.4 Layers of living provenance in socia-lised decision enactment.

■ The *representation layer:* comprising four levels of (increasing) abstraction and semantics, i.e., objective; descriptive; interpretive and exploratory. It addresses provenance-related data in text, image, and audio-visual forms.

■ The *Synthetic layer:* addressing features enabling provenance exploration, anticipation, and improvement.

■ The *Socialising layer:* addressing Living Provenance, networked consensus building, and enactment within ecosystems supported by SIlubi.io.

9.14.2 Functions and Capabilities that are Implemented in the Representation Layer

Within the representation layer, semantic data (text, images, audio-visual) is produced and re-presented at the objective, descriptive, interpretive, and exploratory levels, as follows:

1. *At the objective level,* the functions implemented include: proof of existence provenance attributes "when," "what," "who," for entities involved in transactions to give a verified ordered sequence of particular transactions that really happened. Content within this layer, upon verification, is stored immutably in the transaction record in the blockchain.

2. *At the descriptive level* (semantic, i.e. generator of meaning): for each transaction, concise meaningful descriptions for provenance attributes, "who," "what," "where," "when," and "how" (descriptive) as seen and approved by validating notaries and explorers, that can be directly parsed by Silubi.io's provenance search engine. These are stored in the SIlubi.io blockchain as immutable text describing verified and validated transaction-provenance attributes.

3. *At the interpretive level:* The provenance attributes "how (interpretive)" and "why (for what purpose)" contain interpretive commentaries relevant to provenance attributes "how" and "why (for what purpose)" made by all kinds of agents (transactors, explorers validating notaries, historian-explorers) who interpret and give their opinion as a comment using their expertise and contextual knowledge. Commentaries are "signed off" (given commentator ID

attributions). They are referenced in the blockchain record for the transaction for which they apply and are stored in the blockchain data store. They are not immutable, and they may be updated in the period after a transaction has been verified and marked as completed.

4. *At the exploratory level*: Explorers and authenticators guided and supported within Silubi.io's provenance-building and authentication view, can investigate the provenance of the transaction records that describes the people, institutions, entities, and activities involved in producing, influencing, or delivering a piece of data (e.g. document, audio visual story, PROV-O relational diagram).

9.14.3 Functions and Capabilities that are Implemented in the Synthetic Layer

Within the synthetic layer, data production, access, and interactive processes (presenting data to the user the appropriate view to meet their requirements) is precisely what is synthesised in SIlubi.io's features enabling provenance exploration, anticipation, and improvement implemented through dynamic views and APIs.

Examples of types of data that are synthesised in this way are;

■ Generation and modelling of PROV-O relationship patterns: with the aid of Silubi.io services foregrounded in the Provenance Building and Authentication view.

■ Entity and agent profiles: with the aid of SIlubi.io services foregrounded in the Transaction Management view.

■ Living Provenance stories relating to transactions and their provenance contexts, in text and audiovisual forms: created with the support of PROFLOURI Expertise and Innovation Promotion App.

9.14.4 Functions and Capabilities that are Implemented in the Socialising Layer

Within the socialising layer, the focus is on actualising Living Provenance, networked consensus building and socialised implementation where all sides participate bottom up. Here the ecosystem supported by Silubi.io is brought alive among its participants, individually and socially, through their multisided use of views provided by SIlubi.io, and the synergy and complementarities that this provides between the activities, resources and outputs in the ecosystem (Alaimo et al., 2019).

This enables processes creating social awareness of the knowledge represented in the provenance tapestry, thus generating more *provenance capital* (combing individual, social, and cultural capital) within the permissioned community (Yu et al., 2017).

Provenance capital can enhance decision enactment engagement: by applying this provenance capital in deciding on how to plan and engage in a future-transaction-organising system (hierarchy or network) that would generate transactions with good anticipated provenance (Humphreys, 2021), the circular process of improving the real-world transaction process by means of provenance-based knowledge and actions is completed (Garcia de la Cerda et al., 2018).

Notes

1. See https://rawcoffeecompany.com/pages/our-story
2. WRT Technologies Ltd and World Reserve Global Ltd are sister companies.
3. The initial name of this traction provenance decision support plaform was "SMART.T". World Reserve Global rebranded it as "Silubi.io" in January, 2021.
4. Details of the specification of the features integrated within the SILubi.io plaform are given in the SIlubi.io White Paper (Hill et al., 2020).
5. CC-BY *Creative commons Share Alike licence:* You allow others to distribute derivative works only under a license identical to the license that governs your work.
6. See Humphreys (2021) for a discussion of techniques for anticipating good provenance within a transaction network.
7. The Principal investigators for this project are Clive Robertson (Real-time's Creative Director), Patrick Humphreys (Real-time's Development Director) and Rosa Bravo (Peru).
8. For details, see https://youtu.be/ZYkot66GG3k.
9. SaRA (Salud reproductiva para Adolescentes) we funded by a Development Project Grant to the London School of Economics and Grupo de Innovación Organizacional, Perú.
10. For example, the SaRA club in Pangoa investigated use of special worms to make community land more fertile so the community could grow vegetables for sale. They developed a worm-breeding facility for soil enrichment, then planted and harvested crops on the that they had thus fertilised organically in a choba-choba fashion – selling the surplus vegetable production in the nearby town's market. You can see the original audiovisual story made by the SaRA "Sonkari" club in Pangoa in 1999, at https://vimeo.com/535282571.
11. See for details https://www.youtube.com/watch?v=7srPY94UP14.

References

Adner, R. (2017). Ecosystem as structure: An actionable construct strategy. *Journal of Management 43*, 39–58.

Alaimo, C., Kallinikos, J., & Vallderama-Venegas, E. (2019). Platforms as service ecosystems: Lessons from social media. *Journal of Information Technology 35*(1).

Berkeley, D., Humphreys, P., & Thomas, R. (1991). Project risk action management. *Construction Management and Economics 9*, 17–23.

Casey, M., & Vigna, P. (2018). *The Truth Machine: The Blockchain and the Future of Everything (Unabridged edition)*. New York: Harper Collins.

Checkland, P. (1981). *Systems Thinking, Systems Practice*. Chichester: Wiley.

Enelow, N. (2012). *Fair Trade, Agrarian Cooperatives, and Rural Livelihood in Peru*. PhD Dissertation University of Massachusetts Amherst.

Garcia de la Cerda, O., Humphreys, P., & Saavedra, M. (2018). Enactive management: A nurturing technology enabling fresh decision making to cope with conflict situations. *Futures 103*, 84–93.

Guillen, M.F. (1994). *Models of Management*. Chicago: University of Chicago Press.

Haight, C. (2011). The problem with fair trade coffee: Action case study. *Stanford Social Innovation Review 3*, 74–79. www.ssireview.org

He, D., Habermeier, K., Leckow, R., Haksar, V., Almeida, Y., & Kashima, M. (2016). *Virtual Currencies and Beyond: Initial Considerations*. Wahington, DC: International Monetary Fund Staff Development Note 16/03.

Hill, S., Humphreys, P., & Leong, G. (2020). SILUBI.IO: Silubi A Multisided Trading, Provenance-building and Economic Development Platform. London, UK: *World Reserve Trust Research Paper Series* Vol 1, no. 2.

Humphreys, P. (2021). Socialising the decision-making process: Transaction provenance decision support. *Journal of Decision Systems 30*, 1. doi: 10.1080/12460125.2020.1868653

Humphreys, P., & Berkeley, D. (1995). Handling uncertainty: Levels of analysis of decision problems. In G. Wright (Ed.). *Behavioural Decision Making*. London: Plenum Press.

Humphreys, P., & Jones G. (2006). The evolution of group decision support systems to enable collaborative authoring of outcomes. *World Futures 193–232*.

Humphreys, P., Lorac, C., & Ramella, M. (2001). Creative support for innovative decision making. *Journal of Decision Systems 10*, 241–264.

Larichev, O. (1984). Psychological validation of decision methods. *Journal of Applied Systems Analysis 11*, 37–46.

Lessig, L. (2008). *Remix: Making Art and Commerce Thrive in the Hybrid Economy*. London: Bloomsbury Academic.

Lyons, T., & Courcelas, L. (2019). *Building Better Supply Chains with Blockchain*. Brussels: European Union Blockchain Observatory and Forum thematic report.

Merkle, J.A. (1980). *Management and Ideology, The Legacy of the International Scientific Movement*. Berkeley: University of California Press.

Moreau, L., & Groth, P. (2013). *Provenance: An Introduction to PROV*. London: Morgan & Maypool Publishers.

Parker, G., Van Alstyne, M., & Choudary, S. (2016). *Platform Revolution*. New York: W.W. Norton and Company.

Pomerol, J-C., & Adam, F. (2008). Understanding the legacy of herbert simon to decision support systems. In F. Adam & P. Humphreys (Eds.). *Encyclopedia of Decision Making and Decision Support Technologies*. Hershey, PA: IGI Global, 930–938.

Rauchs, M., Glidden, A., Gordon, B., Pieters, G., Recanatini, M., Rostand, F., Vagneur, K., & Zhang, B. (2018). *Distributed Ledger Technology Systems: A Conceptual Framework*. Cambridge: Cambridge Centre for Alternative Finance.

Vari, A., Vecsenyi, J., & Paprika, Z. (1986). Supporting problem structuring in high level decisions. In B. Brehmer, H. Jungermann, P. Lourens & G. Sevon (Eds.). *New Directions in Research in Decision Making*. North Holland: Amsterdam.

Yang, Y., Cullomosse, J., Manohar, A., Briggs, J., & Steane, J. (2018). *TAPESTRY: Visualizing Interwoven Identities for Trust Provenance*. Los Alamitos: IEEE Symposium on Visualization for Cyber Security.

Yu, A., Garcia-Lorenzo, L., & Kourti, I. (2017). The role of intellectual capital reporting (ICR) in organizational transformation: A discursive practice perspective. *Critical Perspectives on Accounting 45*, 48–62.

Chapter 10

Machine-Learning Solutions in the Management of a Contemporary Business Organisation: A Case Study Approach in a Banking Sector

Leszek Ziora

Czestochowa University of Technology, Czestochowa, Poland

Contents

10.1 Introduction

Machine learning belonging to the artificial intelligence field is nowadays applied in multiple business activity areas. Contemporary business organisations very often apply a holistic approach

DOI: 10.1201/9781003030966-14

to the management process using hybrid solutions such as big data analytics, business intelligence (BI) systems, and artificial intelligence (AI) solutions to improve the efficiency and efficacy of business and decision-making processes.

The quality of input data, including big data sets that can constitute the basis for model training, is an especially important factor as far as quality of the whole decision-making process is concerned. The main advantages of machine-learning application in the management of contemporary enterprise can be classified as the increasing value of the entire decision-making and business processes, improvement and support in the business strategy creation, and improvement of enterprise functionality depending on the branch, e.g. automation of tasks. All of these mentioned benefits may also lead to gaining a competitive advantage in the market. The research methodology of case studies included asking eight questions to the managers of selected banking institutions, which concerned such dimensions as an impact of ML/AI solutions on the acceleration of the decision-making process, its efficacy and efficiency, improvement of business strategy creation, the efficiency of conducted analyses and manager's work, future development trends and challenges faced during its implementation, or its influence on the quality of business decisions.

10.2 The Characteristic, Construction, and Advantages of Machine-Learning Solutions Application

As far as the notion of machine learning is concerned, it is worth mentioning IBM's definition, which emphasises its main feature and advantage as "building applications that learn from data and improve their accuracy over time without being programmed to do so" (IBM Cloud Education 2020). The crucial feature of machine learning is underlined by Pyle and San Jose who confirm that this solution "is based on algorithms that can learn from data without relying on rules-based programming" (Pyle and San Jose, 2015). P. Dangeti states that "machine learning (ML) is a branch of study in which a model can learn automatically from the experiences based on data without exclusively being modelled like in statistical models and over a period and with more data, model predictions will become better" (Dangeti, 2017, p. 7).

In the case of deep learning, it is "more useful when the amount of available training data was increased and it allows to solve more complicated applications with increased accuracy over time" (Goodfellow et al., 2017, p. 12). The same authors underline the fact that "deep learning enables to build complex concepts out of simpler concepts," and provide an example of multilayer perceptron, which is "mathematical function mapping some set of input values to output values" (Goodfellow et al., 2017, p. 12). Alpaydin confirms the fact that "the goal of machine learning is to program computers to use example data or past experience to solve a given problem" (Alpaydin, 2020). The creation of hybrid analyses is also enabled thanks to the application of machine-learning solutions (Teich, 2018).

As far as forms of learning are concerned, there can be distinguished supervised, semi-supervised, unsupervised, and reinforcement learning. S. Russel and P. Norvig state that there can be distinguished "three types of feedback that can accompany the inputs that can determine three main types of learning." The authors provide an example of image recognition where, in supervised learning, "the agent observes input-output pairs and learns a function that maps from input to output and the inputs could be camera images, each one accompanied by an output e.g. bus and this output is called a label. The agent learns a function that, when given a new image, predicts the appropriate label. In unsupervised learning, the agent learns patterns in the input without any explicit feedback. In reinforcement learning the agent learns from a series of re-inforcements: reward and punishment e.g. the winning in chess might be a reward and losing a punishment" (Russel and Norvig, 2021, p. 651). Supervised learning includes such key components as regression analysis, which can be conducted with the use of linear, local, and least squares methods and/or classification applying decision trees, Naive Bayes, support vector machines, and k-nearest neighbours. The unsupervised learning may embrace cluster analysis with hierarchical, k-means, neural networks, and hidden Markov model (Ziora, 2020). Its usage depends on the specificity of a business branch where a given method, technique, or tool is applied. M. Ganiyu states that "regression is used to predict continuous numerical data and classification is used to predict categorical data sets including k-nearest neighbours" (Ganiyu, 2020). R. E. Neapolitan and X. Jiang underline the fact that "supervised learning involves learning a function from a training set and the function learned is called a model of the underlying system generating the data" (Neapolitan and Jiang, 2018, p. 89).

Y. Roh, G. Heo, and S.E. Whang underline another fact that the "major bottleneck in machine learning is constituted by data collection, which is a critical issue and is connected with the emergence of new applications which do not possess enough labelled data" (Roh et al., 2019).

A. Burkov confirms that in the case of supervised learning, there is applied the data set that is the collection of labelled examples; in the case of unsupervised learning, there are unlabelled examples put into practice, and in the case of semi-supervised learning, the data set contains both labelled and unlabelled examples (Burkov, 2019, pp. 3–4).

The crucial issue is to ensure appropriate data quality based on which the machine-learning model is trained; it is also important to ensure that the size of such training set is appropriate (Jelonek et al., 2019, pp. 361–368).

J. G. Carbonell, R. S. Michalski, and T.M. Mitchell enlist a three-dimensional taxonomy of machine-learning research where a classification can be "based on the underlying learning strategy used, classification on the basis of the representation of knowledge or skill acquired by the learner and classification in terms of the application domain of the performance system for which knowledge is acquired" (Carbonell et al., 2015, p. 13).

Mehryar et al. describes standard learning tasks as a classification which is "the problem of assigning a category to each item e.g. document classification; regression which is the problem of predicting a real value for each item e.g. prediction of stock values; ranking which is the problem of learning to order items according to some criterion e.g. web search; clustering which is the problem of portioning a set of items into homogenous subsets e.g. analysing huge data sets, like in case of social networks; dimensionality reduction which consists of transforming an initial representation of items into a lower-dimensional representation" (Mohri et al., 2018, p. 4). The same authors provide fundamental definitions used in machine learning, such as: "examples – items or instances of data used for learning or evaluation, features – the set of attributes, often represented as a vector, associated to an example, labels – values or categories assigned to examples, hyperparameters – free parameters that are not determined by the learning algorithm, training sample – examples used to train a learning algorithm, validation sample – examples used to tune the parameters of a learning algorithm, test sample – examples used to evaluate the performance of a learning algorithm, loss function – a function that measures the difference or loss between a predicted label and a true label and hypothesis set – a set of functions mapping features to the set of labels" (Mohri et al., 2018, p. 4). The further development of machine learning may include deep learning and bio-inspired adaptive systems. Its development is possible due to more powerful computers and, in this case, it is possible to "train bigger models with multilayer networks to solve such problems as image classification, real-time visual tracking, autonomous card driving, logistic optimisation, bioinformatics or speech recognition. Deep learning outperforms classical approaches in this scope" (Bonaccorso, 2017, pp. 14–18). Machine learning is often accompanied with big data, e.g. using Hadoop and MapReduce algorithm, and it can be applied for collaborative filtering using Apache Spark or Naïve Bayes classification (Bonaccorso, 2017, pp. 16–18). The machine-learning process is described by S. Marsland, who enumerates such stages as: "data collection and preparation taking into consideration appropriate quantity of data; feature selection consisting of identifying the features that are most useful for the problem under examination; the choice of appropriate algorithm; parameter and model selection which may require experimentation to identify appropriate values; training which should use computational resources in order to build a model of the data to predict the outputs on new data; evaluation which is testing for accuracy on data that it was not trained on" (Marsland, 2015, pp. 10–11).

The machine-learning (ML) solutions include, besides decision support and its improvement, business processes optimisation that are applied in other areas such as image recognition and classification, self-driving cars development, logistics area, healthcare, and telecommunication. The hybrid approach combines "statistical methods with neural networks, machine learning, big data solutions, Business Intelligence and Management Information Systems, sentiment analysis" (Jelonek et al., 2020, pp. 319–327). The sentiment analysis or opinions mining deploys especially supervised-learning solutions such as decision trees, support vector machines, neural networks, and Bayesian networks (Ziora, 2016, pp. 234–241). ML may find its application in economics. Mullainathan et al. claim that machine learning "not only provides new tools, but it also solves different problems and revolves around the problem of prediction while many economic applications revolve around parameter estimation" (Mullainathan and Spiess, 2017, pp. 87–106). An example of machine learning in the Natural Language Processing domain is the GPT-2 model created by OpenAI. It is a large-scale, unsupervised language model generating coherent paragraphs of text, trained on a dataset of 8 million web pages. GPT-2 is able to generate high-quality conditional synthetic text samples allowing such things as question answering, reading comprehension, summarisation, and translation. According to OpenAI, such systems could be used to create AI writing assistants, more capable dialogue agents, unsupervised translations between languages, and better speech-recognition systems. There can also be dangers resulting from its application, such as the generation of misleading news articles, impersonating others online, and automating the production of spam or faked content (Solaiman et al., 2019). In technological terms, the most popular machine-learning platforms are Google's Tensor Flow open source solution using data flow graphs, Caffe allowing for layers definition with appropriate parameters, IBM Watson Machine Learning and IBM Watson Studio, Google Cloud AI Platform, Azure Machine Learning Studio, Alteryx, Anaconda Enterprise, Peltarion Platform, Explorium, Kraken, H20, BigML, Deep Cognition, and Oracle Data Science Cloud Service.

10.3 Review of Practical Examples and Researches

Multiple benefits can result from the application of machine-learning solutions in the management of a contemporary business organisation. Machine learning is applied in such domains as finances, banks, telecommunication, retail trade, and healthcare. R.C. Pozen and J. Ruane indicate three such ML features that are especially applicable to assets management: "finding new patterns in existing data sets, making new forms of data analysable and reduction of the negative effects of human biases on investment decisions" (Pozen and Ruane, 2019). B. Marr underlines the most important application areas of ML, such as data security, including malware detection and cloud data access patterns; financial trading in predicting and fast executing of trades; healthcare domain, especially in spotting patterns in computer-assisted diagnosis; marketing personalisation with recommendations functions; and fraud detection; (Marr 2016).

J. de Hoog et al. underline the importance of the fact that data quality "can be evaluated based on Key Performance Indicators such as the accuracy of the data, the representation consistency and completeness (de Hoog et al., 2019).

A Deloitte Access Economics report entitled "Busines impacts of machine learning" states that machine learning "is a method of data analysis that automates the building of analytical models" (Dangeti, 2017). The authors of the report underline such benefits of ML as "the ability to discover patterns and correlations, improve customer segmentation and targeting and ultimately increasing a business' revenue, growth and market position." The report presents an MIT Technology Review survey of 375 leading businesses in over 30 countries, which found that 60% of respondents had already implemented an ML strategy and had committed to ongoing investment in ML. It is estimated that global market revenue for ML as a service or vendor platform will reach US$20 billion by 2025. Return on investment on most standard machine-learning projects in the first year is 2–5 times the cost. The report underlines that "global businesses incorporate ML into their core processes for a variety of strategic reasons to deliver benefits to performance outcomes and improve a business position in the market" (Dangeti, 2017). The report presents a few case studies in different branches where, for example, in the case of Airbus company, ML helps in achieving efficiency in operations. One of its ML applications is the detection and correction of satellite images with imperfections, such as the presence of clouds. The company also uses ML for big-data styles analysis for use in other applications, such as engineering, agricultural, or environmental purposes. Three main categories of benefits were defined, such as: achieving things that were not previously thought possible, developing algorithms where the required technology was not previously available, and improving existing processes, which is the most important in terms of business operations (Dangeti, 2017). Another report prepared by Netguru and entitled "The state of Machine Learning in Fintech" states that "machine learning is one of the key forces driving the transformation of the financial services from predictive analytics and fraud detection to personalised customer engagement. The report confirms that large and mid-sized companies are most advanced in ML adoption, and staff and budget limitations are the two primary factors stopping smaller companies from leveraging ML. According to the report, the three top use cases for machine learning in Fintech are advanced analytics, forecasting and fraud detection, and prevention. Some 54% of surveyed companies cited extracting better information from their data as their key driver for adopting machine learning. The institutions make their decisions based on a data-driven approach. The main challenge in adopting ML concerns shortages of skills required within the organisation (S. Al-Sefou, Netguru report 2020).

As far as analysis of foreign case studies is concerned, it is worth mentioning the Data Flair case studies and describing ML application in the Dell technological company, which partnered with Persado to "harness the power of words in their email channel and garner data-driven analytics for each of their key audiences. The company uses ML to improve the marketing copy of their promotional and lifecycle emails, Facebook ads, display banners, direct mail, and even radio content" (Data Flair 2020). The other example presented, also by Data Flair, is ML application in Sky UK media corporation, which has 22.5 million customers. ML framework helped the company to recommend its clients appropriate products and services, improve the relationship with customers, understand what matters to customers, and use ML to deliver actionable intelligence (Data Flair 2020). Another example of using ML in the management of a contemporary business organisation is the Harley Davidson company, which implemented Albert – an artificial intelligence-powered robot. According to this case study, "Albert can be applied to various marketing channels including social media and email. The software predicts which consumers are most likely to convert and adjusts personal creative copies on its own" (Data Flair 2020). "The company analysed customer data to determine the behaviour of previous customers whose actions were positive in terms of purchasing and spending more than the average amount of time on browsing through the website. By the use of Albert Harley Davidson increased its sale by 40% and the brand also observed 2,93% increase in leads" (Data Flair 2020).

One of the most common applications of machine learning includes natural language processing solutions, such as chatbots, voice assistants like Google Assistant, Apple's Siri, Amazon's Alexa, Microsoft's Cortana, or Samsung's Bixby. Another one is image and pattern recognition, e.g. identification of car registration plate numbers, e-mail filtering, spam detection, fraud detection in banking institutions, recommendation and review algorithms in video and audio streaming services leading to greater satisfaction of customers. It is worth mentioning the study conducted in 2020, which aimed to discover and become familiarised with the trends connected to the development of machine-learning solutions. The research sample embraced 50 respondents, the intramural students of the Czestochowa University of Technology. In this opinion survey, the respondents had to indicate the advantages resulting from the application of a machine-learning solution in the area of management and primarily managerial decisions improvement, as well as to show its disadvantages. The most frequent answers indicated such benefits as continuous improvement and increased accuracy and efficiency of the decision-making process (75%), increased work efficiency (70%), automation of tasks (65%), improvement of business analyses (e.g. market, financial analyses) (60%) emphasising fast identification of trends and patterns related to sales of products and services, and the possibility to optimise business decisions (e.g. in case of regression application) (40%). The other responses involved the ability to improve over time (e.g. algorithm's self-improvements) (30%) (Ziora, 2020) (see Figure 10.1).

The disadvantages that respondents indicated included security issues, the vulnerability of machine-learning solutions to attacks (60%), the necessity to ensure proper data quality for training sets (55%), susceptibility to errors (45%), and the requirement of enormous computing power (45%) (Ziora, 2020). Certain limitations of the study might be caused by the fact that the research was conducted in the academic environment.

10.4 Case Study Methodology and Analysis

The methodology of the research included a qualitative approach where the selected research tool embraced case studies with eight questions. The case studies were conducted among five big international banks with headquarters in Warsaw, and all of them belonging to the category of big business organisations defined as employing more than 250 staff. Due to the pandemic situation, the interviews in the banking area were conducted in March 2021 over the telephone. The respondents were the managers of tactical and strategic levels, which apply a different bunch of AI solutions, including machine learning and reinforcement learning on a daily basis. The open questions raised multiple aspects concerning the role of artificial intelligence and machine learning

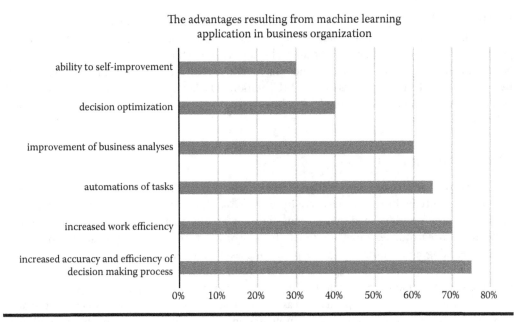

The advantages resulting from machine learning application in business organization

Figure 10.1   **Advantages resulting from the application of machine learning in a business organisation.**

Source: L. Ziora Machine learning solutions in the management of a contemporary business organisation, Journal of Decision Systems, Taylor & Francis Group, 2020.

solutions in the process of contemporary business organisation management. After indicating the type of implemented AI/ML tool, the first question aimed to specify the areas of management and to what extent it is supported by implementing the artificial intelligence/machine-learning tool; it also sought to determine whether and to what extent the solution is useful for conducting business. The second research question indicated the benefits of implementing AI solutions for the company and showed whether the competitive advantage of the business organisation increased (measured as a market share) and whether implemented solutions improved and perfected the company's innovativeness, the company's business processes, and its business strategy. In case of confirmation, the respondents had to briefly specify how and to what extent the situation after the implementation of the AI/ML tool was improved. The third question concerned the problem of supporting decision-making processes at the strategic, tactical, and operational levels of management. In this case, respondents had to indicate whether decision-making processes at all levels and stages were accelerated thanks to the implementation of artificial intelligence/machine-learning solutions; they aslo had to indicate whether such features as effectiveness and efficiency of decisions led to an increase in the business value of decisions. Thay had to indicate whether the mentioned solution had a significant and positive impact on generating value for a business organisation. Question number 4 was devoted to data quality, where respondents had to state whether the quality of data improved the quality of the decision-making process and business analyses carried out with the use of AI/ML solutions, and to what extent (significantly/insignificantly) it was improved. The next open question had to determine whether effectiveness and scope of decision-making analyses (e.g. customer/supplier/environment analysis) based on large data sets (big data and/or Internet of Things solutions) was increased after the implementation of the AI/ML tool. In response to the sixth question, the respondents had to express how they perceive the future of AI/ML solutions in business organisation management. The seventh question raised the issue of how artificial intelligence and machine-learning solutions allowed to increase the manager's work efficiency and what challenges/difficulties needed to be overcome in the process of implementing an AI and/or ML solution. The last question concerned indication of any existing disadvantages of the implemented AI and/or ML solution and areas in which it could be improved.

10.4.1 Case Study 1

Case study no 1 was conducted in one of the largest banks in Poland. This institution started applying AI solutions in its business activity in 2009, and, during the course of the survey, the interviewed manager indicated bots, spam filters, and digital assistants as the types of implemented AI/machine-learning solutions. It is worth mentioning that chatbots are using machine-learning and natural language processing as a basis of their functioning. In the first question, which concerned the identification of management areas and the extent to which implemented AI/machine-learning solution supports management of a given organisation, the respondent indicated such supported areas as customer and employee service, automated accounting, and primarily automated documentation processing. The implemented solution is useful to a large extent in daily business activity. The next question was related to benefits resulting from the implementation of AI solution, and the respondents confirmed that thanks to the implementation of AI/ML, the competitive advantage of the business organisation has increased and it has improved the company's innovativeness as well. Another question was devoted to the issue of whether AI/ML improved business processes and business strategy of the business organisation, and, if yes, to what extent (comparing to the situation before implementation of the AI solution). Response to this particular question confirmed that the business strategy, as well as business processes, were improved. The respondent also confirmed that increased data quality has a significant impact on the quality of the decision-making process and on the quality of conducted analyses. The efficacy and the scope of decision analyses, which are conducted on the huge data sets, were increased. The bank is ready for further development of the ML tool. The respondent also mentioned the advantage of using AI/ML to gain an increase in work efficiency. As far as challenges and difficulties to overcome are concerned, the respondent mentioned the cost of employee training. The respondent did not observe any disadvantages resulting from the implementation of the mentioned solution.

10.4.2 Case Study 2

The second banking industry institution is also one of the biggest functioning in Poland and dealing with finances, leasing, and auctions, and cooperating with insurance institutions. The respondent, similar to the first case study, named bots, digital assistants, and spam filters as applied AI/ML solutions implemented in 2016. The areas of management supported by AI/ML included business and retail customer service, human resources, accounting or even departments responsible for cleaning offices and room access control. The implemented solution is useful to a large degree in the business activity of the bank, and it improved its innovativeness. The business strategy and business processes were improved to a great extent, and the decision-making process was accelerated at all of its stages. The quality of data on the basis of which the analyses are conducted had a positive influence on the speed of conducted analyses. The scope and efficacy of business analyses were increased. An increase in manager's work efficiency was also observed. The respondent underlined that despite high costs connected with AI/ML tools implementation, the costs of its daily usage, maintenance, and staff training, this solution will be developed in the future.

10.4.3 Case Study 3

The third case study was conducted in another banking institution that implemented chatbots answering clients' questions as a machine-learning solution. The respondent stated that "thanks to bots and chatbots, the client can quickly contact us and we will react to his questions and expectations regarding our facility. Thanks to machine learning, our employees can quickly assess the credit risk for each incoming application from a potential borrower, and monitor the creditworthiness of our applicant on an ongoing basis." In the question devoted to the usefulness of the AI/ML solution, the respondent claims that "such solutions are very useful in our business, they help in our daily work analysing lots of data for us, and thus the employees can also focus on other important tasks during their work when the rest of activities is analysed by artificial intelligence." In response to the question related to benefits resulting from ML implementation, it was stated that "for sure, thanks to the implementation of such solutions, employees are more efficient and effective. Our market share has also increased because thanks to the innovative activities we have become more accessible to a potential client and thus our market share has increased a lot." The answer to the question of whether business processes were perfected and improved was positive, and the business stated that "of course, as it has improved the business processes, we have more time for customers. Before the implementation of such innovations, we could not meet the expectations of every potential client. At the moment, we can analyse each inquiry." The decision processes "were also accelerated thanks to the use of automation. The effectiveness and efficiency as well as the speed of decisions made increased, and thus the efficiency of employees work." The increase of data quality also significantly increased the quality of the decision-making process and the conducted business analyses helped in gaining more clients. The scope of business analyses concerning customers has increased thanks to the large data sets used in the case of bot applications. As far as future development plans are concerned, the institution is going to certainly introduce more AI solutions because it helps them in their daily activities, significantly helping employees and allowing them to focus on many other activities. The manager's daily work was improved. In response to challenges, the respondent pinpointed "many tests that the program must pass to implement applications for corporate use and the second issue is conducting employee training, which is not always easy, especially in pandemic times." In case of disadvantages, the indicated drawbacks mention that "sometimes the application does not work properly, it is not able to fully analyse the information provided by the client, so a human must watch over it all the time, it could be improved in such a way that artificial intelligence would be more self-sufficient."

10.4.4 Case Study 4

This case study was conducted in the Polish branch of an international bank that recently launched chatbots applied to communicate with clients. The institution uses an intelligent assistant that answers questions related to the bank's functionality in two ways – by text or by voice – and according to the respondent, this innovative solution understands questions asked naturally, just like in a conversation with another human being. This solution also improved and accelerated communication and, after its implementation, the efficacy, efficiency, and speed of the decision-making process was increased. The data quality influenced the increase of work efficiency as well since it had some impact on the efficiency of conducted customer analyses; also, the scope of the chatbots application was increased. The respondent additionally indicated that "thanks to intelligent solutions, bank employees are less busy and the implementation of artificial intelligence will primarily bring savings for everyone." Challenges to be faced included the requirements of AI/ML tools.

10.4.5 Case Study 5

The last bank institution, which is also a Polish branch of a multinational bank, similar to the previous organisation, also indicated internet bots as an example of an implemented AI/ML solution. The respondent mentioned that "the bot helps us a lot in direct contact with the client. It is not always possible to talk to a consultant, so such a tool helps to answer basic customer inquiries for us consultants. It is equipped with all kinds of responses to meet bank customers expectations." The respondent also indicated that "the solution is very useful in banking as it helps us in our daily work and answers the questions of our future clients. It helps us in our daily work and facilitates some of our activities." It helps us and replaces some of our activities." Taking into account the question regarding the improvement of business strategy and processes, the respondent stated that "it certainly improved the company's functionality and business strategy, and thus influenced a greater number of acquired customers, because we have automated customer service, and earlier it was less effective because there were not enough people to talk to everyone and to present the offer and the range of services provided." Also, thanks to the application of AI/ML solutions, the decision-making process has been accelerated, the effectiveness of employees has increased, and the bank institution gained more clients, which also affects its business position. The quality of the decision-making process was improved, similar to the quality of conducted analyses, and as a result, the number of clients increased. The enhanced scope of client analysis enabled a greater ability to track and save outcomes thanks to the usage of the Internet of Things tools. When the challenges and opportunities are concerned, the respondent claimed that "I think we will be introducing even more AI solutions to manage the company. Thanks to such solutions, we work better, we have higher profits, and generally this solution is very helpful in our industry." The solution allowed for increasing the efficiency of manager's work due to the fact that "the manager who handles everything and is properly trained, becomes more open to new ideas as well as to contacts with other banking representatives." The challenge the bank had to face was a large number of trainings among employees who were not always positive toward this solution. As far as the disadvantages of AI/ML solution is concerned, the respondent noticed that "like any electronic system, it also has disadvantages, it is not always able to recognize human questions. Unfortunately, the truth is that the bot is not always able to replace the human."

The selected advantages and disadvantages resulting from implementation of ML/AI solutions in a banking industry were presented in Table 10.1, where special attention was paid to the problem of ML impact on decision-making support, especially on the quality of decisions and conducted analyses.

Table 10.1 Selected advantages and disadvantages of ML solutions implemented in the banking industry management

Research results in areas common to all research subjects	Impact of implemented ML solution on decision making and supported areas of management	Impact of data quality on the quality of decision-making process and the quality of business analyses	Main advantages resulting from implementation of ML solution	Main disadvantages resulting from implementation of ML solution
Banking intitutions 1–5	Acceleration of decision-making process at strategic, tactical and operational level of managementIncrease of efficiency and efficacy of decisions makingIncrease of decision's business valueUsefulness of implemented solution.	Observed significant and positive effect of ML solutions on the quality of decision making at all levels of managementObserved increase in the quality of conducted analyses	Increase of competitive advantageBetter innovativeness of the whole banking institutionImprovement of business and decision-making processesGeneral increase in work effeciency of a managerPerfected business strategyPositive influence of big data on the quality of decision-making process	Cost of trainingsCost of implementation and maintenance of ML solutions e.g. chatbots, digital assistants.

Source: Author's study.

10.5 Conclusions

The chapter emphasises ML applicability in contemporary business organisation's management area. The supervised, unsupervised, reinforcement, and deep-learning solutions are applied to improve the quality of decision making, increase efficiency, and improve the efficacy of such processes; improve and optimise business processes; automate daily tasks, finally leading to a reduction of operating costs and a gain in competitive advantage. On the basis of literature of a subject review, as well as case studies analysis, we can draw the conclusion that the AI and machine-learning solutions are more often used in medium-sized and big business organisations. Its scope of application depends on the type and specificity of a given branch. The analysis of five case studies showed that AI/ML solutions have many advantages, of which the most essential are the improvement in quality of decision-making processes, general improvement of business processes, improvement and automation of some daily tasks, and support in the creation of business strategy. The big data solutions with the Internet of Things also play an important role in increasing the quality of the whole decision-making process.

As future research, it is planned to enhance the scope of case studies to other industry branches, such as finance and insurance, telecommunications, fast-moving consumer goods (FMCG), car manufacturing and development industry, e-commerce, healthcare, and software development branch.

References

Alpaydin, E. (2020). *Introduction to Machine Learning*. Cambridge, Massachusetts: The MIT Press.

Al-Sefou, S. (2020). The state of machine learning in Fintech. *Netguru report*. https://www.netguru.com/machine-learning-in-fintech-report

Bonaccorso, G. (2017). *Machine Learning Algorithms*. Birmingham, UK: Packt Publishing.

Burkov, A. (2019). *The Hundred-Page Machine Learning Book* (Vol. 1, pp. 3–5). Canada: Andriy Burkov.

Carbonell, J.G., Michalski, R.S., & Mitchell, T.M. (2015). *Machine Learning: An Artificial Intelligence Approach*. Los Altos, CA: Morgan Kaufman Publishers.

Dangeti, P. (2017). *Statistics for Machine Learning: Techniques for Exploring Supervised, Unsupervised and Reinforcement Learning Models with Python and R* (p. 7). Birmingham, UK: Packt Publishing.

Dar, P. (July 15, 2019). Popular machine learning applications and use cases in our daily life. https://www.analyticsvidhya.com/blog/2019/07/ultimate-list-popular-machine-learning-use-cases/

Data Flair case studies, 5 Machine Learning case studies to explore the Power of Technology: https://data-flair.training/blogs/machine-learning-case-studies/2020

Deloitte Access Economics report, Business impacts of machine learning. 2017, https://www2.deloitte.com/tr/en/pages/strategy-operations/articles/business-impacts-of-machine-learning.html

Ganiyu, M. How machine learning works: An introduction into machine learning terminologies centred around regression and classification. https://towardsdatascience.com/how-machine-learning-works-b801303b1a19

Goodfellow, I., Bengio, Y., & Courville, A. (2017). *Deep Learning* (p. 12). Cambridge, Massachusetts: MIT Press.

de Hoog, J., Mercelis, S., & Hellinckx, P. (2019). Improving machine learning-based decision-making through inclusion of data quality. CEUR-WS.org/Vol-2491/short14.pdf

IBM Cloud Education - Machine Learning, (15th July 2020), https://www.ibm.com/cloud/learn/machine-learning

Jelonek, D., Mesjasz-Lech, A., Stępniak, C., Turek, T., & Ziora, L. (2020) The artificial intelligence application in the management of contemporary organization: Theoretical assumptions, current practices and research review. *Lecture Notes in Networks and Systems 69*, 319–327, Springer.

Jelonek, D., Stępniak, C., & Ziora, L. (2019) The meaning of big data in the support of managerial decisions in contemporary organisations: Review of selected research. Future of Information and Communication Conference (FICC 2018, Singapore), Advances in Information and Communication Networks (red.) Arai K., Kapoor S., Bhatia R., Springer, Cham, 361–368

Marr, B. The amazing ways verizon uses AI and machine learning to improve performance. https://bernardmarr.com/default.asp?contentID=1511

Marr, B. The Top 10 AI and machine learning use cases everyone should know about. https://www.forbes.com/sites/bernardmarr/2016/09/30/what-are-the-top-10-use-cases-for-machine-learning-and-ai/#3f2e73c394c92017

Marsland, S. (2015). *Machine Learning: An Algorithmic Perspective.* 2nd edn., pp. 10–11. New York, NY: CRC Press, Taylor & Francis Group.

Mohri, M., Rostamizadeh A., & Talwalkar, A. (2018). *Foundations of Machine Learning* (p. 4). Cambridge, MA: The MIT Press.

Mullainathan, S., & Spiess, J. (2017). Machine learning: An applied econometric approach. *Journal of Economic Perspectives 31*(2), 87–106.

Neapolitan, R.E., & Jiang, X. (2018). *Artificial Intelligence with an Introduction to Machine Learning* (p. 89). New York, NY: CRC Press.

Pozen, R.C., & Ruane, J. (December 2019). What machine learning will mean for asset managers Harvard Business Review https://www.hbr.org/2019/12/what-machine-learning-will-mean-for-asset-managers

Pyle, D., & San Jose, C. (June 2015). *An Executive's Guide to Machine Learning.* Seattle, Washington: McKinsey Quarterly.

Roh, Y, Heo, G., & Whang, S.E. (October 2019). A survey on data collection for machine learning: A big data – AI integration perspective. *IEEE Transactions on Kno+wledge and Data Engineering 99*, 1–1.

Russel, S., & Norvig, P. (2021). *Artificial Intelligence: A modern Approach* (p. 651, 4th edn.). New York City, NY: Pearson.

Solaiman, I., Brundage, M., Clark, J., Askell, A., Herbert-Voss, A., Wu, J. ... & Wang, J. (2019). Release strategies and the social impacts of language models. arXiv preprint arXiv:1908.09203.

Teich, D.A. (July 6, 2018). Management AI: Types of machine learning systems. https://www.forbes.com/sites/davidteich/2018/07/06/management-ai-types-of-machine-learning-systems/#51634c6432fb.

Ziora, L. (2016). The Sentiment Analysis as a Tool of Business Analytics in Contemporary Organisations. Economics Studies. University of Economics in Katowice Research Papers, no 281, Katowice, pp. 234–241.

Ziora, L. (2020). Machine learning solutions in the management of a contemporary business organisation. *Journal of Decision Systems.*

Chapter 11

Integration of the Decision Support System with the Human Resources Management and Identity and Access Management Systems in an Enterprise

Miljenko Hajnić
Faculty of Information studies in Novo mesto, Slovenia

Biljana Mileva Boshkoska
Faculty of Information studies in Novo mesto, Slovenia
Jožef Stefan Institute, Ljubljana, Slovenia

Contents

DOI: 10.1201/9781003030966-15

11.1 Introduction

Managing human resources (HR) within an organization requires engaging proper resources on a daily basis. With the growth of the organization, more resources are required to manage the HR potential. To establish a solid and reliable foundation for an organization's progress, organizational expenses must be carefully planned, organized, and reduced to fulfil the organization's needs while keeping expenses as low as possible. Strategic planning enables better prerequisites for resolving an organization's activities in the future and reaching its objectives. To establish better prerequisites for the success and progress of a large organization, we conducted research on a real business process (BP). We set two hypotheses:

I. Integration of a decision support system (DSS) for HR management (HRM) into a large organization's information system (IS) decreases organizational operational expenses and forms prerequisites for increasing organizational income.
II. Integration of DSS and HRM with Identity and Access Management (IDAM) into the large organization's IS decreases organizational operational expenses and forms prerequisites for higher organizational income.

The continuous operations of HRM and IDAM take a significant part of HR employees' and IT administrators' working time (Weishäupl et al., 2015). By digitalizing the process of making business decisions, we manage to speed up the process of employee (re)deployment and secure granting access rights to the organization's information system (IS). The digitalization of these tasks allows transparent and easier compliance with the constant changes performed by the HR and IT departments in a more effective, secure, and consistent way to preserve the business momentum and to achieve the organization's objectives through collaboration between employees and IS (Weske, 2019).

We modelled and simulated the BP, and we confirm decreasing costs of administration tasks and respectively increasing organization revenue. By simulating activities with parameters from a real-life organization (Table 11.1 and Table 11.2) using appropriate simulation software, we can produce very good indicators of the possible performance of the future system.

Choosing appropriate employees among many others, and their (re)deployment is a complex problem and requires evaluation according to many attributes. Conceptually, multi-criteria decision analysis (MCDA) has been extensively used for supporting complex decisions in public and private organizations (Montibeller and Franco, 2010). In the past years, MCDA has been used to solve complex decision-making problems in the industry (Kikaj and Bohanec, 2019; Nusev et al., 2018), health care (Chen et al., 2020), public administration, agronomy (Rozman et al., 2017), food production (Boshkoska et al., 2019; Hidayati et al., 2017), ecology (Brelih et al., 2018), land-use planning (Bampa et al., 2019), tourism (Puška et al., 2020), housing (Ferreira et al.,

Table 11.1 Parameters' values used for BPM simulation

Parameter	Value
1 Simulation cycle time frame	1 year (365 days)
Simulation cycles[2]	100
1 Workday = 7,5 work hours	= 450 work minutes
260 workdays per year	= 260 x 450 = 117.000 minutes
Employees sample	5.800 (exchange of 2.900 employees twice a year)
Collecting information activity takes	5 minutes
Decision-making (HR department) activity takes	20 minutes
Decision-making (manager) activity takes	15 minutes
HR updating data activity takes	5 minutes
Email notification activity takes	2 minutes
Assigning authorizations activity takes	10 minutes
Checking authorizations activity takes	10 minutes
Authorization successful ratio (probability)[3]	98% successful

Table 11.2 Resources (role) availability and cost per hour

Resources	Cost per hour	Availability
Employee	10 Euro	2900[4]
Manager	20 Euro	208[5]
IT admin	15 Euro	1
HR employee	10 Euro	2

2017), and sports (Delibašić et al., 2018). We also applied the MCDA method Decision Expert (DEX) for developing a decision support (DS) model for HR management (Hajnić & Boshkoska, a decision support model for the operational management of employee redeployment in large governmental organizations, 2020).

Upon the developed DEX model, we built a decision-support (DS) platform (Hajnić & Boshkoska, a disruptive decision support platform for reengineering the strategic transfer of employees, 2021) to utilize the full functionality of the DEX model in a DS system (DSS) that supports organizational HR management. The DSS is a computerized system that provides the necessary information to analyze and evaluate alternatives to make the right choice. DSS should meet all requirements for helping operators to prepare alternatives and make decisions (Tunčikiene et al., 2010). DSS integrations with the HRM software generally, through the years, bring the same role of DSS to assist in the HRM decision-making process (Chack, 2013; Ciancimino et al., 1992; Davis and Meinert, 1989; Jantan et al., 2010).

Identity and access management (IDAM) is considered a stand-alone technology that contributes to businesses' security, securing the organization's IT environment. With IDAM, HRM must initiate employees' activation to make an account and grant appropriate access rights. Integration or interoperability of IDAM and HR can automate the process and enable employees' quick start, on their first day, without waiting for IT services. Therefore, the organization's business can turn into a profitable contribution faster than ever. In that way, employees only acquire permissions they may need while maintaining IT security (Canner, 2020).

IDAM needs to ensure that access rights granted are controlled in a secure and compliant way while ensuring employees can be as productive as possible. One of the IDAM goals is to generate prerequisites that all employees can access the business applications they need to do their jobs. Any time lost in that process will be reflected in the organization's income (Hunt, 2018).

HRM has a business function of choosing appropriate or best employees for an organization or within the organization. The HR department has a detailed view of employees' data, but their main function is not to create employees' identity data. Data provided by the HR department is a good resource, but joining it with other descriptive data collected outside the HR department can create a more accurate employee IDAM record (Williams, 2017).

Based on our previous work and related works we researched, in the next section, we describe the methodology used in this research.

To present research work, we organized this paper as follows. In the following section, we introduce the methodology followed by the real case study. Next, we provide research results from the simulations, and we continue with the discussion of research results. Finally, in the last section, we provide the conclusion.

11.2 Methodology

To prove the feasibility and the effectiveness of integrating DSS with HRM and IDAM into the organization IS, we work out a methodology for testing and analyzing BP improvements. The methodology defines four repetitive steps of BP improvement, as shown in Figure 11.1, in three cycles of improvement. The first cycle is the implementation of the DSS. The second cycle of

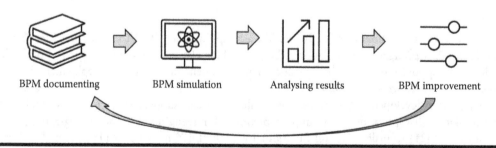

BPM documenting   BPM simulation   Analysing results   BPM improvement

Figure 11.1   Schematic representation of the research methodology.

improvement represents the integration of DSS and HRM. The third cycle of improvement represents the integration of HRM and IDAM.

The final goal is to get results of BPM simulations that can demonstrate the future effects of DSS integration with the HRM and IDAM systems in an organization.

11.2.1 BPM Documenting

Documenting and analyzing BPs is a fundamental task before conducting research. All HRM BPs performed in the organization and used for research are documented and interpreted in the paper according to the BPMN 2.0 standard (Business Process Model and Notation). Business-process management (BPM) is a key technology for the automation and support of processes in medium-sized and large organizations (Becker et al., 2008). It adopts a comprehensive view covering automated coordination of processes, their monitoring, continuous analysis, and improvement for both human tasks and integration of information and software systems (Dumas, 2017).

11.2.2 BPM Simulation

Simulation as a tool is widely used for analyzing steady-state BPs. Different types of analyses are used for the initial design of a BPM and decision-making or continuous improvement. Typically, a model simulation is run repeatedly to identify the limitations and to discuss possible solutions and availability of resources. The erroneous BP design may cause poor performance, uncontrolled utilization of resources, and generally low service levels, so it is very important to analyze processes to find design weak spots, defects, and errors (Van Der Aalst et al., 2010).

We used Bizagi software for computer-based simulation, which follows the "Business Process Simulation Interchange Standard" (BPSim) standard,[1] to observe and validate the BP workflow, to identify the weakness of the process and points for improvements, to conduct various experiments with different resource utilization, to predict the performance and effect of changes, and to find adequate process parameters for optimal efficiency before implementation. One Bizagi simulation cycle comprises four subsequent levels, process validation, time analysis, resource analysis, and calendar analysis, as presented in Figure 11.2. Each subsequent level covers more information than the previous, providing a detailed analysis of the process.

"Process Validation" is the first level to evaluate the structure of the process workflow. In the second level, "Time Analysis," simulation measures the processing time of each activity. In the third level, "Resource Analysis," the simulation predicts process performance according to allocated resources. The fourth level, "Calendar analysis," reflects the resource availability over a defined period. Results of BP simulation are presented by simulation report and activity log.

This approach allows a better understanding of the process behavior. Simulations allow observing the way the system can operate in the future without interrupting the organization's operations (Elliman et al., 2008).

Figure 11.2 Bizagi simulation levels.

11.2.3 Analyzing Results

We performed causal data analysis (explanatory data analysis) to determine the cause-and-effect relationship between variables we change because we cannot be certain that other variables influencing the causal relationship are constant. By causal data analysis, we can see what would happen to another variable if one variable would change, recognize BPs' weak spots and bottlenecks, and generally point out process activities that have to be redefined, improved, and corrected to support business continuity, as expected.

The analysis is based on simulation reports and activity logs that interpret the execution of these activities. The activity log should uniquely identify different process instances of every simulation cycle, and all process activities register in the order in which they perform (Celino et al., 2007).

Some of the important parameters we have to monitor during analysis are accessibility of necessary infrastructure, adequate resource availability and capacity, policy and process compliance, the operational cost of each activity, and many other process-specific parameters. If any of these parameters does not meet expectations, it can be considered as a weakness.

11.2.4 BPM Improvement

Business process improvement (BPI) is an essential factor in organizational development and progress. To keep the business dynamic with the changing environment, organizations need the capability to adapt and align with the new circumstances. BPI is a well-planned change of the BP motivated by the analysis of the existing process and improved to the state where enhancements (automation where applicable) result in a better process.

To enhance organizational efficiency and to transform the way the organization works, the focus is set to the modification and improvement of BPs upraised from dissatisfaction with current processes, feedback from process performers, desire to change the method of organizational works, enhancement of IT and knowledge resources, analysis results, and quality-assurance reports.

To improve the BPM, we first identified the process activities that are creating bottlenecks, the activities that are the most time consuming, and identified the strange or unknown cost and engaged resources, etc. Mitigation of the effects caused by identified bottlenecks can be supported by automation of certain activities or optimization of workflow and resources that lead to the BPM redesign and improvement. Redesign of the BP should meet at least one of the following purposes: enhanced functionality, increased quality, increased flexibility, reduced operation (cycle) time, and reduced cost (Shtub and Karni, 2010).

11.3 Use Case

The use case includes a real organization with almost 3000 employees, which operates across the whole country in fields of finance, post-control, billing, risk analysis, IT support, etc. Besides the organization's specific security policy, which defines occasional redeployments of employees, the organization has to follow business dynamics and be ready for instant changes of locations where business activities must be done. Such a change of focus results in engaging a large portion of the resources needed for employees' redeployment and HRM on-time support. While employees wait for redeployment, the organization increases the unallocated potential, recognized as an expense or mortgage. To find the key performance indicators (KPI) of the initial BP, we documented the initial BP of (re)deploying employees into an organizational unit using the business process model (BPM), as presented in Figure 11.3.

In the *preparation* phase, the HR department decides whether to redeploy an employee into (another) OU. In the second phase (*processing*), the HR employee updates data in the HR application and sends an e-mail notification to the manager. The manager makes a decision on which application roles have to be assigned to an employee. The manager notifies the IT

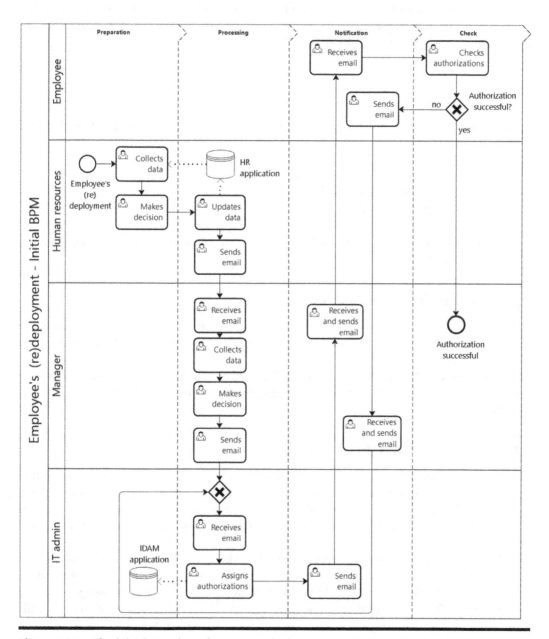

Figure 11.3 The initial BP of employee's (re)deployment in the organizational unit.

administrator about it, and, finally, the IT administrator updates employee authorizations. In the third phase (*notification*), the IT administrator informs the manager about granted authorizations; the manager then forwards that information to the employee. In the fourth phase (*check*), an employee verifies updated authorizations. If updating authorizations is not successful, the process returns to the third phase, *notification*.

The precondition for future automation of described BP is well-defined and analyzed BP. In continuation, we performed the following analysis: (i) we validated that the initial process behaves as expected, (ii) we verified a process definition correctness, (iii) we simulated resource utilization (performance) to meet requirements (Van der Aalst, 2008) by interactive simulation with the corresponding tool - Bizagi Modeler (BizAgi Ltd).

11.4 Results

After documenting the BP, we simulated and analyzed the initial BP, which was followed by BPI in three stages:

    I. by implementing a DEX model into DSS
    II. by the integration of DSS and HRM
    III. by the integration of HRM and IDAM

The simulation and results of the initial BP, as well as improvements obtained in each stage, are presented in continuation.

11.4.1 Initial BPM Simulation Parameters

In continuation, in Table 11.1 and Table 11.2 we present values of the parameters used in the simulation. All anomalies and unusually long processing are defined through 2% of unsuccessful process endings.

For completing all tasks of employees' (re)deployment in one year, the organization has to designate minimally one IT administrator employee and two employees from the HR department.

11.4.2 Results of Initial BPM Simulation

We conducted a simulation to get an existing BP explanation by values of KPIs needed for future references of the BP optimizations and improvements, presented here as follows in Table 11.3 and Table 11.4. We conducted simulation of 100 cycles completed successfully for an average of 5919,97 cases per cycle, with an average of 119,97 (2,03%) unsuccessfully completed cases per cycle.

The cost of employees' management is also reflected through the overhead expense for employees while they wait for their user account to be updated. To calculate the overhead expenses, we used the organization's statistical information that every employee makes an average income of 147 € hourly. The initial BPM simulation generates 1,193,355.8 EUR loss of income while employees wait for their user account to be updated, as presented in (11.1).

Table 11.3 Total work time spent and Total cost of employees' work in the initial BPM simulation

	Resource/role (availability)	Minutes	Utilization	Total cost EUR
1	HR (2)	185.600	79,96%	30.933,33
2	Manager (208)	139.439,94	0,60%	48.493,29
3	IT administrator (1)	84.757,12	71,41%	20.719,90
4	Employee (2900)	71.279,58	0,02%	11.879,93
	Total (Σ1–4)	481.076,64		112.026,45

Table 11.4 Initial simulation times for completing one (re)deployment case

Completing one (re)deployment case	Time
Shortest time	83 minutes
Longest time	203 minutes
Average time	83,98 minutes

$$5,800 * 83.98 \; minutes \; per \; case/60 \; minutes \; per \; hour * 147 \; EUR \qquad (11.1)$$

The stated calculations (1), (2), (3), and (4) do not say that the remaining income would necessarily be made but rather show an extrapolated estimation of loss, which can be expected under similar conditions.

11.4.3 Implementing a DEX Model into DSS

The first stage of BPI is already completed by the DEX model implementation in the DSS to help decision makers in the HR department. This DSS platform retrieves all relevant information about employees and uses those data in the decision-making process (Hajnić and Boshkoska, A disruptive decision support platform for reengineering the strategic transfer of employees, 2021). We documented Stage 1 BPM and performed a simulation to present the improvement process in detail.

We managed to accelerate the data collection and processing by substituting the HR manual work with the DSS platform, including evaluations and proposing suggestions of a possible decision.

Improvement of Stage 1 according to the initial BP is visible in the elimination of the employee's manual tasks, collecting and processing employee data, as presented in Figure 11.4. From Stage 1 onward, this task is automated and operated by the DSS platform.

After documenting the BPM, we set all parameters in the Bizagi software needed for the Stage 1 simulation process. All parameters described in Table 11.1 and Table 11.2 used in the

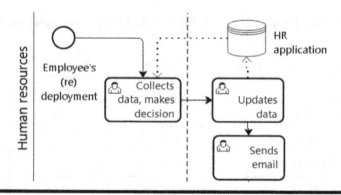

Figure 11.4 Stage 1 improvement of collecting and processing data.

simulation of the initial BPM (Section 2.1), remain the same in the Stage 1 simulation, except "Collecting information activity," which is automated and takes 2 minutes (reduced from 5 minutes). Also, Stage 1 utilizes only one HR employee to complete the tasks.

Stage 1 simulation of 100 cycles completed successfully for an average of 5.918,02 cases per cycle, with an average of 118,02 (1,99%) unsuccessfully completed cases per cycle (possible error range is 0,03%).

Comparing to the previous initial stage, Stage 1 improvements yielded an additional reduction of the total time needed for completing (re)deployment tasks of all employees twice a year, as presented in Table 11.5.

Times for completing one (re)deployment task are also additionally reduced by Stage 1 improvements, when compared to the previous initial stage, as presented in Table 11.6.

Table 11.7 presents Stage 1 improvement comparing to the previous stage, described in the section *Use case*, reflected in the organization's cost savings yielded from the reduction of total time and resources needed for completing all (re)deployment tasks through the one year.

Stage 1 improvement also reduces the possible loss of income on 866.383,70 EUR while employees wait for their user account to be updated, as presented in (11.2), which can be projected as an additional possible income of 326.972,10 EUR per year, compared to the initial stage.

$$(5,800 * 60,97 \text{ } minutes \text{ } per \text{ } case/60 \text{ } minutes \text{ } per \text{ } hour * 147 \text{ } EUR) \qquad (11.2)$$

Table 11.5 Total work time spent in the Stage 1 BPM simulation

Role	Minutes	Employees	Utilization	Improvement[6]
HR	52.200	1	44,98%	−133.400
Manager	139.436,04	208	0,60%	−3,9
IT admin	84.698,78	1	71,40%	−58,34
Employees	71.252,28	2900	0,02%	−27,3
Total	**347.587,10**			**−133.489,54**

Table 11.6 Stage 1 BPM simulation times for completing one (re)deployment case

Completing one (re)deployment case	Time	Improvement
Shortest time	60 minutes	−23 minutes
Longest time	206 minutes	+3 minutes
Average time	60,97 minutes	−23,01 minutes

Table 11.7 Total cost of employees' work in the Stage 1 BPM simulation

Role	Total cost EUR	Improvement EUR
HR	8.700,00	−22.233,33
Manager	48.490,69	−2,6
IT admin	20.713,07	−6,83
Employee	11.875,38	−4,55
Total	**89.779,14**	**−22.247,31**

The completed simulation process of Stage 1 improvement resulted in the possibility for additional process improvement, which is described in Section 5.2.

11.4.4 Integration of DSS and HRM

BPI Stage 2 includes integration of DSS platform with HRM application, which will enable automated data storage in the HRM application once one of the proposals for a new employee scheduling decision is accepted in the DSS. We designed the process to automate the sending of email messages to stakeholders who continue their activities in this process. If HRM software does not have this functionality of automated email sending, this precondition should be met so we can terminate the manager's role and manager's activities because all necessary information for the assignment of new authorizations is delivered directly to the IT department (administrator). In this stage of improvement, the manager's role lost all activities from the previous stage and only an email message is sent to the manager as a notification that a new employee is (re)deployed to the manager's organizational unit. From Stage 2 onward, the manager's tasks are reduced only to receiving email notifications. Improved BPM is presented in Figure 11.5.

All parameters used in the simulation of the Stage 1 improvement (Section 5.1), remain the same values, except "decision making (manager) activity," which is terminated now; "HR Updating data activity," which is automated now and takes 5 seconds (reduced from 5 minutes); and "email notification activity," which is automated now and takes 5 seconds (reduced from 2 minutes).

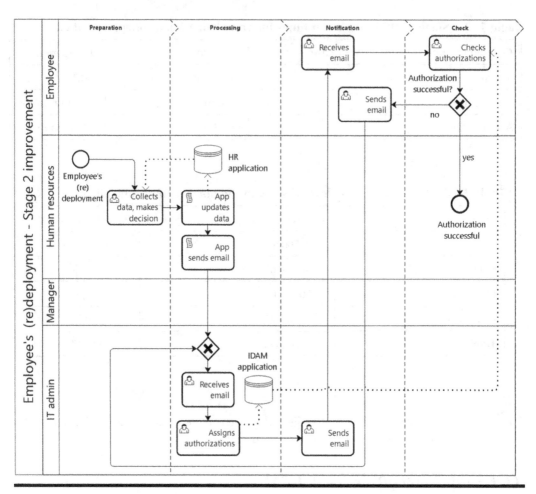

Figure 11.5   Stage 2 improvement of employee's (re)deployment BPM.

Conducted Stage 2 simulation of 100 cycles completed successfully for an average of 5918,93 cases per cycle, with an average of 118,93 (2%) unsuccessfully completed cases per cycle (possible error range is 0,02%).

Comparing to the previous Stage 1, Stage 2 improvements yielded an additional reduction of the total time needed for completing (re)deployment tasks of all employees twice a year, as presented in Table 11.8.

Times for completing one (re)deployment task are also additionally reduced by Stage 2 improvements comparing to the previous Stage 1, as presented in Table 11.9.

Table 11.10 presents Stage 2 improvement comparing to the previous Stage 1 reflected in the organization's cost savings yielded from the reduction of total time and resources needed for completing all (re)deployment tasks through the one year.

Stage 2 improvement also reduces the possible loss of income on 414.505,70 EUR, while employees wait for their user account to be updated, as presented in (11.3), which can be projected as an additional possible income of 451.878,00 EUR per year, compared to the Stage 1.

Table 11.8 Total work time spent in the Stage 2 BPM simulation

Role	Minutes	Employees	Utilization	Improvement[7]
HR	12.566,67	1	10,00%	−39.633,33
Manager	0	0	0%	−139.436,04
IT admin	85.361,10	1	71,43%	+662,32
Employees	71.265,02	2900	0,02%	+12,74
Total	**169.192,79**			**−178.394,31**

Table 11.9 Stage 2 BPM simulation times for completing one (re)deployment case

Completing one (re)deployment case	Time	Improvement
Shortest time	28,17 minutes	−31,83 minutes
Longest time	148,17 minutes	−57,83 minutes
Average time	29,17 minutes	−31,80 minutes

$$(5,800 * 29,17 \; \textit{minutes per case} / 60 \; \textit{minutes per hour} * 147 \; \textit{EUR}) \qquad (11.3)$$

Section 5.3 describes the additional improvement of Stage 2 developed after the analysis of recorded data.

11.4.5 Integration of HRM and IDAM

Stage 3 improves includes improvements of both Stage 1 and Stage 2. In this stage, integration of DSS and HRM application with IDAM application will enable automatically assigning authorizations on the employee user account once the proposed decision is accepted in the DSS application and data is automatically stored in the HRM application, as presented in Figure 11.6.

Table 11.10 Total cost of employees' work in the Stage 2 BPM simulation

Role	Total cost EUR	Improvement EUR
HR	1.933,33	−6.766,67
Manager	0	−48.490,69
IT admin	20.716,26	+3,19
Employee	11.877,50	+2,12
Total	**34.527,09**	**−55.252,05**

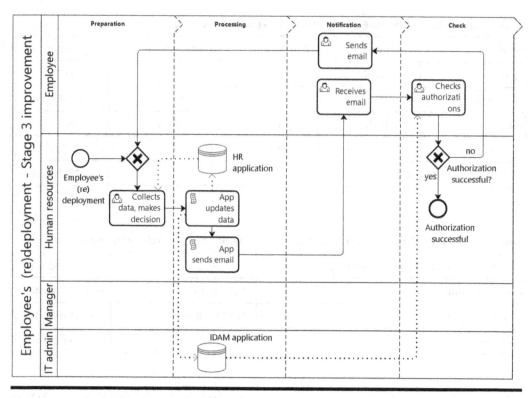

Figure 11.6 Stage 3 improvement of employee's (re)deployment BPM.

This integration removes the need for the IT administrator role, and the IT administrator's activities are terminated because the assignment of new authorizations to the employee user account is performed automatically.

An email message is sent to the manager as a notification that a new employee is redeployed to the manager's organizational unit. Another email message is sent to the IT administrator as a notification that authorizations are assigned to the employee's user account.

All values used in the simulation of the Stage 2 improvement (Section 5.2), remain the same, except "Assigning authorizations activity," which is automated and instant upon HRM data update.

Stage 3 simulation of 100 cycles completed successfully for an average of 5.919,5 cases per cycle, with an average of 119,5 (2,02%) unsuccessfully completed cases per cycle (possible error range is 0,01%).

Comparing to the previous Stage 2, Stage 3 improvements yielded an additional reduction of the total time needed for completing (re)deployment tasks of all employees twice a year, as presented in Table 11.11.

Times for completing one (re)deployment task are also additionally reduced by Stage 3 improvements comparing to the previous Stage 2, as presented in Table 11.12.

Table 11.13 presents Stage 3 improvement comparing to the previous Stage 2 reflected in the organization's cost savings yielded from the reduction of total time and resources needed for completing all (re)deployment tasks through the one year.

Table 11.11   Total work time spent in the Stage 3 BPM simulation

Role	Minutes	Employees	Utilization	Improvement
HR	13.054,85	1	67,99%	+488,18
Manager	0	0	0%	0
IT admin	0	0	0%	−85.361,10
Employees	71.273,00	2900	0,14%	0
Total	**84.327,85**			**−84.864,94**

Table 11.12   Stage 3 BPM simulation times for completing one (re)deployment case

Completing one (re)deployment case	Time	Improvement
Shortest time	14,17 minutes	−14 minutes
Longest time	67,33 minutes	−80,84 minutes
Average time	14,54 minutes	−14,63 minutes

Stage 3 improvement additionally reduces the possible loss of income on 206.613,40 EUR, while employees wait for their user account to be updated, which can be projected as an additional possible income of 207.892,30 EUR per year, as presented in (11.4).

$$(5,800 * 14,54 \; minutes \; per \; case/60 \; minutes \; per \; hour * 147 \; EUR) \qquad (11.4)$$

Stage 3 is the final stage of BPM improvement in this research.

Finally, we grouped simulations' results from Table 11.3, Tables 11.5, 11.7, 11.8, 11.10, 11.11 and 11.13, (1), (2), (3), and (4) to graphically present improvements through time and cost decreasing and the potential rise of income, as presented in Figure 11.7.

Table 11.13   Total cost of employees' work in the Stage 3 BPM simulation

Role	Total cost EUR	Improvement EUR
HR	1.973,17	+39,84
Manager	0	0
IT admin	0	−20.716,26
Employee	11.878,83	+1,33
Total	13.852,00	−20.675,09

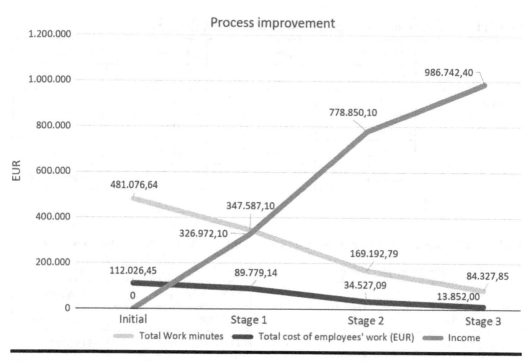

Figure 11.7 **Results of all stages of BPM improvements compared to the initial stage.**

In continuation, we will discuss all BPM improvements we developed and simulated to gain real numbers for making conclusions.

11.5 Discussion

Many companies and organizations around the world operate simultaneously in many locations distributed over the country, continent, or whole world. Occasionally, unexpected and unplanned events occur that disturb normal business activities. Service-oriented organizations should immediately reorganize their activities to support uninterrupted deliveries; they need to quickly respond to unexpected and unplanned events. For example, proposed DSS-HRM-IDAM integration may be helpful in organizations that want to prevent corruption and prevent undesirable relationships between employees and parties involved in business processes that could cause material damage to the corporate or government budget. There are more examples of proposed integrations usage in various business fields that require immediate action and the transfer of employees to another location where current employees suffer due to increased activity (summer/winter tourist season, epidemic health care, life-saving services, etc.).

These research results should be taken into account when considering how to speed up HRM and IDAM processes in an organization by integrating DSS, HRM, and IDAM standalone software into the effective and efficient IS, or make interoperability between software to achieve the same objectives. The research results provide a new perception of the relationship between DSS, HRM, and IDAM and contribute a clearer understanding of the organization's operational costs generated by HR and IT departments' activities. Interpreted results support the organization's financial motivation to start an analysis of potential investment in IT integrations to establish a solid base for an organization's prosperity. These results matter because they are grounded on the real organizational use case, on the real sample, and the real BP of (re)deployment. From yielded research results, we can see practical implications in large organizations where the organizational assessment of investing in the IT integrations covers the cost of HRM and IDAM activities.

We did not include the organization's monthly expenses on electricity, network and computer maintenance, costs of software licences, and any other operational expenses needed for keeping the organization's business continuity because many of these expenses are already present, with or without HRM and IDAM. We estimated the automation processes of "updating data in HR software" and automation of "e-mail notification" to last 5 seconds, although this time varies. Software utilization and network bandwidth are not always at the same level of availability. Additional costs caused by employees' redeployment, such as higher employee travel expenses or employee separate living allowance are not in the scope of this research simulation, and they are not part of the research results because those data are unknown at the time of research.

Despite those limitations, we estimate that costs generated by these unknown factors cannot have a significant impact on the estimated efficiency of investment in IT integrations.

11.6 Conclusion

We conducted a BPI on a real organization by digitalizing the HR process of employee redeployment and integrating a DSS with IDAM. The performed simulations' results show that implementation of a DSS brings improvement that can be recognized in the reduction of time needed for manual employees' activities, particularly collecting and processing employees' data for preparing propositions of (re)deployment cases to decision makers.

The first improvement, enabling the automation of data updating in the HRM application and enabling automation of sending email messages to stakeholders who continue their activities, reduces the processing time by 51,32%, operational expenses by 61,54%, and up to 52,16% in compensation of the projected loss of income. The second stage simulations results give strong motivation for the next process upgrade: integration of DSS and HRM application. DSS integration with HRM into IS stimulates creating prerequisite to enhance IT service's on-time operations to follow and support HRM tasks and activities.

Integrating IDAM software with HRM and DSS into IS enable updating authorizations directly from HRM software to reduce the processing time by 50,16% and gets further operational expense savings by 59,88%, and up to 50,15% compensation of the projected loss of income.

The comparison of the final improvement to the initial state of the BP before any improvements shows that integration of the DEX model in the DSS platform, and integration of DSS with HRM and IDAM software into IS can result in up to 82,74% time savings, up to 87,64% of operational expenses savings, and decrease up to 82,69% the projected loss of income.

Acknowledgement

The work of the last author was supported by the HECAT project, funded within the EU Framework Programme for Research and Innovation Horizon 2020, under grant number

870702, and was partially supported by the Slovenian Research Agency (ARRS) core research programme (P1–0383).

Notes

1. BPSim (bpsim.org) is Workflow Management Coalition (wfmc.org) standard. It defines a specification for the parameterization and interchange of process analysis data allowing structural and capacity analysis of a process model providing for pre-execution and post-execution optimization.
2. Bizagi recommends using min. 30 replications (cycles) to make sure the simulation reaches a stable state, but conducting research it turned out that 100 replications or more yield acceptable results for later comparison and analysis. Reason for that lies in the Probability ratio.
3. Probability ratio is set to 2% of unsuccessful endings through 100 cycles. It varies from 1,5% to 2,5%. Average probability ratio of unsuccessful endings stabilizes on 2% at the end of the simulation, as configured. Deployment unsuccessfulness is caused by unusually long processing interval because of HR employees' sickness, vacations or holidays and those events from the real world we replicated into the simulation.
4. Count of employees for simulation purpose is rounded to a hundred.
5. Count of managers for simulation purpose is equal to the number of organizational units that have manager work position.
6. Improvements according to the previous initial BPM.
7. Improvements according to the previous Stage 1.

References

Bampa, F., O'Sullivan, L., Madena, K., Sandén, T., Spiegel, H., Henriksen, C., & Debeljak, M. (2019). Harvesting European knowledge on soil functions and land management using multi-criteria decision analysis. *Soil Use and Management 35*(1), 6–20. doi: 10.1111/sum.12506

Becker, A., Fisteus, J., & Delgado-Kloos, C. (2008). Business process analysis. In A. Becker (Ed.). *Electronic Commerce: Concepts, Methodologies, Tools, and Applications*. Hershey, Pennsylvania, USA: IGI Global, 691–697. doi: 10.4018/978-1-59904-943-4.ch056.

Boshkoska, B., Liu, S., Zhao, G., Fernandez, A., Gamboa, S., del Pino, M., & Chen, H. (2019). A decision support system for evaluation of the knowledge sharing crossing boundaries in agri-food value chains. *Computers in Industry 110*, 64–80. doi: 10.1016/j.compind.2019.04.012

Brelih, M., Rajkovič, U., Ružič, T., Rodič, B., & Kozelj, D. (2018). Modelling decision knowledge for the evaluation of water management investment projects. *Central European Journal of Operations Research 27*, 759–781. doi: 10.1007/s10100-018-0600-5

Canner, B. (2020). *Solutions Review - Identity and Access Management*. (Solutions Review). Retrieved February 24, 2021, from Solutions Review: https://solutionsreview.com/identity-management/how-identity-management-interacts-with-human-resources-hr/

Celino, I., Medeiros, A., Zeissler, G., Oppitz, M., Facca, F., & Zoeller, S. (2007). Semantic business process analysis. *Proceedings of the Workshop on Semantic Business Process and Product Lifecycle Management SBPM 2007. 251*. CEUR-WS.org. Retrieved December 10, 2020, from http://ceur-ws.org/Vol-251/paper6.pdf

Chack, D. (2013). Decision support system for human resource management of the organization. *International Journal of Management Research and Business Strategy 2*(3), 105–111.

Chen, Y., Ding, S., Zheng, H., Zhang, Y., & Yang, S. (2020). Decision support for personalized hospital choice using the DEX hierarchical model with SMAA. *Knowledge and Information Systems 62*, 3059–3082. doi: 10.1007/s10115-020-01448-1

Ciancimino, A., Lari, I., Nicolo, F., & Lucertini, M. (1992). A decision support system for human resource management: Strategic and tactical planning flow network models. *7th IFAC Symposium on Information Control Problems in Manufacturing Technology (INCOM'92)*. 25, pp. 421–427. Toronto, Ontario, Canada: Elsevier. doi: 10.1016/S1474–6670(17)52403-9

Davis, D., & Meinert, D. (1989). Human resource decision support systems HRDSS: Integrating decision support and human resource information systems. *Information Resources Management Journal 2*(1), 41–48. doi: 10.4018/irmj.1989010104

Delibašić, B., Radovanović, S., Jovanović, M., Bohanec, M., & Suknović, M. (2018). Integrating knowledge from DEX hierarchies into a logistic regression stacking model for predicting ski injuries. *Journal of Decision Systems 27*, 201–208. doi: 10.1080/12460125.2018.1460164

Dumas, M. (2017). Business process modeling. In *Encyclopedia of Database Systems*. New York, NY: Springer Science, Business Media LLC, 1–8. doi: 10.1007/978-1-4899-7993-3_260-2

Elliman, T., Hatzakis, T., & Serrano, A. (2008). Business process simulation: An alternative modelling technique for the information system development process. *International Journal of Enterprise Information Systems (IJEIS) 2*(3), 43–58. doi: 10.4018/jeis.2006070104

Ferreira, F.A., Spahr, R.W., Sunderman, M.A., Banaitis, A., & Ferreira, J.J. (2017). A learning-oriented decision-making process for real estate brokerage service evaluation. *Service Business 11*, 453–474. doi: 10.1007/s11628-016-0315-4

Hajnić, M., & Boshkoska, B. (2021). A disruptive decision support platform for reengineering the strategic transfer of employees. *IEEE Access 9*, 29921–29928. doi: 10.1109/ACCESS.2021.3059895

Hajnić, M., & Boshkoska, B.M. (2020). A decision support model for the operational management of employee redeployment in large governmental organisations. *Journal of Decision Systems*, 1–9. doi: 10.1080/12460125.2020.1768681

Hidayati, A., Juyuspan, F., Novianty, C., & Bima, D. (2017). Implementation of decision expert (DEX) in the "SALADGARDEN" application. *4th International Conference on Electrical Engineering, Computer Science and Informatics (EECSI)*Yogyakarta: Institute of Electrical and Electronics Engineers (IEEE), 1–5. doi: 10.1109/EECSI.2017.8239156

Hunt, R. (2018). *Understanding the role of HR in identity and access management*. (Turnkey Consulting Ltd) Retrieved February 21, 2021, from Turnkey: https://www.turnkeyconsulting.com/keyview/understanding-the-role-of-hr-in-identity-and-access-management

Jantan, H., Hamdan, A., & Othman, Z. (2010). Intelligent techniques for decision support system in human resource management. In Ger Devlin (Ed.). *Decision Support Systems*. Rijeka: IntechOpen. doi: 10.5772/39401

Kikaj, A., & Bohanec, M. (2019). Towards web-based decision modeling software. *Proceedings of the Central European Conference on Information and Intelligent Systems* (pp. 333–340). Varaždin, Croatia: The Faculty of Organization and Informatics (FOI). Retrieved January 10, 2021, from https://kt.ijs.si/MarkoBohanec/pub/2019_CECIIS_DEX2Web.pdf

Montibeller, G., & Franco, L. (2010). Multi-criteria decision analysis for strategic decision making. In C. Zopounidis & P. Pardalos (Eds.). *Handbook of Multicriteria Analysis* (Vol. 103). Berlin, Heidelberg: Springer-Verlag, 25–48. doi: 10.1007/978-3-540-92828-7_2

Nusev, G., Boškoski, P., Bohanec, M., & Mileva Boshkoska, B. (2018). A DSS model for selection of computer on module based on PROMETHEE and DEX methods. In *ICDSST 2018: Decision Support Systems VIII: Sustainable Data-Driven and Evidence-Based Decision Support 313*. Cham, Switzerland: Springer International Publishing AG, 157–168. doi: 10.1007/978-3-319-90315-6_13

Puška, A., Šadić, S., Maksimović, A., & Stojanović, I. (2020). Decision support model in the determination of rural touristic destination attractiveness in the Brčko District of Bosnia and Herzegovina. *Tourism and Hospitality Research 20*(4), 387–405. doi: 10.1177/1467358420904100

Rozman, Č., Maksimović, A., Puška, A., Grgić, Z., Pazek, K., Prevolšek, B., & Cejvanović, F. (2017). The use of multi criteria models for decision support system in fruit production. *Erwerbs-Obstbau 59*, 235–243. doi: 10.1007/s10341-017-0320-3

Shtub, A., & Karni, R. (2010). Business process improvement. In A. Shtub & R. Karni (Eds.). *ERP - The Dynamics of Supply Chain* (2nd edn.). New York, NY: Springer Science+Business Media, LLC, 249–254. doi: 10.1007/978-0-387-74526-8

Tunčikiene, Ž., Bivainis, J., & Drejeris, R. (2010). Integrated DSS for strategic planning in public institutions. *Journal of Business Economics and Management 11*(4), 671–688. doi: 10.3846/jbem.2 010.33

Van der Aalst, W. (2008). Challenges in business process analysis. In *Lecture Notes in Business Information Processing 12*. Funchal, Madeira: Springer-Verlag Berlin Heidelberg, 27-42. doi: 10.1007/978-3-540-88710-2_3

Van Der Aalst, W.M., Nakatumba, J., Rozinat, A., & Russell, N. (2010). Business process simulation. In J. Brocke & M. Rosemann (Eds.). *Handbook on Business Process Management 1: Introduction, Methods, and Information Systems*. Berlin, Heidelberg: Springer, 313–338. doi: 10.1007/978-3-642-0041 6-2_15

Weishäupl, E., Kunz, M., Yasasin, E., Wagner, G., Prester, J., Schryen, G., & Pernul, G. (2015). Towards an economic approach to identity and access management systems using decision theory. *2nd International Workshop on Security in highly connected IT Systems*. Vienna, Austria: IWSEC 2015. Retrieved May 02, 2020, https://epub.uni-regensburg.de/32143/1/SHCIS_MK.pdf

Weske, M. (2019). Part I foundation. In M. Weske (Ed.). *Business Process Management, Concepts, Languages, Architectures* (3rd edn.). Berlin, Heidelberg: Springer, 3–21. doi: 10.1007/978-3-662-59432-2_3

Williams, C. (2017, February 20). *Yin and Yang: Two Views on IAM - HR vs Identity Management*. (RSA Security LLC, Bedford, MA 01730). Retrieved February 24, 2021, from RSA: https://www.rsa.com/en-us/blog/2017-04/yin-and-yang-two-views-on-iam-hr-vs-identity-management

Conclusions

This book has presented recent developments in various aspects of decision-making support, with the emphasis on rational decision making in organisations. The authors led us through the meanders of psychological, organisational, and technological aspects of decision making, not forgetting about the constant problems of decision making: uncertainty and pressure.

The chapters making up this book show us not only the variety of perspectives involved in decision making, but also the variety of domains where rational decision support systems are needed. In the case studies presented here, we had the opportunity to consider medical doctors, students, and managers of various universities, IT project teams, construction companies, banks, coffee trade representatives, small and large manufacturing companies, etc.

We have also been shown the richness of relationships in which the decisions should and have to be taken nowadays. Modern organisations operate in chains and networks, and they have multiple responsibilities: social, legal, business, ethical, etc. Thanks to new possibilities, discussed in this book we can take transparent decisions, taking into account a multitude of stakeholders and their diverse features, incorporating diverse criteria, using multiple types and drivers of information and decision-making patterns and referring to numerous lessons learned. The marriage of theoretical ideas with the possibilities offered by the technology will make the decisions in our organisations more rational and, at the same time, more human.

Index